Re

MANCHESTER
UNIVERSITY PRESS

Rewriting Scotland

Welsh, McLean, Warner, Banks, Galloway, and Kennedy

CRISTIE L. MARCH

Manchester University Press

Manchester and New York

distributed exclusively in the USA by Palgrave

Published by Manchester University Press
Oxford Road, Manchester M13 9NR, UK
and Room 400, 175 Fifth Avenue, New York, NY 10010, USA
www.manchesteruniversitypress.co.uk

Distributed exclusively in the USA by
Palgrave, 175 Fifth Avenue, New York, NY 10010, USA

Distributed exclusively in Canada by
UBC Press, University of British Columbia, 2029 West Mall, Vancouver, BC, Canada V6T 1Z2

British Library Cataloguing-in-Publication Data
A catalogue record for this book is available from the British Library

Library of Congress Cataloging-in-Publication Data applied for

ISBN 0 7190 6032 x *hardback*
     0 7190 6033 8 *paperback*

First published 2002

10 09 08 07 06 05 04 03 02   10 9 8 7 6 5 4 3 2 1

Typeset in Caslon and Rotis Sans
by Koinonia Ltd, Manchester
Printed in Great Britain
by Bell & Bain Ltd, Glasgow

to Scott, for all of his help and support

Contents

Foreword

This text serves as an introduction to some of the contemporary Scottish writers who have brought Scottish writing closer to the centre stage of literature. As the following chapters reveal, their works play on a variety of themes that belie what many readers see as 'traditional' Scottish literature. In many instances, Scotland and Scottishness figure largely in the writing. At other times, however, concepts of Scottish identity move backstage as writers explore other issues of narrative construction. Iain Banks, for example, writes 'space opera' science fiction or explores the more sinister side of his characters in ways that have little to do with 'Scottishness' per se.

Although this text offers critical and theoretical interpretations of these writers' works, it aims to make the writers accessible to readers who may be unfamiliar with much contemporary Scottish writing and who are likely to be unfamiliar with much literary theory. Each chapter is devoted to a single author – Irvine Welsh, Duncan McLean, Alan Warner, Iain Banks, Janice Galloway, and A. L. Kennedy – and presents the themes they explore in their works as well as explaining the works themselves. In the process, the text offers readers some perspective on the development of contemporary Scottish literature.

Acknowledgements

Many thanks to the staff at Manchester University Press, to Linda Wagner-Martin, to Rebecca Davison, to my family, and to my husband.

Introduction

Concepts of 'Scottishness'

The picture of 'Scotland' that occurs to many, if not most, people involves kilts, bagpipes, green hills, and thick Scottish brogues that appear in films such as *Braveheart* (with the occasional Highland cow thrown in for good measure). Similarly, the picture of Scottish writing that occurs involves Robert Burns' romanticised visions of rustic love in the heather and Sir Walter Scott's historical novels celebrating the Highlands and Scottish heroes such as Bonnie Prince Charlie. Alternatively, those a bit more familiar with twentieth-century Scotland recognise the impact of the Industrial Revolution's shift to the cities, where Glasgow and its working-class population offer an 'urban and gritty'[1] vision of Scotland. Novelists detailing the squalor of Glaswegian slums and the impoverished, alcoholic lives of male Scottish labourers at once rejected the singularity of the rural Scottish life and replaced it with an urban vision of Scotland. Thus, on the one hand 'Scotland' is perceived as a 'conglomeration of phoney representations and spurious traditions, with false mythologies of land and community', Douglas Gifford comments, 'while on the other its cities are dumb, unrelated, unimagined'.[2]

Yet both of these visions offer only single facets of Scotland and Scottish writing and ignore the complexity of identifying what Scottishness is, socially and imaginatively. Increasingly, contemporary Scottish writing involves complicated negotiations among the Scottish 'identities' that have proliferated since the 1970s and 1980s as writers reject the need to fit within either of these two literary paradigms. Where literary Scotland once was what 'people who don't know Scotland' think: 'it's got lots of hills, it's very green, it's very pretty', and people would write about it 'as if that almost existed', A. L. Kennedy explains, the late twentieth century has altered that image. 'The towns began to exist and now the whole place exists and it doesn't matter and you don't have to worry about it at all', she comments. 'You can write about Peru.'[3]

Although some contemporary Scottish writers have turned away from Scotland as subject matter in order to write about such diverse non-Scottish topics as Texas swing music culture, like Duncan McLean does, all have offered new visions of Scotland that play between the traditional rural and urban models of Scottishness. Writers are drawing from various elements of these models and combining them to create new images of Scotland that defy easy categorisation at the same time that they reflect significant elements of contemporary Scottish life. Irvine Welsh, for example, writes about drug users in the Edinburgh/Leith area, drawing on Edinburgh's status as one of the peak drug-using cities in the 1990s.

Ironically, this mixing of urban and rural, traditional and modern, even Highland and Lowland belies what many contemporary writers see as a national history lost in the limbo of 'Britain'. Keith Dixon notes that contemporary Scottish writers 'have gone to pains to point out that they are writing from what they see as a national literary vacuum, and that their inspiration in cultural terms is more North American or European than Scottish or even British'.[4] A. L. Kennedy echoes this sentiment, noting that 'the cultural history of Scotland has been a lot about having no identity'.[5] As the following sections illustrate, however, contemporary Scottish writing springs out of, as much as it may depart from, Scottish literary developments in the 1970s and 1980s formed through Scotland's socio-cultural transformation from a compliant British territory to a defiant Scottish 'nation'. Yet contemporary writers transform these developments into their own visions of what Scottish literature is, selecting and discarding various stylistic and thematic elements to create a myriad of literary possibilities.

The Scottish socio-political scene since World War II

During the late 1930s and early 1940s the idea of an overarching 'British' identity, encompassing Scotland and England, dominated social thinking, as British war propaganda emphasised the need for British unification in the face of a common European enemy. Economically, the war machine built up Scotland's concentration on heavy industry and shipbuilding, particularly in Glasgow, both during the war and afterwards in Britain's rebuilding period.

Yet when the post-war boom ended, a dramatically altered economic landscape confronted Scotland. The markets controlled by the now defunct British Empire had disappeared and foreign competition for such key Scottish industries as coal and steel production destabilised Scotland's economy. The image of the working-class urban labourer who had replaced the earlier centuries' rural image of the Highland crofter as a repository of laudable Scottish values now became an image of disillusionment and failure. Despite this disillusionment, the Attlee government's creation of the Welfare State in the late 1940s, with its policies of public ownership, encouraged Scottish approval of Britishness because the Scottish economy benefited.

However, by the early 1960s these programs had failed to check Scotland's rising unemployment, and the ensuing British economic crisis of the late 1960s and early 1970s created scepticism about Scotland's future and prompted a surge in Scottish nationalist sentiment. Writers such as George Friel, Robin Jenkins, and James Kelman emphasised 'the spiritual bleakness and hopelessness of modern Scotland' and viewed the Scottish past as 'utterly irrelevant for the majority of people living in arid non-communities and employed, if at all, in soul-destroying monotony'.[6]

These dire visions echoed the failure in 1979 of a vote for Scottish devolution as well as the instalment of a new Conservative British government under Margaret Thatcher, whose push for privatisation and a dismantling of the Welfare State Scotland had come to rely on made her a fitting figure for Scottish disdain. Scots felt they were inadequately represented in British government. To many, Thatcher's government displayed a disregard for Scottish concerns and led to a feeling of alienation and a subsequent rise in nationalist sentiment. Such decisions as the allocation of income from the North Sea oil fields to English counties when widespread belief in Scotland was that Scottish oil should be used for Scottish projects furthered this alienation, as did Thatcher's stated commitment to reining in the vocal and resistant Scottish labour unions and her use of Scotland as a testing ground for the poll tax a year before it was enacted in England. In the face of such actions, Scots were forced to 'reassess the power of the British state apparatus in Scottish society'[7] and recognise the erosion of a common ground of Britishness, Gerry Hassan explains. This resentment fostered the explosion of what came to be called the New Scottish Renaissance as writers began to explore Scottish identity and experiment with narratives that allowed such exploration. Such experimentation was inevitable, Ian Bell suggests, because 'in a climate where there are no formal arenas for debate and no institutions of national self-identity other than a rather faceless Scottish Office, literature takes on greater importance'.[8] At the beginnings of this revived

interest in Scottish writing, Alasdair Gray and James Kelman emerged
as the leaders of a new direction for Scottish literature.

Alasdair Gray, James Kelman, and the new Scottish renaissance

Alasdair Gray and James Kelman re-directed the predominantly urban,
Glaswegian, working-class novel in the late 1970s and 1980s through
their experimentation with alternative narrative and linguistic structures.
During the pessimistic 1960s and 1970s, the Scottish novel had become
largely synonymous with the working-class urban novel, a phenomenon
explained by Manfred Malzhan as the rejection of the English middle-
class novel. 'Working-class features are important [to the Scottish novel]
because they are more identifiably Scottish than their more anglicised
urban middle-class counterparts', Malzhan explains. 'Consequently, the
assertion of a working-class identity in a Scottish context is likely to
appear also as the assertion of a Scottish identity.'[9] Novels such as
Gordon Williams' *From Scenes Like These* revealed the transformation of
young men with hopes and aspirations into more hardened men resigned
to shoddy work conditions and the threat of unemployment. In addition,
the urban landscape offered by writers such as Robin Jenkins, George
Friel, and, to some extent, William McIlvenney was de-industrialised,
full of poverty, alcoholism, and 'hard men' – a 'barren Scotland'[10] that, in
the wake of the 1979 defeat of the Scottish devolution vote and economic
hardship, seemed all too real.

Gray and Kelman, however, offer re-readings of the urban Scot,
suggesting that Glasgow is merely an 'emblematic figure of the Scottish
urban experience',[11] creating a more wide-reaching vision of a downtrodden Scotland. The characters they present do not engage in 'grand
movements of history', but instead are divorced from a meaningful Scottish history entirely. They act only in what Keith Dixon calls the 'small
movements of individuals trapped in a history-less present' of 'confinement, imprisonment, isolation'.[12] In the process, as Gavin Wallace claims,
they 'transcended' the boundaries of 'working-class urban realism',[13]
galvanised to a large extent by the same 1979 voting defeat that had
seemed a nail in the coffin of Scottish identity. The two writers reject
blanket perceptions of Scottishness as either the rural crofter or the
unemployed, working-class urban labourer. Instead, they focus on
characters who struggle with the fragmentations of identity that such
stereotypes of Scottishness, and other concerns of modern life, have
created. Through their narrative innovations, both Kelman and Gray

challenge 'received images of Scotland', particularly, as Susanne Hage-mann notes, urban culture.[14] Kelman in particular has begun to move beyond a Scottish context, instead exploring what Janice Galloway notes is less and less Glasgow and increasingly an abstract landscape – a move-ment away from the Scottish landscape that A. L. Kennedy's *Everything You Need* and Duncan McLean's *Lone Star Swing* also undertake in order to explore non-Scottish issues such as the process of writing or music historiography.

Kelman, as Douglas Gifford explains, 'wages war on cultural imper-ialism and "Eng Lit"'. By excluding 'issues of landscape, race, tradition', Gifford continues, his vaguely recognisable 'post-industrial Scotland' offers more general concerns about 'economic and social deprivation'.[15] In the process, Kelman's works break out of the genre of the working-class novel, whose pointed message aims at socio-political reform, and instead present characters 'marginalised from traditional working-class values, who do not believe in the possibilities of communal political action'.[16] In *The Busconductor Hines* and *A Chancer*, he confronts readers with an 'uncertainty of direction', and 'passive beings incapable of initi-ative or of instigating independent planned courses of action'.[17] Although *How Late It Was, How Late* offers more direction and, perhaps, a bit of optimism in Sammy's attempts to cope alone with a sudden blindness caused by a police beating, the fact that Sammy is alone, without the support of an urban community in which he has lived all of his life, illustrates the pervasiveness of Kelman's sense of a disempowered and disinterested working class that lives without meaning. 'Ye just battered on, that was what ye did man ye battered on, what else can ye do?' Sammy thinks. 'There's nothing else. No when ye come to think about it.'[18] The stream-of-consciousness narrative, displaying what various scholars have recognised as a movement to an existential writing style focusing on the everyday existence of marginalised individuals, highlights his break from the themes of working-class solidarity and calls to social action that previously characterised the Scottish working-class urban novel.

Similarly, Kelman's writing experiments with everyday vernacular break from both a middle-class, English novel tradition and from a Scottish urban novel tradition which uses that same English as a narra-tive framework to explain and contain the working-class dialogue. Kelman refuses to confine himself to a middle-class English or a working-class Glaswegian, but instead to work with language as a 'mixing of the register of which real speech consists', comments Alan Freeman. If, as

Freeman continues, social strata are not 'unified entit[ies]',[19] then the
speech Kelman offers suggests the marginalised position most of his
characters hold – between a perception of Scottish culture confined to
the unemployed, urban working class, and a perception of middle-class
sensibilities and language as being only English, not Scottish. Simon
Baker points to an excerpt from *Greyhound for Breakfast* as an illustration
of what Cairns Craig calls a 'unity of voice replac[ing] unity of political
or social purpose as the foundation of solidarity', when the first-person
narrator commingles his reading list of Kafka and John William Draper
with his announcement that he is 'on the broo [unemployment] now'.[20]

Kelman increasingly 'disregard[s] all conventional adornments,
including most of the punctuation',[21] Baker notes, stripping the narrative
down to its naked language so that, for example, in *How Late It Was,
How Late*, the only voice in the narrative is Sammy's own. In this way,
Kelman strives to shed the third person narrative voice that pretends to
be objective, but instead recreates a privileging of middle-class English
as the language of explanation and authorial voice. In the process, he
aims 'to write and remain a member of [his] own community'[22] – a dual
position rarely achieved by Scottish writers from the previous decades.

Gray also offers characters downtrodden by a disconnection with a
'Scottish' community on the same individualised level as Kelman does.
Yet, Wallace notes, in the painful process of exploring their sense of
hopelessness and lack of social identity, he leaves open opportunities for
self-expression and the ultimate recovery of self-esteem emancipated
'from the obsessive restrictions of the past'.[23] Where Kelman offers
characters unwilling or, more often, unable, to lobby for social reform,
Gray presents the potential for seemingly paralysed characters to act in
meaningfully social ways, ranging from Jock's realisation of his need to
act rather than wallow in self-pity at the end of *1982, Janine* to the
politically active, socially reformist working-class characters that have
transformed the derelict city of Unthank in Book Four of *Lanark*.

Gray also engages in experimenting with language and 'problem-
atising the whole process of authoritative story-telling'[24] as in *Lanark*,
and *Poor Things*. Where Kelman peels away his narrative, revealing the
bare structure and character language, Gray adds layer upon layer of text,
purposefully intruding an authorial voice, and sometimes more than one,
on the story. His play with narrative structure, illustrations, and the im-
possibility of crafting a story that stands alone creates voluptuous texts.
In his ground-breaking *Lanark*, for example, he conflates two storylines,
rearranging the sections of the novel so that his epilogue, in which a self-

proclaimed 'author' makes an appearance, precedes the last of the four books in the novel, and his third and fourth chapters bookend the first and second. In addition, he provides marginalia detailing the various 'plagarisms' that either influenced or found their way directly into the story's creation. Even the 'author' who appears in the Epilogue cannot control the text, as events from the characters' lives hurtle pell-mell into the narrative without his knowing, much to his chagrin and annoyance.

Contemporary Scottish writers acknowledge the literary modes developed by Gray and Kelman. Kevin Williamson, who has acted as publisher and mentor-peer of such writers as Irvine Welsh and Alan Warner, notes that Kelman's work gave working-class Scots confidence in their identity by championing Scots language and suggesting how that language had been marginalised.[25] Janice Galloway comments that her first encounter with Gray, through his *Lanark*, offered 'something free-ing. It knew words, syntax, and places I also knew yet used them without any tang of apology'.[26] Alan Warner recalls 'how completely I believed there was nobody alive in Scotland writing a book' and 'the deep shock and amazement Alasdair Gray's mighty *Lanark*' gave him.[27] Similarly, Iain Banks remembers *Lanark* as 'one of the best pieces of Scottish literature at least since the second world war and possibly this century'.[28]

Yet these contemporary Scottish writers have not simply embraced these innovations. Instead, they tease out underlying questions and concerns of interest to them. McLean and Warner, for example, transport the problems and concerns of urban culture to rural areas in Scotland, blurring the traditionally perceived bifurcation of the two. Kennedy and Galloway investigate the lives of urban Scottish women largely invisible in Kelman's writing. Kelman and Gray present what Keith Dixon suggests are 'post-feminist' men who engage in 'almost Calvinist self-flagellation in their relations with women',[29] such as Jock's solitary and lonely sexual fantasies intended to mask his lost relationships in Gray's *1982, Janine*. Similarly, Galloway offers 'post-feminist' women who over-analyse and second-guess themselves in their attempts to build stable relationships with men, assuming the burdens of both feminist and traditional agendas but successfully carrying neither.

Contemporary Scottish novelists

The following chapters examine the ways in which such character-isations of the Scottish landscape, youth culture, gender, and the complexities of Scottish identity play out in the narratives of some of

Scotland's most striking, and often most shocking, contemporary fiction writers. Chapter 1 focuses on Irvine Welsh and his establishment as an icon of youth culture both within and without Scotland, including his participation in popular media and the impact of the film version of his novel, *Trainspotting*. In the process, Welsh writes through the voice of urban Scottish youth that defies the solitary voice of Kelman's Glasgow. Welsh's narrative experimentation also provides an avenue for rewriting working-class narratives and exploring gender issues, particularly as both relate to urban lifestyles. In the process, Welsh imbues his writing with elements of the grotesque that subvert 'safe' narrative forms.

Chapter 2 offers Alan Warner's transferral of the manifestations of youth culture into the Scottish Highlands and Islands, exploring the means by which distinctions between urban and rural break down as categorisations of Scottishness. The fragmentation that characterises contemporary and urbanised youth culture is juxtaposed literally onto more traditional and rural Scottish landscapes, revealing at once the similarities and the disparities between the two. In addition, Warner's oblique but striking rescripting of the role Scottish gender traditionally plays out in narratives and his use of music culture, particularly the rave phenomenon of the 1990s, introduces additional elements of the 'Scottish experience'.

In Chapter 3, the reconstruction of rural Scotland through blurred boundaries between the urban and the rural experience continues in Duncan McLean's works. Although much of McLean's writing relies on grotesque and violent images of troubled individuals and individual relationships to suggest social fragmentation on a larger scale, he also explores issues of gender anxiety, the upheaval of traditional working-class culture, and the struggles of Scottish youth to locate meaningful cultural identities. Finally, an investigation of his later work reveals a departure from Scottish material entirely.

Chapter 4 addresses the alternative narratives employed by Iain Banks. It examines the deceptively simple division of his work into science fiction 'cult' novels and more mainstream novels to reveal the breakdown of such narrative delineations in his hybrid novels that employ the narrative techniques of both genres. In addition, the chapter explores the problems of gender in Banks' works as well as the blurring of urban and rural landscapes and the theatre of the macabre prevalent in McLean's and Welsh's writing.

The discussion of Janice Galloway's writing in Chapter 5 shifts focus away from contemporary male writers to contemporary female writers.

Galloway's novels centre around women who try to erect, often futilely, structures of social signification that include them as women within a male-dominant Scottish social, and literary, tradition. Her vision of urban Scotland plays on the bleak image Kelman's work creates, inverting it to expose the gender assumptions that drive her characters.

Such troubled or absent cultural affiliations drive A. L. Kennedy's characters, as Chapter 6 suggests. Like Galloway she presents women struggling to identify themselves within the expectations of urban working-class life, and like McLean she departs from Scottish material in her most recent work, instead situating the writing process at the centre of her text.

Finally, this text ends by linking these various themes and writers to other contemporary Scottish fiction writers such as Dilys Rose, Ajay Close, Jimmy Boyle, and Des Dillon. In addition, the chapter introduces other branches of contemporary Scottish writing such as the fiction of Allan Massie, Robin Jenkins, and Iain Crichton Smith, which reveal the wealth of possible narratives available to the contemporary Scottish novel.[30]

Notes

1 C. March, 'An interview with Janice Galloway', *Edinburgh Review* 101 (1999), 92.

2 D. Gifford, 'Contemporary Scottish fiction I', in D. Gifford and D. McMillan (eds), *A History of Scottish Women's Writing* (Edinburgh, Edinburgh University Press, 1997), 590–1.

3 C. March, 'An interview with A. L. Kennedy', *Edinburgh Review* 101 (1999), 103.

4 K. Dixon, 'Talking to the people: a reflection on recent Glasgow fiction', *Studies in Scottish Literature* 28 (1993), 97.

5 March, 'An interview with A. L. Kennedy', 102–3.

6 Gifford, 'Contemporary Scottish fiction I', 595.

7 G. Hassan, *The New Scotland* (London, The Fabian Society, 1998), 4.

8 I. A. Bell, 'New writing in Scotland', *British Book News* (Feb. 1987), 72.

9 M. Malzhan, 'The industrial novel', in C. Craig (ed.), *The History of Scottish Literature, v. 4: Twentieth Century* (Aberdeen, Aberdeen University Press, 1987), 230.

10 G. Wallace, 'Introduction', in G. Wallace and R. Stevenson (eds), *The Scottish Novel Since the Seventies: New Visions, Old Dreams* (Edinburgh, Edinburgh University Press, 1993), 3.

11 K. Dixon, 'Making sense of ourselves: nation and community in modern Scottish writing', *Forum for Modern Language Studies* 29.4 (Oct. 1993), 363.

12 *Ibid.*, 364.

13 Wallace, 'Introduction', 3.
14 S. Hagemann, 'Introduction', in S. Hagemann (ed.), *Studies in Scottish Fiction: 1945 to Present* (Frankfurt am Main, Peter Lang, 1996), 12.
15 D. Gifford, 'The return to mythology in modern Scottish fiction', in S. Hagemann (ed.), *Studies in Scottish Fiction: 1945 to Present* (Frankfurt am Main, Peter Lang, 1996), 30.
16 C. Craig, 'Resisting arrest: James Kelman', in G. Wallace and R. Stevenson (eds), *The Scottish Novel Since the Seventies: New Visions, Old Dreams* (Edinburgh, Edinburgh University Press, 1993), 101.
17 I. A. Bell, 'Form and ideology in contemporary Scottish fiction', in S. Hagemann (ed.), *Studies in Scottish Fiction: 1945 to Present* (Frankfurt am Main, Peter Lang, 1996), 231.
18 J. Kelman, *How Late It Was, How Late* (London, Secker & Warburg, 1994), 52.
19 A. Freeman, 'Ghosts in sunny Leith: Irvine Welsh's *Trainspotting*', in S. Hagemann (ed.), *Studies in Scottish Fiction: 1945 to Present* (Frankfurt am Main, Peter Lang, 1996), 254.
20 S. Baker, '"Wee stories with a working-class theme": urban realism in the fiction of James Kelman', in S. Hagemann (ed.), *Studies in Scottish Fiction: 1945 to Present* (Frankfurt am Main, Peter Lang, 1996), 247.
21 *Ibid.*
22 J. Kelman, *Some Recent Attacks* (Stirling, A. K. Press, 1992), 82.
23 G. Wallace, 'Voices in empty houses: the novel of damaged identity', in G. Wallace and R. Stevenson (eds), *The Scottish Novel Since the Seventies: New Visions, Old Dreams* (Edinburgh, Edinburgh University Press, 1993), 225.
24 Bell, 'Form and ideology', 227.
25 S. Redhead, 'Rebel, rebel: Kevin Williamson', in S. Redhead (ed.), *Repetitive Beat Generation* (Edinburgh, Rebel Inc., 2000), 157.
26 J. Galloway, 'Different oracles: Me and Alasdair Gray', *Review of Contemporary Fiction* 15.2 (Summer 1995), 194–5.
27 S. Redhead, 'Celtic trails: Alan Warner', in S. Redhead (ed.), *Repetitive Beat Generation* (Edinburgh, Rebel Inc., 2000), 130.
28 J. Robertson, 'Bridging styles: A conversation with Iain Banks', *Radical Scotland* 42 (Dec. 1989/Jan. 1990), 11 July 2000, available at www.phlebas.com/text/interv4.html.
29 Dixon, 'Talking to the people', 103.
30 As Andrew Greig has exclaimed, 'Glasgow and Scotland are not synonymous, nor is Edinburgh!' D. McMillan, 'Constructed out of bewilderment: stories of Scotland', in I. A. Bell (ed.), *Peripheral Visions: Images of Nationhood in Contemporary British Fiction* (Cardiff, University of Wales Press, 1995), 80.

1

Irvine Welsh's cultural rave

Rebel Welsh

Irvine Welsh's writing first reached a wide audience at the inception of Kevin Williamson's *Rebel Inc.*, one of 'Scotland's first literary fanzine[s]',[1] although his first published story appeared in a *New Writing Scotland* anthology in 1991. That story, 'First Day of the Edinburgh Festival', interested Duncan McLean, whose anthology booklet series, *Clocktower Press*, eventually published some of Welsh's stories. In 1992, a *Clocktower* booklet, *Past Tense: Four Stories from a Novel*, contained four Welsh stories that would later become part of *Trainspotting*, although at the time it was the slowest selling of the booklets thus far. 'To write about heroin addicts on a run-down Edinburgh estate',[2] McLean notes, was far from the commercialism of which critics later accused Welsh. Rather, the topic did not seem to interest many readers at all. Yet Welsh's work did spark Williamson's interest, and when *Rebel Inc.*'s first issue came out, it included one of his stories. When *Rebel Inc.* became an imprint a short time later and began publishing books, Welsh's stories appeared in its first volume, *Children of Albion Rovers*, alongside stories by Alan Warner.

Welsh's first novel, *Trainspotting*, met with unexpectedly high critical acclaim and was long-listed for the Booker Prize, although it reached only a limited audience. After the theatre version of the novel played, however, interest in the novel accelerated. When the film version of *Trainspotting* was distributed in the United States and Europe in 1996, Welsh's popularity as a writer soared globally. This new popularity also changed expectations about who 'literary' audiences were. Welsh notes, for instance, that when the theatre version of *Trainspotting* played in London, the box office was unsure how to deal with the numerous young cash-paying patrons and had to delay the performance.[3]

Linguistic and narrative play

Part of Welsh's narrative innovation is his use of language. He creates narrative forms that both challenge non-Scottish readers and speak familiarly to those who recognise the lives his fiction characterises. *Trainspotting*, for example, generated a London *Times* glossary explaining the language Welsh's characters use. This glossary is reminiscent of Anthony Burgess' *A Clockwork Orange*, except the language Welsh presents is not a fictional youth culture language, but the real, day-to-day language of young, working-class urban Scots. Ironically, the film version translates and dubs this language at certain points for an American audience, partially disrupting, in turn, the linguistic disruption Welsh's commitment to this working-class dialogue enacts on Standard English as the appropriate narrative form.

In this use of dialogue, Welsh's work echoes James Kelman's linguistic innovations, although Welsh explains that his writing reacts against Kelman's increasingly nihilistic direction and commitment to downtrodden urban working-class characters.[4] Alan Freeman sees Welsh's use of dialect as a means of evoking 'form over content', so that the words characters use come to represent the social environment in which they live, rather than the individualised thoughts characters have. As a result, the language Welsh uses is both freeing, expressing a social group on the periphery of English language and the English text, and confining – what Freeman suggests is 'undermining the concept of selfhood' as a stable element in an inherently unstable social medium.[5] Susanne Hagemann notes that Welsh's fiction presents characters who 'inhabit the geographical and social margins of Edinburgh', suggesting the 'fragmentation of their personal and social identities'.[6] His use of dialect exhibits this instability, as characters struggle with language to express emotions often foreign to them. At times, characters are incapable of communicating at all. In 'Across the Hall', a double-column page format separates the experiences of Stephanie and Frank, who masturbate while thinking of each other at night, vocalising their desires in each other's absence. Yet when they meet in the hall outside their apartments, they are too shy to speak more than painfully stammered comments about the weather.

At other times, Welsh's characters wrestle to articulate concepts largely alien to their experiences. In *Trainspotting*, for example, Spud's attempts to explain why Renton and Sick Boy should not kill a squirrel in the park come close to illustrating his sense of a cohesive environment, but fall short of fully explaining his emotional reaction. The squirrel 'scampers a bit away, moving really weird, archin its whole boady likesay. Magic wee silvery grey thing … ken?' The squirrel is 'batherin nae cunt likesay! Ah hate it the wey Mark's intae hurtin animals … it's wrong man. Ye cannae love girsel if ye want tae hurt things like that … ah mean … what hope is thir?'[7] Welsh offers an environment in which self-interest is prominent and 'community and continuity' are so 'conspicuously absent'[8] that characters like Spud often clash such fleeting ideas against characters such as Renton and Sick Boy. Yet Welsh's characters, though they often lack direction, still possess a vibrancy that his use of language amplifies, however disturbing his readers may find it.

Often, Welsh marks the discrepancy between Standard English and Scots English, suggesting a disconnect between the two languages that reflects a social estrangement as well. In 'A Smart Cunt', for example, when Dave and his friends rob a middle-class English house he puts on a Scots accent, noting that 'people always used to say to my old man – who's Scotch – people like this smarmy scumbag, that they never understood the Jock accent. Funny thing is, when I do these little jobs, they always seem to get the message loud n clear and no mistake.'[9] Here Dave points not only to the linguistic difference between his gang and the people they rob, but also to the social difference between the middle- and working-class as he confronts the English homeowners.

Welsh offers a similar clash of Scottish and non-Scottish in 'The Two Philosophers'. In the story, two rival philosophy professors, Lou Ornstein from the United States and Gus McGlone from Scotland, decide to present their metaphysical argument of 'magic' versus 'unknown science' to a Scottish pub audience to settle which one is more believable to the layperson, but eventually get into a fistfight in the streets and are arrested for brawling. McGlone is a Conservative who rejects working-class activism and Marxist theories. Yet he is beaten and booked for drunken disorderliness while the radically liberal, working-class champion Ornstein is released because the police believe his story – and his accent. To them he's not just one of the 'animals … that terrorise the public',[10] as they assume the drunk and dishevelled McGlone is. Despite McGlone's embrace of the classical liberal tradition of Hume and Ferguson, such Scottish history is out of place in the Glasgow police station, or, the story suggests, in modern Glasgow itself. Instead, the contemporary Scottish image is the drunken ruffian the police assume McGlone is.

The end of the story reiterates the perceived social schism between McGlone and Ornstein through another linguistic play. When Ornstein emerges, uncharged and unruffled, from his interview at the police station, a boy tells him, 'ah saw you fightin this eftirnin, big man. Ye were magic, so ye wir', to which Ornstein replies, 'no, I was unknown science'.[11] The uncomprehending Ornstein does not recognise the boy's reference to 'magic' as a compliment, crystallising the disconnect between the language that allows him to walk free while McGlone is confined by his accent and, consequently, his forced membership in the urban working class.

In his play, 'You'll Have Had Your Hole', though, Welsh combines middle- and working-class language to reveal the tension in Scottish conceptualisations of sex and masculinity. As Willy Maley notes, 'you'll have had your hole' conflates the middle-class Edinburgh woman's 'you'll have had your tea' with the working-class man's reference to sex as 'having your hole'.[12] The first statement is one of refusal – a comment meant to indicate that tea is not forthcoming from the hostess. The second statement is one of acquisition – of sexual fulfilment that is, or is desired to be, forthcoming. The combination acts as a backdrop to a play about anal rape, reflecting the woman's refusal and the man's violent sexual desire that represent not only a break in social class, but also in gendered forms of expression.

Welsh also suggests ways in which the working-class Scottish accent binds characters into sounding uneducated and undeveloped – much like a Brooklyn accent in the United States came to denote the dull, lumbering urban working-class man in the late twentieth century. In 'Lorraine Goes to Livingston', Welsh presents Rebecca, a wealthy writer of romance novels, and Lorraine, her young Scottish nurse. Rebecca complements Lorraine's appearance enthusiastically, deciding to include her in a romance novel. She announces that she has a vision of Lorraine as 'a consort of Lady Caroline Lamb, at one of those grand regency balls, pursued by suitors', but Lorraine says 'Naw, ah'm intae house, especially jungle n that likes. Dinnae mind trancey n garage n techno n that, bit ah like it tae kick but ken?' When Rebecca pursues the idea of Lorraine waltzing, Lorraine can only repeat, 'Mair intae house, eh. Jungle likes.'[13] Lorraine's comments create a disconnect of language and appearance – although Lorraine aesthetically belongs in the nineteenth century 'bodicerippers' that Rebecca writes, her dialogue reveals an inability to adequately express herself so that Rebecca can understand her. This difficulty echoes Dave's comment in 'A Smart Cunt' concerning the English ability to understand Scottish language.

Despite this representation of working-class Scottish language as aligned with the downtrodden and the inferior, Welsh plays with middle-class accents as well to create dichotomies of appearance and reality. In

'Lorraine Goes to Livingston', the English middle class is nothing to be envied. At one point, the wealthy businessman and philanthropist, Freddy Royle, comments on a hardcore pornographic shop he frequents. 'Oi got moiself a noice little vist-vuckin magazine the other week there', he drawls. 'Ow zum of them there girlz an boyz can take one of them vists up their doo-daas oi don't know.'[4] His statements, presented in a phonetic middle-class accent, are all the more repulsive because he is a necrophiliac who donates money to the local hospital in order to have his choice from the hospital morgue. Compared to Freddy, Lorraine and her working-class accent and rave culture music tastes suddenly seem more elevated than her conversation with Rebecca would have the reader believe. Welsh clearly takes sides on this disparity – Rebecca eventually leaves her similarly perverted leech of a husband and joins Lorraine on the rave scene.

Narrative manipulation and role play

Welsh experiments with narrative structure as well in order to expose his characters and offer fuller explanations of their often disturbing behaviour. In *Trainspotting*, he splinters the narrative into a series of vignettes in which various characters frankly present their points of view on events that have occurred to them or to others – who in turn receive the opportunity to speak in their own short snatches of narrative. As a result, characters who comment negatively on their friends in turn garner criticism, revealing the deep personal and social flaws each experiences. For example, Renton notes that his group has created a series of myths about their resident and self-proclaimed 'hard man', Begbie, that prevents them from earning his anger and attention and binds them to him even in their disgust with him:

> Myth: Begbie backs up his mates.
> Reality: Begbie smashes fuck oot ay innocent wee daft cunts whae accidently spill your pint or bump intae ye. Psychopaths who terrorise Begbie's mates usually dae so wi impunity, as they tend tae be closer mates ay Begbie's than the punters he hings aboot wi. He kens thum aw through approved school, prison n the casuals' networks, the freemasonaries that bams share.[5]

Yet Begbie has his opportunity to retort, noting that Renton has changed into someone who tries to act above his class, putting on a middle-class accent to speak with women on their trip to London. Later Begbie counters his posturing about being a vegetarian when they are at breakfast

with a woman in whom Renton is interested by reminding him about
the animals they used to torture when they were children. In the process
of these exchanges, Welsh exposes not only the personal flaws of Renton
and Begbie, but also the social constructs of class and masculinity.

Trainspotting's combination of first-person and third-person narratives also serves to further illustrate the variety of perspectives and
fragmentation of personalities that confront the reader. Only at the end
of the novel does the third-person account of Renton's betrayal and
flight from his friends in a London drug deal tie together many of the
narrative's strands. After stealing the money from the drug sale and taking
a boat to Amsterdam, Renton reflects on the primary characteristics of
Sick Boy, Second Prize, Spud, and Begbie, and what they might mean
for his possible return to Edinburgh. He suspects that Sick Boy, a 'born
exploiter' would have a 'grudging admiration' for his actions, so similar
to what he himself would do.[16] He sees Second Prize as a junkie too bent
on his own destruction to remember the betrayal beyond his next hit of
heroin. Although he feels truly guilty for betraying Spud, who because of
his good nature and more developed sense of morality than the others
has been a natural victim, Renton recognises that Begbie's violence and
misguided sense of honour will prevent his ever returning. In the process
of these introspections, Welsh summarises some of the splintered
identities that loosely characterise the darker side of Scottish urban
culture – exposing problems of violence, drug use, self-centeredness, and
apathy.

Welsh's *Filth* also manipulates narrative forms to explore the life of
Bruce Robertson, an Edinburgh policeman. Bruce's drug use, pornography, corruption, and disregard for the police system and the people
he is hired to protect embody the variety of negative characteristics
Trainspotting offers. As the novel progresses, the thoughts of a tapeworm
Bruce is harbouring offer a growing moral consciousness and introspection on Bruce's childhood. The worm literally is inscribed on the
pages of the novel overlapping with Bruce's narrative and blocking out
bits and pieces of Bruce's text. As a result, it textually and visually over-
rides Bruce's hedonism and sadism with moral commentary, eventually
resulting in Bruce's overwhelming guilt and suicide.

Marabou Stork Nightmares offers a different narrative play as Roy, in
a suicide-attempt-coma induced by his sense of guilt from gang-raping
Kirstie, moves between consciousness of his family around his bedside,
semi-conscious memories of his life, and unconscious fantasy construc-
tions about going on safari in colonial Africa. As Roy shifts from level to

level of consciousness, the text's font changes on the page, emulating that shift and interspersing fragments of narrative from other levels to create a montage of text, illustrating Roy's attempts to escape full consciousness and his unwanted memories by dwelling in the fantasy Africa his 'Jamboland' creates. Yet the gaps between the texts are the spaces into which the unwanted memories intrude. Roy's conversations in Jamboland become infiltrated with his memories of life in Scotland, so that a conversation with his fictional travel companion, Sandy, about the African landscape, turns into a conversation about Scottish football. Later, his guilty memories of the gang-rape translate a 'boys only'[17] excursion with Sandy into a squalid and predatory sexual encounter with two women who appear along the dusty trail.

In addition, his homophobia and memories of being abused by his uncle taint a harmless swim with Sandy, who looks at the Vaseline Roy applies to his sunburnt lips and smirks, 'one could think of other uses for that, Roy'.[18] The fantasy world further unravels when, after he and Sandy find their employer, Dawson, has captured some thieves, the three men prepare to rape them – a gang-rape that echoes Roy's rape of Kirstie. Although Roy manages to wrest control of his fantasy away from his memories, the near breakdown of the fantasy structure spells the end of Roy's ability to evade the consequences of his actions in 'real life'. Eventually Roy's fractured mental states coalesce into consciousness, just in time to witness his mutilation and death at Kirstie's vengeful hand.

Much as Roy's fantasy Jamboland purports to offer escape from painful personal memories, the colonial African setting allows Roy to escape his feelings of degradation in Scotland and recall the feelings of racial superiority and empowerment that his few childhood years in South Africa offered him. In the Jamboland setting, the language Welsh employs shifts from the familiar Scottish dialogue to a more formal Standard English with echoes of nineteenth-century benevolent racism, sharply contrasting with Roy's more usual language. When commenting on his African porter's theft of supplies, he notes, 'I find this attitude of "something for nothing" sadly prevalent amongst the non-white races, but I put the blame fairly and squarely on the shoulders of the white colonialists.' Immediately afterward, though, he defeats a struggle toward consciousness, exclaiming, 'Naw, cause I'm too quick for youse, you'll never find ays in here.'[19] Yet the high English Roy uses in Jamboland also reveals cracks in his consciousness as Scottish language slips into his narrative, suggesting the breakdown of the fantasy to which he has tried to escape. When he and Sandy need to escape a mob of native men, he admits to feeling a 'wee bitty paranoid'[20] – a premonitory feeling that infiltrates his entire fantasy and unravels it.

The use of formal language also appears in 'Lorraine Goes To Livingston' as Rebecca writes her romance novel. 'In the eyes of her hostess she saw such a look of glowing approval that, indeed, a mirror was superfluous', the novel says. 'She looked heavenly and striking in a red dress made from imported Indian silk'.[21] Yet, as in *Marabou Stork Nightmares*, Welsh compromises this style as the novel's subject matter transforms into a nineteenth-century pornographic text upon Rebecca's discovery of her husband's embezzling and hardcore pornography pursuits.

The 'role playing' that Roy uses to evade reality in *Marabou Stork Nightmares* appears in many of Welsh's stories. As with his linguistic play, Welsh offers characters who defy expected categorisations to illustrate discrepancies in social structures and perceived notions of character types. In 'Where the Debris Meets the Sea', for example, Welsh juxtaposes football hooligan culture with Hollywood glamour figures. Kim Basinger, Kylie Minogue, Madonna, and Victoria Principal lounge in their Santa Monica, California penthouse, pining over centrefolds, write-ups, and television interviews of football casuals, rather than the other way around. In addition, the women speak in the working-class Scottish language that the casuals themselves would use as they peruse the photographs and stories. 'Total fuckin ride' Victoria announces of Deek Prentice, who is 'resplendent in a purple, aqua and black shell-suit'.[22] Meanwhile, the interviews with the casuals juxtapose their pubs and pool-playing with the language reserved for celebrity interviews while Welsh pokes fun at a strong work ethic so lacking in many of his characters. Deek denies involvement in,

> an altercation at a stag night in Fox's Box. It's not a boozer I use, and in any case I was working overtime that night! If I was in the pub as often as certain gossip columnists claim, I'd hardly be able to hold down my driving job with Northern Removals. With three million people unemployed, I've certainly no intention of resting on my laurels.[23]

In its shifting of social roles, the story also reveals Welsh's disdain for the figures mass media promotes as influential or instrumental celebrities. 'It's like people might read the *Record* or *Sun* or *Mirror* or something but it's got absolutely no real influence in their lives in any kind of meaningful way', Welsh comments.[24]

Welsh offers a similar disruption of expected character roles in his depiction of God in 'The Granton Star Cause'. When God confronts a wastrel Boab in a pub, he angrily rejects Boab's admonitions that his attention is better focused on starving children. 'Every fuckin time ah come doon here, some wide-o pills ays up aboot what ah should n shouldnae be fuckin daein. Either that or ah huv tae enter intae some philosophical fuckin discourse wi some wee undergraduate twat aboot the nature ay masel, the extent ay ma omnipotence n aw that shite', he says. 'It's no for yous cunts tae criticise me. Ah made yous cunts in ma ain image. Yous git oan wi it; yous fuckin well sort it oot. That cunt Nietzsche wis wide ay the mark whin he sais ah wis deid. Ah'm no deid; ah jist dinnae gie a fuck. It's no fir me tae sort every cunt's problems oot. Nae other cunt gies a fuck so how should ah? Eh?'[25] That God expresses the careless and unconcerned attitude which Boab, among others of Welsh's characters, has, contrasts to the benevolent image of a caring and patriarchal figure. Here, the patriarch is as likely to lash out in spite – as he transforms Boab into a housefly – as he is to offer solace and sustenance to those in need. Welsh's God is entirely at home in the pubs his characters frequent.

Such role shifting also occurs in 'Disnae Matter' to emphasise, rather than conflate, character types, as a nameless 'hard man' talks about taking his child to Disneyland. While there, he complains about the weak beer available, then explains how he punched one of the cartoon characters because, as he tells security, 'cunt jumped oot in front ay the bairn. Well ootay fuckin order.'[26] When the guard, the employee, and the management offer their apologies and the management threatens to fire the employee, he takes their overtures not as public relations concerns, but as consideration and respect for his hard man status. Much like Begbie's reaction to placating behaviour in *Trainspotting*, he becomes forgiving and magnanimous, telling management not to fire the employee after all, although he is tempted to beat him in retaliation. 'Boy's entitled tae keep ehs joab; that wis ma good deed fir the day,' he comments. 'Ah jist goes: Aye, you n aw, mate.'[27]

Welsh also offers a conflation of American media-induced stories and Scottish working-class reality in 'Snowman Building Parts for Rico the Squirrel' to emphasise a similar stereotype. Rico the talking squirrel has just completed a combination Lassie/Mary Poppins reformation of a somewhat dysfunctional American family. Their teary-eyed, heartfelt farewells to him – seemingly straight out of a happy Hollywood ending – are interspersed with scenes from a television show, The Skatch Femilee Rabirtsin, that reveal sexual and emotional depravity, physical abuse, and squalor in a Scottish working-class home. When a happy American boy hopes that Rico or one of his squirrel friends will help the Scottish children on the television and his mother assures him they will, Rico mutters 'don't hold your fuckin breath on that one honey'.[28] Although the American family was worth, and capable of, being saved, even the miraculous Rico acknowledges defeat in the face of the bleak and unchanging image of a Scottish working-class family that the show depicts.

Youth culture, drug culture, and the Scottish raves

The character role play that Welsh depicts in his works reflects a dichotomy of visions, both amusing and dark. A similar dichotomy appears in his accounts of the youth culture scene among the Scottish working class. Welsh notes that drugs are such an integral part of Scottish urban life that to leave them out of his stories would be disingenuous and false.[29] As a result, much of his fiction explores, even if peripherally, the role of drug use in the lives of his characters. On the one hand is the rave culture, characterised by Ecstasy and speed, dance clubs and characters almost overwhelmed by chemical-induced love and emotion. On the other hand is the heroin and cocaine culture, characterised by withdrawal, theft, AIDS, and deconstructed relationships. Through this discrepancy of rave and heroin culture, Welsh illustrates the two avenues of Scottish youth culture and the disparate impact a choice of one or the other may have.

The characters who embrace rave culture find that, despite the drawbacks, the lifestyle offers an initial freedom of experience that allows them to change dead-end lives and revel in a sense of self as well as a search for new direction and meaning. In 'Lorraine Goes to Livingston', for example, the shut-in, overweight, romance novelist Rebecca finds a way to cope with her discovery of her husband's embezzling and pornographic pursuits by shifting her attentions to Lorraine and the rave clubs Lorraine frequents. By the end of the story, she has become an independent, svelte young woman on the rave scene. Heather has a similar experience in 'The Undefeated' when she visits her university friend, Marie, for a weekend without her husband, Hugh. When she and Marie go to a club and take Ecstasy, Heather feels vibrant and alive. 'It was like I'd died and was moving through heaven,' she explains. 'All those beautiful people were smiling and looking like I was feeling. The thing was, they didn't look any different, you just saw the joy in them.'[30] These emotions contrast to her staid and dull life with Hugh, whom she now sees as a complacent and smug capitalist stooge. Her desire to have something more than this lifestyle is catalysed by her evening with Marie. Afterward, she quits her job, leaves Hugh, and enrols in a teaching course.

To a large extent drugs like Ecstasy, and to a lesser extent speed and acid, entail relatively mild comedowns and non-habit forming drug highs. As a result, characters such as Marie and Heather are often 'weekend ravers', abstaining during the week and holding regular employment, then partying at the weekend. The ability to lead relatively 'normal' lives offers more flexibility, as well as drug reactions that lend themselves toward feelings of community and support. In 'Lorraine Goes to Livingston', Glen watches the world around him with the same glow of optimism Heather experiences in 'The Undefeated':

> All the joy of love for everything good was in him, though he could see all the bad things in Britain; in fact this twentieth-century urban blues music defined and illustrated them more sharply than ever. Yet he wasn't scared and he wasn't down about it: he could see what needed to be done to get away from them. It was the party: he felt you had to party … it was the only way.[31]

This optimism acts as a temporary panacea for Roy in *Marabou Stork Nightmares* as well. After fleeing Edinburgh in guilt and fear about his participation in Kirstie's rape, he comes to Manchester where he finds acceptance in the local rave scene and eventually creates a life of work, weekend raving, friends, and a girlfriend. Although he succumbs to guilt after seeing public service posters and fliers advocating a new anti-sexual violence campaign, during his time in the Manchester rave scene he lives, for the first and only time, the relatively undisturbed and peaceful life he has always craved.

Yet Welsh offers the darker side of drug use, particularly heroin use, as well. The characters of *Trainspotting* move in and out of heroin use, occasionally quitting and suffering through withdrawal, but eventually returning to heroin. In the process, they resort to stealing, running public assistance scams to defraud the government and collecting additional unemployment benefits to fund their drug purchases. Renton and Spud, for example, are caught stealing books from a local bookstore, and Renton is constantly moving between Leith, London, and other towns to keep his unemployment claims viable and to escape suspicion from the authorities. When Renton needs something to ease his withdrawal, he endures Forrester's taunts and jibes in order to buy whatever Forrester has to offer. 'Ah'd walk oan ma hands and knees through broken gless fir a thousand miles tae use the cunt's shite as toothpaste and we baith know it,' he says.[32]

In addition, the heroin use takes an emotional toll by offering a means of escaping any painful emotions, allowing them to disengage from their environments. When Leslie's infant daughter, Dawn, dies of SIDS through neglect, the entire group, including Leslie, inject more heroin to blot out the experience. Heroin also becomes a substitute for love and sex – the preferred means of physical stimulus. 'That beats any meat injection … that beats any fuckin cock in the world', Ali exclaims.[33] The need to avoid withdrawal leads the characters to any action necessary for the next purchase, without regard for the consequences.

The heroin use also levies dramatic physical tolls as well. The withdrawal Sick Boy suffers through at the beginning of the novel has him retching and shaking as he drags himself to Swanney's to buy more. At another point, Renton's forced withdrawal at his parents' house generates hallucinations about Dawn's death as the infant, swollen and misshapen, screams accusingly at him. In addition, the heroin emaciates its users, causing loss of appetite and constipation. The primary risk heroin poses, though, is the ever-present spectre of HIV and AIDS. Matty dies alone of toxoplasmosis in his apartment, Davie becomes infected through a woman with whom Venters had sex, knowing he was HIV positive, and Julie leaves behind a now-orphaned, though HIV-free, infant. As a result of these effects of heroin, the users in *Trainspotting* seem to inhabit a nightmare world centred on the next fix.

Yet even the rave scene offers its own problems, as Welsh points out. When characters move from weekend raves to weekday drug use, they begin to lose perspective and become like Renton and the other heroin users in *Trainspotting*. Lloyd, in 'The Undefeated', is an unemployed drug dealer, acting as go-between for upper level dealers and spending most of his time using whatever non-injection drugs are available. Although Heather initially finds the rave experience freeing, she recognises that Lloyd's overcommitment to it will destroy both him and their relationship. She demands that he stop using if he wants to stay with her – a demand to which he acquiesces by the end of the story. Although Chris Mitchell sees this as 'a peculiarly conservative twist – that the natural high of love is better than a chemical one',[34] the ending offers Welsh's statement that the drugs of the rave culture – Ecstasy, acid, and speed, may be freeing in moderation, but are crippling in overuse.

Alan Freeman suggests that drugs in general offer Welsh's characters individual expression, but do so through a self-interested system in which there are, as Swanney, one of the drug-dealers in *Trainspotting*, suggests, 'nae friends in the game. Jist associates'.[35] At the same time, Freeman notes, this individuality is merely a façade for drug users who have become 'a product, a commodity bought and sold ... both consumer and consumed'.[36] This process occurs with both the heroin and the rave cultures. The overwhelming love and sense of community that occurs at the rave clubs breaks down individuality and autonomy so that people, such as Lloyd, Hazel, Amber, and Ally in 'The Undefeated', exchange themselves among one another with abandon, not caring who they are with or what they do with their bodies. Similarly, in 'Lorraine Goes to Livingston', Glen finds himself attracted initially to Lorraine, but after seeing her roommate, Yvonne, at a club through Ecstasy-clouded eyes, he decides he is in love with her at the same time she decides the same about him, although their attraction to each other is based entirely on the amplified sensations they feel because of the drugs.

This sort of easy substitution de-individualises characters, resulting in their almost puppet-like reactions to the stimuli around them. The DJs at the local clubs and at popular rave resort areas like Ibiza manipulate these emotions through music, bringing the crowds to a frenzy of dancing and then allowing them to cycle down before bringing them up again. In 'Lorraine Goes to Livingston', Glen reacts to the music from the club after his Ecstasy kicks in. 'The music, which he had had a resistance to, was getting into him from all sides, surging through his body in waves, defining his emotions', Welsh writes. 'Now he was going with it, his body bubbling and flowing in all ways to the roaring bass-lines and the tearing dub plates.'[37] Lloyd has a similar reaction in 'The Undefeated', noting that the 'music is in me around me and everywhere, it's just leaking from my body, this is the game this is the game and ah look around and we're all going phoah and our eyes are just big black pools of love and energy'.[38]

Music figures in Welsh's works as more than an illustration of the effects of Ecstasy. It creates a backdrop against which events unfold and to which characters relate, reflecting Welsh's own fascination with music. In *Trainspotting*, the titles of some of the sections echo some of the punk rock and early 1980s music. For example, 'London Crawling' plays on The Clash's 'London Calling', and a line from an Iggy Pop song, 'America takes drugs in psychic defense', is translated into the title, 'Scotland Takes Drugs in Psychic Defense'. In 'The Undefeated', Heather sees Hugh's humming Dire Straits' 'Money for Nothing' as indicative of his changed, and now pretentious and boring, character. Steve Redhead sees the use of 'house rhythms'[39] reflected in the narrative structure of Welsh's works, particularly the characters' dialogue. The short staccato speech of characters such as Renton as he rants against life outside of heroin has the urgency of a rave techno beat. 'Nae money, cannae git pished. Goat money, drinkin too much. Cannae git a burd, nae chance ay a ride. Git a burd, too much hassle, cannae breath withoot her gittin oan yir case.'[40] This use of music, Redhead suggests, further indicates the close ties between the youth culture music scene and the new literary modes for contemporary novelists, such as Welsh, that reflect the same youth culture.

Working-class culture

Despite this focus on the youth and rave cultures, though, Welsh sees his work as stemming from working-class culture more generally. Politically he has been linked with the New Labour party of the late 1990s and has been identified as part of the recent 'Britlit' movement, but Welsh's characters belie the success story New Labour tries to promote. At the same time, Welsh tries to avoid overt exploration of a socio-political betrayal of the urban working class. 'I kind of take all that as a given', he says. 'I'm more interested in what the "Thatcher's Children" generations of forty and under of the working class get up to – how they survive in the current economy and society.'[41]

Although Welsh offers bits and pieces of anti-English/anti-British sentiment, such sentiments are merely the backdrop, the assumed state of things, of his characters' lives. In 'Eurotrash', for example, Euan, recently recovered from heroin addiction, wanders around Amsterdam, finally landing in a bar with Richard and Chrissie. While discussing the historical ill-treatment of the Dutch, Richard accuses the British of colonial hatred and includes Euan in that 'you British'. Euan comments that he 'was almost tempted to go into a spiel about how I was Scottish, not British, and that the Scots were the last oppressed colony of the British Empire. I don't really believe it, though; the Scots oppress themselves by their obsession with the English which breeds negatives of hatred, fear, servility, contempt and dependency.'[42]

Similarly, Welsh rejects the politically active working-class figure as emblematic of the urban working class. In 'The Undefeated', Heather recognises her disillusions about her husband, Hugh, and her expectations of him during university. 'He was what I thought a rebel was: working-class, into student politics', she explains. 'What a lot of fucking non-sense.'[43] Instead, Hugh has moved up the corporate scale, transforming from 'First-rung-on-the-ladder Professional Employee Hugh' who is committed to 'defending and improving the services working people are entitled to' into 'Private Sector Manager Hugh' who is committed to 'maximising profit through cost efficiency, resource effectiveness and expanding into new markets'.[44] Although this transformation irritates Heather, what disturbs her more is his abandonment of previous beliefs and affiliations in order to more closely resemble the middle-class profile he aspires to achieve. During a political discussion with Heather's parents, for example, he talks about privatising some areas of the NHS, where previously during university he had been committed to socialist politics for working-class benefit. The final straw for Heather, though, is his change of football affiliations when he dismisses his previous team, Dunfermline, for the Glasgow Rangers. 'They know how to put a good corporate hospitality package together at Ibrox', he says. For Heather, this shift has 'done it. A man who changes his women you can forgive, but a man who changes his teams ... that shows a lack of character. That's a man who has lost all sight of things that are important in life. I couldn't ever be with someone like that.'[45] Disgusted, she finally leaves him.

Hugh's progression from working-class life into a middle-class business environment charts a social movement that causes anxiety and isolation in others of Welsh's characters, most notably Roy in *Marabou Stork Nightmares*. Part of Roy's disorientation concerns his eventual movement out of the estate, and the life it represents, with which he is so familiar. Gill Jamieson sees Welsh's writing as conflating issues of place – the geographical delineations of the run-down estates in which Welsh's characters live – and space – a negotiation of ideas about community and identity.[46] Roy remembers going with his friend into more affluent areas of the city, where the 'people in the big hooses, hooses that were the same size as our block, which sixty families lived in' would 'phone the polis' and have the boys removed from the neighbourhood.[47] These images of affluence contrast with the pretensions of class for which his family aims. The colour television, video recorder, and satellite dish that his father thinks makes them 'different from the rest of the families in the scheme, a cut above the others. Middle-class' are what Roy sees as defining them as 'prototype schemies' sucked into the delusion that conspicuous consumption breeds class.[48]

After his family moves temporarily to South Africa, he becomes interested in the better school system and achieves as a student, which allows him to train for a white-collar job as a computer program designer after the family returns to Scotland and to move to a better neighbourhood and out of the scheme. Yet his familial roots and his membership in a football casual gang bind him back to the scheme. This dichotomy of experiences leaves him in a cultural limbo, bound on the one side by the close affiliations with working-class family and friends, and on the other side by the new life he has created by his eventual move to Manchester into a white-collar environment. The working-class world, complete with its violence, culminating in Kirstie's rape, haunts him and leads to his eventual suicide attempt.

Even the fantasy world Roy constructs for himself during his coma becomes inextricably linked with his attachments to working-class Scotland. His 'Jamboland' evokes working-class Edinburgh, Jamieson notes, because Jambo is a slang Hiberian term for a Hearts supporter in football.[49] Kevin Williamson notes that Welsh's works offer fictionalised snippets of 'unofficial' Scottish history that has been 'written out' of the official history. In *Marabou Stork Nightmares*, for example, the football riot in which Roy participates in fact details the Hearts takeover of the Hiberians. Such events, Williamson points out, more deeply affect working-class people than the European summit meeting in Edinburgh in the late 1990s or even the instalment of the 1990s Scottish Parliament.[50]

This micro-revision of Scottish history reflects a larger tendency to localise working-class experience, as characters are often confined by the boundaries of education, economics, and the views of those around them. In 'A Smart Cunt', for example, Brian contemplates his own personality after being rebuffed by some of his friends and his family. In the process, he realises that he has only limited ways of describing himself. 'It seemed that drug-taking over the years had reduced me to the sum total of the negative and positive strokes I received from people; a big blank canvas others completed', he notes. 'Whenever I tried to find a broader sense of self the term: A SMART CUNT would come back to mind.'[51] Roy similarly finds himself haunted by his family history and the taunting he suffered in the scheme for his leg, mangled by the family dog, and his overlarge ears, which makes him lash out first at Caroline, a girl in his secondary school class who teases him, and then later Kirstie, who he thinks has sneered at his overtures. Such identity formation occurs in *Trainspotting* as well, when Begbie, who as a boy had earned the mock reputation among his friends as a 'hard man', has grown into someone who now believes those myths and embarks on increasingly sadistic and ill-tempered capers to reinforce that impression.

This need to appear ultra-masculine effectually breaks down communication among Welsh's characters. Women, for example, have difficulty relating to such men, and the men in turn fear being considered soft by spending too much time with them. Begbie, for example, resists the pregnant June's efforts to 'domesticate' him – to the point that he becomes angry when she asks him where he is going and begins hitting and kicking her in the groin and stomach. The grounds for communication among men are even more treacherous. Begbie's friends are careful to dance around him verbally, or try to divert his attention on a new target by reminding him of past situations when he bested them, all the while hoping not to become his next target themselves. Renton remembers when Begbie used to be 'lighter … before he started tae believe his ain, and it must be said, oor, propaganda aboot him bein a total psychopath'.[52] Begbie has become so enamoured of his own power that when Renton refuses to have a full breakfast because he does not want to eat the meat, Begbie tells him angrily that he has ruined the entire breakfast and threatens him.

Although Lloyd in 'The Undefeated' is on less dangerous terms with his friend Nukes, the two also have difficulty communicating at times. Nukes is willing to discuss some of Lloyd's emotional doubts and concerns, but does so in a way that preserves his sense of masculinity. In defining love, he comments that 'love is when ye want yir hole every night, but offay the same lassie'. When Lloyd objects that 'thir's some lassies that ye it yir hole offay, and there's others that ye make love tae. Ken what ah mean?' Nukes somewhat abashedly replies, 'Ah ken that, ah ken that … ah just use the expression "git yir hole" cause it's shorthand and sounds a bit less poofy, eh.'[53] Despite these attempts to discuss emotions, however, Lloyd recognises the boundaries of Nukes' willingness to endure such conversations. When Lloyd thinks about the intimacy he has with Heather and how it differs from other sexual relationships, he notes that this is the sort of discussion he wants to have with Nukes. But when Nukes arrives, Lloyd balks. 'Glad ye came ower, mate, thir was something ah wanted tae talk tae ye aboot,' he begins, but when Nukes asks what it is, Lloyd says 'ah jist wanted tae see if ye fancied comin up tae McDiarmid Park for the BP Youth games the moarn's night. Ally's taking the car, eh.' Nukes' response epitomises their inability to speak on the same level about women. As he asks 'you cowped that bird yit, Lloyd?' Lloyd comments that 'Ah like Nukes, ah lap the cunt up, but see the day? The day ah wish it wis Ally or Amber that had come around.'[54]

This need to appear masculine and tough appears in 'A Smart Cunt', where, although he has been hit in the face with a pint glass by an acknowledged hard man without any retaliation on his part, Brian's scar creates the impression of masculinity he craves. 'People would think I was a hard man', he notes with satisfaction. 'It's okay for Yul Brynner to say, in *The Magnificent Seven*: It's the guy that gave him the scars you have to worry about, he never drank in the Gunner, the shitein cunt.'[55]

Characters such as Begbie and Brian's friend Roxy are inured to the harm they create. At one point, Begbie throws a pint glass off a balcony into a pub in order to cause a barroom brawl. When Roxy and Brian inadvertently kill a blind man from the neighbourhood as they steal his wallet, Brian is racked by guilt while Roxy not only is unfazed, but finds the man's grave and urinates on it. The prevalence of such characters in Welsh's novels and short stories both recognises and attacks such images of working-class culture, exposing at once the danger and the pettiness of such claims to masculinity.

Welsh prefers characters who have these extreme 'guy-in-the-pub' views and who are not empathetic figures because they challenge his writing and make his readers question the assumptions about the urban working class that he presents.[56] In *Filth*, he offers Bruce, a violently bigoted and misogynistic policeman who does cocaine, engages in sexual blackmail, hires prostitutes and sleeps with his friends' wives, and, we learn, commits a racially-motivated murder before finally committing suicide. 'I wanted to take somebody who was a real reactionary, respectable figure doing the things that most authoritarian personalities do subconsciously, using his power in that organisation, very nakedly', Welsh explains. Bruce's actions cover for a 'spoiled idealism' about the role of such people and the society that mis-forms them when 'things should and can be better'.[57] The pervasiveness of such attitudes create almost brutish men so thickly protected from emotional expressions other than anger and arrogance that they verge on the caricaturistic and the ridiculous, in the process exposing the meaninglessness of 'hard man' models.

In 'A Fault On the Line', for example, Welsh over-embodies his main character with such characteristics. The speaker laments his wife's train accident, in which both of her legs were amputated, but only because it means he cannot watch the football game at home with his beer. Eventually he calls for an ambulance at the station only because 'ah gits tae thinking thit the ambulance'll maist likely huv tae go past oor bit oan its wey op tae the hoaspital n ah could bail oot n catch up wi her back up thair, eftir the game likes'.[58] In addition, he refuses to console his children, instead threatening them if they bother him too much with their worries about their mother. Although he wonders briefly if he is being too harsh with his son, he shrugs the momentary concern off, noting that 'ah goat it aw, the very fuckin same treatment fae ma auld man n it did me nae fuckin herm at aw ... ah'm livin proof thit it's the best wey'.[59] His reaction to the accident and his concerns about the game and his wife's ability to have sex without any legs is humorous, because it seems that no one could be so callous. At the same time, though, the images are disturbing because the speaker's treatment of his children and his willingness to abandon his wife are representative of the Scottish experience Welsh's writing recreates. That his son may grow into the same self-interested adult offers a bleak backdrop that echoes the game's relative unimportance – 'not anything tae write hame aboot ... another fuckin nil-nil draw but, eh'.[60] Such ultra-masculine attitudes lend themselves to violence both within the family and within the community.

The violent and the macabre

The tendency toward a hard man culture that dominates Welsh's writing leads to a series of violent images in most of his works. In *Trainspotting*, for example, such images range from Begbie's beating of a man in the street after seeing his drunken father making a fool of himself earlier in the evening, to Sick Boy shooting a dog and then throttling it after it turns on its owner in confused pain, to Davie arranging to look like Venter's son has been tortured and murdered, showing Venter photographs of the scene, then murdering him. In 'The Shooter', Gal convinces Jock to help him beat up a fellow thief who owes them money, but when they arrive, Gal shoots the man for sleeping with his wife while he was in jail. He then turns on Jock with the same accusation, pulling the trigger as the story ends. Roy, in *Marabou Stork Nightmares*, belongs to a gang of football casuals who cause riots at the football games. Similar images appear in 'Stoke Newington Blues', in which two drug-users are beaten by the police until they sign confessions stating that a black friend of theirs in custody is a drug kingpin, in return for some drugs and a release. In 'The House of John Deaf', John is beaten and his beloved pet mouse is crushed by one boy who finds out that John has been having sex with his sister and is angry that he will be teased by his friends about it.

Welsh also offers detailed images of the grotesque and macabre that stray from the run-of-the-mill pub fights, muggings, and other drug-induced mayhem, revealing a society fraught with uncertainty and danger. At one point in *Trainspotting*, for instance, a desperate Renton in withdrawal digs through his diarrhoea in a filthy public bathroom to retrieve the opium suppositories he has just lost. Earlier, a hungover

Davie, who has vomited, urinated, and defecated on the bed while passed out in his girlfriend's mother's house, wraps up the sheets to wash them at home. When he resists Mrs Houston's attempts to wrest the sheets from him so she can wash them herself, the sheets fly open, dousing all of them and the entire kitchen and breakfast table with their contents. In 'Snowman Building Parts for Rico the Squirrel', the image of the 'Skatch Femilee Rabirtsin' on the screen reveals a woman whose underwear is stained with a 'combination of a severe UTI and a non-specific sexual disease'.[61] Such detail also plays out in 'Lorraine Goes to Livingston' in the descriptions of the corpses Freddy molests in the morgue, and in the pornographic story Rebecca writes to retaliate against her husband. In 'A Smart Cunt', Brian and his friends abuse Ronnie's body while he is in a drug-stupor on the couch. They stick their erections in his ears and take photographs, cover him with food, and, as they get carried away, urine, vomit, and faeces, then leave him behind while they go to a club.

The prevalence of such images has given Welsh the reputation of a nightmarish writer concerned more with shock value than with por-traying working-class life as it really is.[62] Yet, these grotesqueries reveal the extremities of human behaviour, reminding us how uncomfortably close to life these events are and how close such 'underground' events run to an often too-inattentive surface. Welsh also reminds readers that the lives people lead are often fraught by the violent or the macabre, forcing individuals to cope or, more often, to bow out, as Roy does in *Marabou Stork Nightmares*.

Even the characters themselves find revealing some of their violent actions difficult. In 'A Smart Cunt', Brian explains that after Roxy has hit the blind man from behind so they could steal his wallet, Brian kicks snow in the man's face before running away. But at the end of the story, wracked with guilt, he reveals that he had kicked the man in the head and so may be the actual murderer. In *Marabou Stork Nightmares*, Roy's explanation of the gang-rape is that he pretended to rape Kirstie but did not have the heart to follow through. When Kirstie appears at the hospital to take her revenge, though, we learn that not only did Roy participate, but that he anally raped her in a particularly brutal way, and that he, not his friend Lexo, was responsible for instigating and planning the attack.

Troubled gender and homosexuality

Much of the violence and hostility that Welsh depicts occurs against women, much like Kirstie's gang-rape in *Marabou Stork Nightmares*. Jamieson sees Welsh's fiction, through these sequences, as depicting the female body with 'great violence and loathing'.[63] Male characters stare at women's bodies, criticising 'fat arses' and typing women they dislike as 'slags'. Many of the women are either portrayed as too grotesque for sex, like the 'Fat Sow' in *Trainspotting* who has 'INSERT COCK HERE' inked onto her inner thigh,[64] or appealing only because of sex, like Tommy's girlfriend, Lizzy. Most of Welsh's male characters are looking for a good 'ride' – although many of the women seek the same, too. In addition, women are either 'come-hither' sex fiends, who generally enjoy anal sex more than vaginal sex, much like their male partners seem to do, or victims who have been raped and therefore are frigid or have succumbed to emotional breakdowns as a result. Sometimes, women are a combination of both types of women, like Lucia in 'A Smart Cunt'. Although she is bloated and aggressive, French-kissing Brian and grabbing Roxy's crotch in front of her boyfriend, The PATH, her actions arouse him. As Brian and Roxy leave a bar, they see The PATH having sex with Lucia on the ground in an alleyway, rolling on the ground naked and hollering.

Yet many, if not most, of Welsh's female characters have suffered through rape and degradation. Donna, Davie's girlfriend in *Train-spotting*, has been raped and HIV-infected by Venters. In *Marabou Stork Nightmares*, Roy masturbates against a school-age Caroline and insti-gates Kirstie's gang-rape in retaliation for his perceived ridicule at their hands. Bruce forces a schoolgirl to give him fellatio in exchange for his promise not to report her drug use to her politician father in *Filth*. And Welsh's play, 'You'll Have Had Your Hole', concerns anal rape in a recording studio.

Welsh occasionally offers men like Dave in 'Fortune's Always Hiding', who resist such violence against women. He says he does not 'hold with hitting a Doris: not like my old man'. Although he is willing to do so on a robbery job because the rule is to hit whoever answers the door, 'punching a Doris ain't something I go for: not in a personal way like. I ain't saying it's really wrong cause I know some Dorises that deserve a fucking good slapping; all I'm saying is that their ain't no real satisfaction in it'.[65] Despite this seeming respect for women, though, he has no compunction about having violent sex with and verbally debasing his ex-wife, who he calls The Slag. In *Trainspotting*, Renton has a moment of realisation in which he recognises the severe gender inequity women suffer when he and Sick Boy conspire to play a phone prank on Kelly while she is tending bar. Sick Boy phones the bar, asking her to page 'Mark Hunt'. As Kelly yells 'ANYBODY SEEN MARK HUNT?' through the bar, the men all laugh, and one responds, 'naw, but ah'd like tae!' Only then does Kelly realise that her yelling 'Mark Hunt' has been, in Scots, 'ma cunt'. She 'feels like a caged animal in a zoo … the joke is on the woman again … the silly wee lassie behind the bar'.[66] When Renton notices her pained reaction, he at first has the 'knee-jerk thought: *Wrong time of the month*', then realises that the men's laughter is 'not funny laughter. It's lynch mob laughter'.[67]

Yet many of the men who gain similar inklings of how hostile the environment is for women become uncomfortable with the implications of that hostility. Euan of 'Stoke Newington Blues' listens to Ange talk about how she was gang-raped by a group of men who lure a woman from the clubs and 'use her like a fucking hanky for as long as they want'. Although he momentarily considers that 'to get close to understanding how it feels you have to think of about a dozen guys giving it Clapham Junction up your arsehole', he becomes unsettled by her talk of how the rape has killed her inside and is grateful that the hit of heroin shuts her up.[68] When Samantha in 'Fortune's Always Hiding' is with Dave, she comments that, with her lack of arms, she is nothing but a 'fuck toy' who can't fight him off.[69] Yet Dave becomes uneasy about the situation and about her talking about sex with him while they sit naked, very unlike his sexual encounters with The Slag. When she offers him the opportunity, 'I couldn't do nothing. I loved her and I wanted to look after her. I needed her to love me, not to talk like some fucking weird slut. I don't go for gels talking like that.'[70] Dave is disturbed by her sexual aggression and by her thirst for revenge – emotions he expects to see only in men.

Jeremy Gilbert argues that even though Welsh's fiction swarms with 'lads, hard-men, schemies and casuals', it usually endorses a 'feminist/ feminised' perspective in the end, often making men such as Dave uncomfortable.[71] In *Marabou Stork Nightmares*, for example, Roy, who has gang-raped Kirstie, in turn has his penis and testicles cut off and stuffed into his mouth before he is stabbed to death by a vengeful Kirstie. Kirstie, who has killed the other rapists already, has recovered from the rape and is now, Roy notes as he dies, 'beautiful. Thank God. Thank God she got it back. What we took.'[72]

In *Trainspotting*, Ali and Kelly, backed by a group of women that gather around them, fight back against some workmen who harass them.

'Have you goat a girlfriend?' Ali hollers. 'Ah doubt it, because yir a fat, ugly prick. Why no just go intae the toilet wi a dirty book and have sex wi the only person crazy enough tae touch ye – yirsel.' When he calls her a 'boot' and tells her to 'fuck off', she stands her ground, noting that once she opens her mouth she transforms from a 'doll' to a 'boot', but that does not change the fact that they are still ugly pricks. Kelly, too, finds the courage to fight back, retorting, when the workmen call them dykes, 'If aw guys wir as repulsive as you, ah'd be fuckin proud tae be a lesbian, son!' Two of the older women watching begin to comment on the exchange. One reprimanding the women for talking that way and using that language, and the other applauding them for handing the men back what they give. 'It's good tae see young lassies stickin up for thirsels. Wish it happened in ma day,' she comments.[73] Later, Hazel, sexually harassed by some men on whom she is waiting in a restaurant, takes her anger out on them through their food. She wrings out her used tampon in their soup, urinates in the wine and on the fish, and defecates in the chocolate sauce on their dessert. Such retaliation, though, comes only rarely for the women in Welsh's works. Instead, most of the women characters, like Begbie's June, suffer in silence and hope for the best. If Welsh offers the strong side of women fighting against the masculinist working-class society he portrays, he also presents the weakened position they hold in such a society.

Homosexuals occupy a similarly ambiguous position in Welsh's works. They are considered weak and unmanly – an antipathy that emerges not only in dialogue, in which various characters accuse each other of being 'poofs' or acting 'poofy' in order to insult their masculinity, but also in the way characters worry about how they are perceived, or about how their behaviour might transform them into homosexuals. In *Trainspotting*, for instance, Venter keeps a *Penthouse* in his hospice room, even though he is dying of AIDS, so that no one will think he contracted the disease through homosexual contact. In 'Fortune's Always Hiding', Dave, after kissing his young son hello, notes that 'I'll have to stop this kissing lark though, he's getting far too bleedin big for that. Could make him soft, that palaver could; even worse, turn him into one of them queer blouses you see hanging around. Ain't natural that.'[74]

This hostility toward homosexuals also translates into physical violence. Brian is beaten by a gang who remembers he was friends with Denise when he visits his childhood neighbourhood in 'A Smart Cunt'. 'If ye hing aboot wi poofs, that makes you a poof, that's the way ah see it,' one of the gang members says.[75] In 'Fortune's Always Hiding', Dave

finds Sturgess' latest gay prostitute and beats him as a warning to
Sturgess. Yet in the process of beating his head against the dashboard
Dave becomes excited, shouting that he's going to 'make your mouth all
nice and soft, just like a nice girl's privates, then I'm gonna get a proper
fucking suck'. The violence further arouses him, and he forces the man
into oral sex, after which, repulsed by his own arousal, he notes that 'for
what he's bleedin well made me do, I should fucking well kill him'.[76]

At the same time, though, Welsh offers homosexual characters and
encounters that display an increasingly tolerant departure from homo-
phobic norms. One such character is Denise, a mixed bag of homosexual
queen campiness and estate-raised hardness, in 'A Smart Cunt'. He out-
queens most homosexuals so that the 'gay punters' who frequent the gay-
friendly pubs and clubs hate him. At the same time, though, he drops
the camp when his authority, particularly among his young gay hangers-
on, is challenged. When one of them plays a jukebox song to which
Denise has claimed propriety, Denise breaks into the hard-man response
so typical of Welsh's characters. 'Batter yir fuckin cunt in, son!' he snarls,
causing his young follower to flee the pub.

Denise also flaunts his homosexuality, using it to brag about female
conquests in much the same way that his heterosexual friends do. While
having sex with one woman, he imagines the gay men he desires, and
then ridicules her for thinking she could possibly change his sexual
orientation. 'This daft hoor turn aroon n sais tae us: Tell ays that wisnae
somthin else, she goes, aw cocky like. Like she'd expected me tae throw
away the tub ay KY!' he says. 'Well, ah hud tae pit hur in the picture; ah
tells her it wisnae even as fuckin good as a bad wank, wi her ah hud tae
use ma imagination mair, tae pretend ah wis shaggin something worth-
while.'[77] By claiming to use women as his heterosexual friends do, Denise
aligns himself as masculine as they are, not as a feminine 'poof'.

At the same time, Brian, the main character of 'A Smart Cunt',
points out that although Denise appears soft but is actually a hard man,
many of the hard men he knows are actually 'big sensitive blouse[s]'. He
notes that 'the Scottish Hardman ladders his tights so he rips open the
face of a passer-by', or 'the Scottish Hardman chips a nail, so he head-
butts some poor fucker'.[78] By pointing out his respect for Denise and his
disdain for the stereotypical Scottish Hardman, Brian displays a relatively novel attitude toward gays, although this friendship with Denise
earns him a beating by others who are not nearly so progressive.[79] The
connection between Brian's tolerance and his social medium at large
remains tenuous at best.

Euan in 'Eurotrash' displays a similar tolerance for homosexuality. While in Amsterdam, he engages in a sexual relationship with Chrissie, who at once disgusts and attracts him. Chrissie's fascination with anal sex does not raise Euan's suspicions, although eventually he abandons her for a younger, more attractive woman. Yet after she commits suicide and he attends her funeral at Richard's prompting, he learns that she was a transsexual, having undergone numerous operations to become a woman. When he returns to see Richard after the event, he sits and talks with him about Chrissie's life instead of attacking him or getting angry. Instead, he recognises Richard and Chrissie as 'just people trying to get by'.[80]

Renton's homosexual encounter in *Trainspotting* also reveals the 'kinder, gentler' side of Welsh's characters. At first repulsed by Giovanni's advances in London, Renton becomes fond of the Italian man as the evening wears on. Although Christopher Whyte sees his comment that 'ah might end up whappin it up the wee cunt's choc-box yet' as reflective of Welsh's commitment to static images of Scottish men,[81] Strachan sees the comment as embracing the possibility of a homosexual identity, or at least the willingness to explore such a possibility. 'Within the social and sexual register of Welsh it is a perfectly acceptable comment, considering the manner in which characters talk about women they fancy, or indeed love,' Strachan notes.[82] That Renton has already had an oral sexual encounter with a gay man in London before suggests a sexual tolerance that even Brian lacks. However, Strachan points out, Renton's comment that such an action is possible in London 'because it isnae Leith' spells out the still-restrictive hyper-masculine society Scotland represents to Welsh's characters. Although Strachan sees such characters as Welsh's attempt to uproot his texts from a traditional Scottish disapproval of homosexuality, the fact that characters such as Denise must prove themselves hard to maintain their right to sexual expression reveals the deep roots such views have. Similarly, the resistance to women and the fear of being thought soft defines so many of Welsh's characters, despite Lloyd in 'The Undefeated'. Like Brian's desire to discuss sex with Nukes, but fear to do it, so much comes down to one's appearance in front of one's mates.

Notes

1 K. Williamson, 'Introducing Rebel Inc.', 1 June 2000, available at www.canongate.net/rebel/rip.taf?_n=6.
2 S. Redhead, 'Introduction: the repetitive beat generation – live', in S. Redhead (ed.), *Repetitive Beat Generation* (Edinburgh, Rebel Inc., 2000), xxv.
3 *Ibid.*, xxii.
4 S. Redhead, 'Post-punk junk: Irvine Welsh', in S. Redhead (ed.), *Repetitive Beat Generation* (Edinburgh, Rebel Inc., 2000), 139.
5 A. Freeman, 'Ghosts in sunny Leith: Irvine Welsh's *Trainspotting*', in S. Hagemann (ed.), *Studies in Scottish Fiction: 1945 to Present* (Frankfurt am Main, Peter Lang, 1996), 255.
6 S. Hagemann, 'Introduction', in S. Hagemann (ed.), *Studies in Scottish Fiction: 1945 to Present* (Frankfurt am Main, Peter Lang, 1996), 13.
7 I. Welsh, *Trainspotting* (New York, W. W. Norton & Company, Inc. [Martin Secker & Warburg Ltd., 1993], 1996), 159.
8 Hagemann, 'Introduction', 13.
9 I. Welsh, 'Fortune's Always Hiding', in *Ecstasy* (London, W. W. Norton & Company, Ltd. [Jonathan Cape Ltd., 1996], 1996), 87.
10 I. Welsh, 'The Two Philosophers', in *The Acid House* (London, W. W. Norton & Company, Ltd. [Jonathan Cape Ltd., 1994], 1995), 116.
11 *Ibid.*, 117.
12 W. Maley, 'You'll have had your theatre', 1 June 2000, available at www.spikemagazine.com/0199welshplay.htm.
13 I. Welsh, 'Lorraine Goes to Livingston', in *Ecstasy* (London, W.W. Norton & Company, Ltd. [Jonathan Cape Ltd., 1994], 1996), 20.
14 *Ibid.*, 23.
15 Welsh, *Trainspotting*, p. 83.
16 *Ibid.*, 342.
17 I. Welsh, *Marabou Stork Nightmares* (London, W. W. Norton & Company, Ltd. [1995], 1997), 123.
18 *Ibid.*, 56.
19 *Ibid.*, 5.
20 *Ibid.*, 8.
21 Welsh, 'Lorraine Goes to Livingston', 36.
22 Welsh, 'Where the Debris Meets the Sea', in *The Acid House* (London, W. W. Norton & Company, Ltd. [Jonathan Cape Ltd., 1994], 1995), 88.
23 *Ibid.*, 90.
24 Redhead, 'Post-punk junk', 138.
25 I. Welsh, 'The Granton Star Cause', in *The Acid House* (London, W. W. Norton & Company, Ltd. [Jonathan Cape Ltd., 1994], 1995), 129.
26 I. Welsh, 'Disnae Matter', in *The Acid House* (London, W. W. Norton & Company, Ltd. [Jonathan Cape Ltd., 1994], 1995), 119.

27 *Ibid.*
28 I. Welsh, 'Snowman Building Parts for Rico the Squirrel', in *The Acid House* (London, W. W. Norton & Company, Ltd. [Jonathan Cape Ltd., 1994], 1995), 144.
29 Redhead, 'Post-punk junk', 149.
30 I. Welsh, 'The Undefeated', in *Ecstasy* (London, W.W. Norton & Company, Ltd. [Jonathan Cape Ltd., 1994], 1996), 230.
31 Welsh, 'Lorraine Goes to Livingston', 26–7.
32 Welsh, *Trainspotting*, 20.
33 *Ibid.*, 9.
34 C. Mitchell, 'Love is a many splintered thing', 1 June 2000, available at www.spikemagazine.com/spikeecs.htm.
35 Welsh, *Trainspotting*, 6.
36 Freeman, 'Ghosts in sunny Leith', 258.
37 Welsh, 'Lorraine Goes to Livingston', 26.
38 Welsh, 'The Undefeated', 155.
39 Redhead, 'Introduction', xxvii.
40 Welsh, *Trainspotting*, 133.
41 Redhead, 'Post-punk junk', 142.
42 I. Welsh, 'Eurotrash', in *The Acid House* (London, W. W. Norton & Company, Ltd. [Jonathan Cape Ltd., 1994], 1995), 17.
43 Welsh, 'The Undefeated', 171.
44 *Ibid.*, 215–16.
45 *Ibid.*, 241.
46 G. Jamieson, 'Fixing the city: arterial and other spaces in Irvine Welsh's fiction', in G. Norquay and G. Smyth (eds), *Space and Place* (Liverpool, John Moores University Press, 1997), 217.
47 Welsh, *Marabou Stork Nightmares*, 26.
48 *Ibid.*, 27.
49 *Ibid.*, 221.
50 S. Redhead, 'Rebel rebel: Kevin Williamson', in S. Redhead (ed.), *Repetitive Beat Generation* (Edinburgh, Rebel Inc., 2000), 159.
51 Welsh, 'A Smart Cunt', in *The Acid House* (London, W. W. Norton & Company, Ltd. [Jonathan Cape Ltd., 1994], 1995), 250.
52 Welsh, *Trainspotting*, 88.
53 Welsh, 'The Undefeated', 259.
54 *Ibid.*, 268.
55 Welsh, 'A Smart Cunt', 235.
56 Redhead, 'Post-punk junk', 149.
57 *Ibid.*, 144.
58 I. Welsh, 'Fault On the Line', H. Ritchie (ed.), *New Scottish Writing* (London, Bloomsbury Publishing PLC, 1996), 51.
59 *Ibid.*, 53.
60 *Ibid.*, 54.
61 Welsh, 'Snowman Building Parts for Rico the Squirrel', 139.

62 G. Marshall, 'Dirty Work', 1 June 2000, available at www.spikemagazine.
    com/0399filth.htm.
63 Jamieson, 'Fixing the city', 224.
64 Welsh, *Trainspotting*, 21.
65 Welsh, 'Fortune's Always Hiding', 89.
66 Welsh, *Trainspotting*, p. 279.
67 *Ibid.*, 279.
68 I. Welsh, 'Stoke Newington Blues', in *The Acid House* (London, W. W.
    Norton & Company, Ltd. [Jonathan Cape Ltd., 1994], 1995), 34.
69 Welsh, 'Fortune's Always Hiding', 125.
70 *Ibid.*, 126.
71 Redhead, 'Introduction', xx.
72 Welsh, *Marabou Stork Nightmares*, 263–4.
73 Welsh, *Trainspotting*, 275.
74 Welsh, 'Fortune's Always Hiding', 93–4.
75 Welsh, 'A Smart Cunt', 287.
76 Welsh, 'Fortune's Always Hiding', 140.
77 Welsh, 'A Smart Cunt', 223.
78 *Ibid.*, 276.
79 Z. Strachan, 'Queerspotting', 1 June 2000, available at www.
    spikemagazine.com/0599queerspotting.htm.
80 Welsh, 'Eurotrash', 31.
81 C. Whyte, Introduction, *Gendering the Nation* (Edinburgh, Edinburgh
    University Press, 1995), xv.
82 Strachan, 'Queerspotting', n. pag.

2

Duncan McLean's Highlands

D. I. Y.

Duncan McLean began his writing career while acting in a stand-up comedy theatre group, the Merry Macs, that performed throughout Scotland in the mid-to-late 1980s. The group's material addressed an assortment of topics, ranging from party politics to social inequity. 'We were very politically motivated',[1] McLean explains. After the group broke up, McLean became a janitor in order to support his more serious attempts at writing. In the early 1990s, he began publishing the *Clocktower Press*, a fanzine akin to the football and music fanzines, published in slim booklets in a 'do-it-yourself vein', much as the later Rebel Inc. began.[2] 'We decided that glossy production and distribution in prestigious outlets was less important than getting our voices heard', McLean comments in his *Clocktower Press* anthology, *Ahead of Its Time*.[3] Yet McLean considers the fanzine simply a vehicle for good writing – for exposing new writers who then can become more established in publishing – rather than as a cultural icon. 'Most periodicals should be put out of their misery after three or four years', he explains, because the important issue is whether interesting work is coming out, not how long a literary magazine has been published.[4]

McLean sees his work as deeply influenced by music and his time in comedy theatre. 'For me it was the DIY ethos of punk', he explains, and 'the wonderfully scabrous, nihilistic monologues of Jerry Sadowitz'.[5] From his experiences with comedic street theatre, he learned that only 'the audience and the performer'[6] are necessary – a realisation that materialised not only in his bare-bones approach to the *Clocktower Press* publications, but also appears in his plays. In the theatre version of his novel, *Blackden*, for example, characters walk one at a time onto the bare stage and give monologues to explain their interactions with the mysteriously disappeared main character, Patrick. Although such a technique heightens the risk of losing the audience should the connection between actor and audience slip, it focuses the audience on the dialogue itself, forcing listeners to imaginatively flesh out the story they hear. It is this 'getting the edge' that McLean sees as instrumental to street busking and as the goal for which Brecht thought the theatre should strive.[7]

At the same time, growing up in the north-east of Scotland exposed him to the same landscapes and people Lewis Grassic Gibbon, a writer of rural Scottish life during the early twentieth century, explored in his trilogy of novels. Gibbon's rural subject matter was 'a place I knew',[8] McLean explains. Also, his exposure to Kelman's *The Busconductor Hines* offered a Scotland McLean recognised as 'the place I lived in right now'.[9] In addition, Gibbon's and Kelman's narrative innovations transformed these seemingly mundane and familiar places into literature-worthy material for McLean. Gibbon's simple yet striking integration of dialogue into the narrative by omitting quotation marks blends the authorial voice with the characters' voices. He similarly merges the two voices by writing the narrative framework to the dialogue in the cadence and phrasing of the characters' own language.

Such use of language greatly affected McLean, who sees himself as more of a rural writer, despite *Bucket of Tongues'* (his short story collection) focus on life in Aberdeen. 'It takes a while for a place to enter into your brain and soak into your bones, or the language going to the roots of your tongue', he explains. 'That's the most important thing: the rhythm of the language and the vocabulary.'[10] Kelman, too, focuses on the thoughts and speech of his characters, minimising the distance between character and authorial framework. Both writers create a closeness between reader and narrative that McLean sees in the street theatre's focus on the audience/performer relationship.

McLean's use of monologue accomplishes a similar task in theatrical works such as *Blackden*. In *One Sure Thing*, the stage adaptation of McLean's short story, 'Dying and Being Alive', only Keith appears on stage to relate a recent incident with his wife and children concerning his fear of death. This first-person monologue, McLean explains, offers a layering that teases out nuances in the story. 'You have the layer of immediate drama – the character standing and talking to you – then you have the once-removed layer – where the character acts out scenes from his memory or imagination', McLean comments. 'Switching back and forth between the two brings interesting contrasts, even contradictions.'[11]

While McLean finds Kelman's work with narrative structure and dialect intriguing and influential, he sees a disconnect between the urban and rural experience that characterise their respective writing. Kelman's work is 'based in the big cities. Glasgow is his place',[12] McLean notes. Yet McLean tries to do 'for the country what Kelman had done for Glasgow. To look at minutiae and every day [sic] life' and to 'convey the atmosphere of the Scottish countryside, and what it was like to grow up there'.[13] In addition, he wants to 'get away from the nostalgic and goofy images of bagpipes and get down to the actual reality of Scottish rural life'.[14] What motivates Scottish writers, he explains, is more often than not these untold stories of life perspectives they have to offer. Scottish writers explain their impetus to write as 'No one has written about my part of the country before. I want to make that voice heard', he suggests.[15] As a result, he focuses on the smaller rural communities, revealing the day-to-day lives through snapshots and vignettes of his characters' actions and conversations.

This difference is part and parcel of what McLean sees as instrumental in contemporary Scottish writing and what may be one of the only unifying forces in that writing. 'There is one thing that ties them all together', he explains, 'which is their adherence to their own voice, or the voice they grew up with. That is the voice that tells the story.' As a result, they all 'believe in the primacy of the spoken individual voice which is the basis of the story that they're telling'.[16]

McLean sees his work as exploring life in the places with which he is most familiar. 'I grew up in the country and spent all my life in the country', he comments. For example, the island of Orkney, where McLean lives, offers a different life perspective than urban locations do for writers. While Irvine Welsh splits his time between London, Amsterdam, and Edinburgh, spinning records at local clubs and writing about the rave culture, McLean notes that in Orkney, 'it doesn't matter if you're a writer. Nobody cares how you make a living. People just care about what type of person you are, whether you're good to your neighbours and friends, and how you treat the animals.'[17]

Hard men and urban apathies

While many of the short stories collected in *Bucket of Tongues* deal with city life, McLean notes that such stories arose from his few years in Aberdeen. The city life these stories explore lies in the shadow of the North Sea oil industry and is a far cry from the relatively sprawling cities of Edinburgh or Glasgow. As a result, his depictions of urban working-class life differ from the severe portraits Irvine Welsh paints, although he does explore some of the more negative ramifications poverty and urban living have on characters' emotional development.

Such violently negative depictions appear in stories such as 'Bod Is Dead', in which Buzby appears in front of his friends, including the narrator, announcing that he is going to kill Bod, another friend who at the moment is having sex with Buzby's mother. During this announcement, the narrator explains Buzby as 'quick to rouse, quick to freeze, he'd punch some bugger's lights out or give them a fucking hug depending on his mood'.[18] Despite knowing this, though, Buzby's friends merely mouth words of disbelief and 'spout shite like a man's got to do whatever the fuck' to further rile Buzby's temper, rather than diffuse the situation, not really believing he actually will do anything to Bod. They see his 'hard man' act as momentary and fleeting, not expecting his anger to last more than the few minutes it has in the past. So when Buzby leaves them to wait outside his apartment they joke about the situation rather than act concerned about what Buzby will do. Yet this refusal to act continues at the end of the story, when the narrator sees Buzby has been waiting for Bod in the dark. 'I think for a minute about going over and helping him kill Bod or stopping him killing Bod, but then I think, Fuck it fuck it fuck it, and head off home for my tea.'[19] The narrator's apathy and unwillingness to get involved may be troubling, but more disturbing is his indifference about the outcome of the incident. He is equally willing to kill or to protect a friend but for the interruption of teatime.

A similar indifference arises in the play *Singing Mrs Murphy*, later staged as *Rug Comes to Shuv*. A drunken Rug and Shuv argue about whether or not they are going to get Shuv's wife drunk and photograph Rug having sex with her unconscious body to provide proof in divorce court that she is both promiscuous and an alcoholic, and therefore not fit to have custody of their daughter. Although Rug's initial refusal results in a fight, by the end his indignation at the concept has transformed into indifference. When Shuv announces that Rug is going 'up my wife's cunt', Rug says, 'wherever'.[20] Both *Singing Mrs Murphy* and 'Bod Is Dead' offer characters whose sensibilities have been stunted by their experiences, resulting in apathy or indifference to the effect of their decisions on others.

The abusive relationship between Rug and Shuv and between Buzby and his mates that emerge in the stories also appears in the 'You Think I'm Thick but It's You that's the Cunt' section of the tryptich story 'Three Nasty Stories', in which the narrator lists out the outrages and indignities committed by his so-called mate. 'It's you that shoves shit through the doors of paki families, you that fucks on the bus, that spits on the necks of old dears in the post-office queue, smokes like a lum in the health centre waiting-room',[21] the narrator accuses. He complains about the money taken and used for drink, the disrespectful treatment of women, and the domineering approach to his own decision-making. Yet, as the diatribe continues, it becomes evident that the narrator's 'pal, mate friend mucker fellow-fenian drinking-partner bastard bosom-buddy chum cunt you cheating bastard you thieving fucker you the smart one the one with the suit the one with the job you cockeyed carrothaired spunktongued cunt' is absent,[22] suggesting the narrator would never muster the nerve to make such accusations to his friend's face for fear of retaliation.

Such images of these hard men, similar to Welsh's Begbie in *Trainspotting*, rarely appear in McLean's works, though, and when they do, the image often cannot withstand the realities facing the characters. In 'The Druids Shite It, Fail To Show', for example, Colin, the leader of the football casual gang, finds his authority questioned by some of the gang, who refuse to sacrifice their personal lives and relationships to his vision of manliness and commitment to the casuals. After they meet at a standing stone ring to revel in their successes at a recent football riot in Dundee, Colin demands that the youths give up their girlfriends so that the women do not interfere with the gang. When Billy begins to object, Colin pins him down on the sacrificial standing stone and threatens him. Yet instead of succumbing, Billy challenges Colin's motivation in isolating the gang from women, accusing him of sexual inadequacy. 'He's no chance of getting a ride for at least three years – I mean look at him, he's a scrotty wee runt – and *we've* all got to live like monks till *his* balls drop and he gives us the nod',[23] Billy comments. When he leaves, two other members leave with him, and although Colin reasserts his authority with the remaining four, suggesting that the three who left are too soft to belong to the gang anymore, he now presides over a diminished group.

Even the tenor of 'A/deen Soccer Thugs Kill All Visiting Fans' differs from the bald depictions of violence that characterise Welsh's soccer casuals in such works as *Marabou Stork Nightmares*. Instead, Davy has left his gang, married, and now works at an offshore oil drilling facility. When he visits with his younger brother, Frank, who has come up from Edinburgh to Aberdeen for a football match and a fight, he remembers his days as a casual with amusement – and with not a little apprehension for Frank, particularly when Frank reveals that the gangs have started using knives as well as fists. 'It's plain fucking daft man:

somebody could get killed! How can you go in and enjoy your fighting if you ken you might be killing somebody any minute?' Davy exclaims. He even draws on the classic adult line, announcing that fighting with knives could even 'tak[e] their eye out'. For Davy, being a casual, particularly in hindsight, was 'only a game' whereas for Frank it is 'something you *are*'.[24]

The distance between the lives Davy and Frank lead appears even greater when Davy's wife arrives and Frank tells her about the accidents on the oil rig Davy has been describing to him but has not told to her. Davy explodes at Frank, shouting, 'I wish you'd grow up and leave people in peace'.[25] Although an avid soccer casual only six years ago, Davy has moved away from the violent casual scene and instead has embraced married life and work.[26] Frank, however, considers his gang a brotherhood, even though the stakes have got higher with the addition of knives. The ominous newpaper-like title, announcing that local fans have killed all those who travelled to the game, suggests that Frank has transformed from casual to casualty.

Just getting by

McLean's depiction of these young working-class men does not always lean toward violence. In 'Cold Kebab Breakfast', for example, the narrator and his friends blow their Christmas bonuses on drink and take-aways, stumbling loudly through the streets and acting raucously in a taxicab, but their behaviour is comparatively mild, resulting only, the narrator tells us, in the usual morning hang-over. Instead of exploring working-class violence, McLean takes common themes of Scottish working-class life, such as unemployment, alcoholism, and poverty, and reveals how characters who do not succumb to the nasty, brutish, and short lives such difficulties often create, function on an everyday basis. Thus, he offers characters who struggle to muddle through, hand-to-mouth, and achieve some sort of short-term security and safety.

In 'When God Comes and Gathers His Jewels', for example, a young unmarried and unemployed couple return home from having their weekly pint at the local pub to find their dingy flat has been burgled. Their only possessions of value, a dozen cassette tapes and the gas canister to their space heater, have been stolen, and they are left without heat and have no money to purchase another gas canister. Yet the two of them try to find ways to make the best of the situation as they attempt to heat the space so they can sleep. When the glass hot water bottles Jackie tries to make fall off the counter and shatter, Robbie manages to stop her crying as he holds her. As they bury themselves uncomfortably under all of the coats and blankets they can find, Robbie comments that 'a fart at this stage of the game could be fatal',[27] lightening their moods. Despite the grim situation, they joke with each other affectionately, rather than avoiding the problem by lashing out at each other.

A similar situation confronts the unnamed young couple in 'Shoebox' when they have only black coffee and lentils left to eat on Sunday morning, with sixty pence and no unemployment money due to them until Tuesday. Although they resort to stealing, the boy spending that last bit of money on milk and a candy bar at the local grocery while the girl steals groceries behind the shopkeeper's back, they accept it as necessary to survive, stealing only what they need to last until Tuesday. With no other options available, they resign themselves to having become thieves.

Mr Angusson in 'Loaves and Fishes, Nah', engages in a similar scheme. With only thirty-seven pence and no prospect of unemployment benefits coming within the week, he sees a notice about a free food disbursement and rushes to the disbursement centre. As he moves through the queue and hands his unemployment card to various officials to get the food, he tries not to dwell on the degradation of his position. 'Take my card, take my whole life too, cause I can't help getting my lunch from you,' he thinks.[28] When he learns that he can rub out the date they have made on his card indicating he has already had a disbursement, he unashamedly catches a bus to the next food depot. Although he recognises his dishonesty, much like the couple in 'Shoebox', he feels he has been left with little choice. McLean's frank depiction neither condones nor condemns such behaviour, instead offering it simply for the reader to make his or her own assessment.

Unlike Welsh's scheming Renton, who makes a living from manipulating the unemployment system in *Trainspotting*, Angusson becomes dishonest only when pushed to the extreme. His inability to get unemployment benefits stems from his honest admittance of having had a few days work in the past week, rather than hiding his work from the unemployment office. Most of McLean's characters are trying to make a living and get by, as Angusson is, rather than dodge responsibility. In 'Quality Control', for example, Gary is hired through the unemployment centre to be a quality control manager of a skateboard factory that turns out to be a family-run cottage industry. Eager to do a good job, he assiduously checks each skateboard by standing on it, breaking most of them in the process. Yet he is fired almost immediately because the company owner realises that Gary actually *is* checking for quality, rather than simply packing the skateboards in crates to be shipped out.

McLean's workers are often used or cheated by their employers. In *Blackden*, for example, Shona works almost incessantly through the novel as a chef for the owner of the local pub, who has expanded the pub's service to include bar-suppers and has volunteered her to make stovies for the bar dance. In 'Headnip', a kitchen assistant who endures regular verbal abuse from the restaurant chef/owner and his wife quits after learning that the owners have been claiming a share of the tips for him from the waitresses every evening, but not giving him the money. At other times McLean's characters endure unsavoury work conditions because they have no other options beside unemployment. In 'Tongue', Dugald works as a butcher's assistant, cleaning the machines and the scraps of meat, and scrubbing down the tongue for the butcher to slice and pickle, under the scathing eye of his employer. Similarly, in 'Lucky to be Alive', the narrator remembers working in a meat-products factory and having to clean out the vats that held mince, holding his breath to avoid the smell of rotting flesh. Despite such indignities, though, these figures are more concerned with keeping their jobs and earning a living than defying their working conditions. McLean's characters are simply trying to get by.

Although some of McLean's characters hold steady, well-paying jobs, other events in their lives intrude to destroy their happiness or their security. Benny reminds the narrator of 'Lucky to be Alive' that they have 'a no bad life really, eh? I mean not working at some shitey job, nearly always plenty to drink: what more could you ask for?'[29] Yet the narrator, who has been on a drinking binge and vomiting blood for the past day, passes out in the pub and finds himself in the hospital, still vomiting up blood and unable to take advantage of the 'no bad life' he has.

McLean's play, *Julie Allardyce*, also offers, at least initially, a character who enjoys and feels empowered by her work. A technician on an oil rig, Julie works the remote-operated camera-mounted ROV that allows her to examine the rig underwater. 'This is where life gets worth living', she announces as she prepares to lower the ROV into the ocean.[30] The well-paying job also allows her to have 'everything! My job. My car. My flat'[31] as well as her engagement to a co-worker.

Yet as the play progresses we learn that she really wants to live and work on the family farm and is embittered towards her brother, who 'decided I'd have to bugger off away from our land and work at something else, only come back for an afternoon once a month and even then not be allowed to have a say in the running of the place'. And why, she asks? 'Just cause I was a quine and he was a loon.'[32] She also learns that her fiancé, David, is angry that Julie wants to stay on the rig and have him take a land job because she makes more money and has better job prospects than he does. 'You say these things now, but what's going to happen when you fall pregnant?' he asks. 'Will you still want to go back offshore after that? The ROV joystick in one hand and jiggling the pram in the other?'[33] As she and David begin to diverge from each other's life goals, she realises that she does not really love him. As a result, she begins to find her seemingly perfect life crumbling around her.

This disintegration hastens when David's hand is caught in the ROV cables and he is hauled into the air, echoing a disturbing dream Julie had earlier in the play about the ROV slicing her hand off at the wrist. When the supervisor, Grant, refuses to sacrifice some of the equipment to save David's hand, Julie ignores his orders and slices the cables even though it means losing her job. Although David sees this as a sacrifice of love, she points out to him that she would have done the same for anyone in his position and breaks their engagement. Stripped of job and fiancé, Julie turns back to her brother and arranges to live on a corner of the farm after all.

Violent insecurities

Grant's refusal to value David's hand over the drilling equipment illustrates one of the ways in which McLean explores the violent or the disturbing in his writing. Hints and undercurrents of the sinister occasionally bubble to the top of the narrative, as in his second novel, *Bunker Man*, *Rug Comes to Shuv*, or 'Three Nasty Stories', but often they simmer under the surface, as in 'Tongue'. Such elements suggest the uncertainty and insecurity most of McLean's characters face in what they see as an unsafe world.

This insecurity runs through *Bunker Man*, as Rob, a secondary school janitor, focuses the social and sexual anxiety he feels onto the Bunker Man, a mentally disturbed man who loiters on school grounds and squats in an abandoned WWII bunker abutting the ocean. Although Rob begins contented with his marriage and his job as a school janitor, his sense of well-being disintegrates as the novel progresses. He and his wife, Karen, have moved back to Karen's childhood town in north-east Scotland so she can accept a lucrative job with an oil company. Rob takes a job as janitor, but he feels his financial and social position are inferior to Karen's white-collar executive position because she earns twice as much as he does and because he feels estranged from her colleagues. This disparity surfaces most keenly at a dinner party with Karen's co-workers. When Andrea asks Rob what he teaches at the school, she is taken aback by his reply that he is a janitor. 'Oh. Andrea pulled a funny face of embarrassment. That must be interesting, she said. Alec snorted, trying to keep in a laugh.'[34] Later Rob castigates Karen for his feelings of inferiority. 'They all look down on me, you ken, they all think I'm a piece of shite cause I'm *just a jannie*.'[35] He also accuses her of scheming to unman him socially and financially. 'You can't just have a normal job, a make-some-cash-to-live-on job', he yells. 'You have to have a high-flying, impress-the-folks-and-neighbours job, a humiliate-the-husband job.'[36]

Rob's response is to find another sexual partner with whom he feels empowered in a way he does not with Karen. Sandra, a fourteen-year-old student at the school, offers such a relationship. Desperate for attention and affection, she allows Rob to dictate the terms of their sexual relationship, permitting him to enact sexual desires in a way that Karen, a very willing sexual partner, will not. Their encounters move from hurried and fumbled sex in the school lavatories after school hours to longer rendezvous on the deserted beaches.

Yet Sandra's sensuality and sexual permissiveness feed Rob's fears about Karen. He begins to think Sandra is dangerous to him and feels it 'essential to take control of the situation'.[37] Sandra's expressions of female sexuality represent Rob's potential inability to control, which in turn worries him about Karen and his ability to control her. Because he cannot dictate her career, he frets about managing her sexually. 'Karen could just be a bit too difficult at times: she had things on her mind he didn't know about, couldn't control',[38] he thinks. That Karen could be a 'dangerous' woman like Sandra consumes him. He becomes convinced she is having an affair with one of her co-workers, at one point rummaging through her clothing searching for the smell of another man's semen. Eventually he refuses sex with her to assert his own sexual control in the face of her supposed lack of control. 'I never ken where your mouth's been, or what's been in it',[39] he shouts at her. Sandra feeds this growing suspicion of Karen's activities, questioning him about Karen's job and the time she devotes to it. 'It's the oldest excuse in the book, isn't it?' she asks when Rob meets her during the school dinner hour. 'Working late! Like you're working over your dinner break!'[40]

Rob's reaction to the sexual and social threats he feels illustrates his feelings of inferiority, resulting in his need to lash out in order to re-establish himself in the sexual and economic foreground. Yet, as he struggles to regain control, his grasp of reality and the control he really possesses over his relationships and his job slips, resulting in increasingly bizarre behaviour. His accusations of Karen lead to accusations and sexual threats against her friend, Susan. 'She's a menace', he tells Karen. 'She's dangerous. A woman like that, living by herself there.'[41] He also begins to draft increasingly demented memos to the school dominie, suggesting, for example, that the school enact a drug redistribution program so that faculty and staff can gain access to the drugs Rob claims all the students are using. At a later point, he seizes the paint rollers Karen is using to repaint the living room and paints over the windows, claiming that securing the house as a bunker will give them secrecy and 'stop the evil bastards from spying on us'.[42]

Rob becomes increasingly paranoiac, feeling the world is hiding 'bad things going on' that are undermining his life and creating an unsafe environment for him.[43] 'None of this business with filth building up in the corners, piling up by skirting boards, gathering everywhere, deeper and fucking deeper till we're smothered in the fucking stuff', he tells Karen. 'Get it out in the open. Let's get a good clear look at it! Then *stamp it out*.'[44] Unable to fulfil the male roles of sexual and social dominance on which he was raised, he feels vulnerable to the women who have usurped his sense of masculinity. Only by asserting himself and re-establishing his importance, which he feels his job and Karen have diminished, does he feel he can create a safe space.[45]

Rob tries to elevate his sense of purpose and importance by catching and punishing the Bunker Man, who he increasingly sees as the root of his problems. After being warned by the dominie to keep an eye out for suspicious characters lurking around the school, he sees Bunker Man as a threatening figure both to the school and to himself. He wins the confidence of Bunker Man, bringing him food and speaking with him, learning about his habits so he can eventually get rid of him. As he tries to find a way to catch Bunker Man in an act that will allow him to take action against the man, this activity becomes entangled with his desire to reassert control in his life, to punish Karen for her supposed infidelity and her superior social position, and to punish Sandra for her sexual permissiveness.

In the process, Rob displaces his own sense of having been wronged onto Bunker Man, but enacts the repression and social deviance he sees Bunker Man as representing. Rob engages in increasingly invasive and aggressive sex with Sandra, pushing her compliancy to the limits. At one point he manipulates an unwitting Sandra into a position for anal intercourse, in which he violently engages, and then forces her to perform fellatio after the intercourse. Later, he inserts a flashlight into her vagina and watches the glow from her abdomen – a sight he finds so arousing that even though she protests and starts screaming, he violently rapes her in order to 'be really inside, in her skin, in control of her'.[46] Only when he tries to make her have sex with the Bunker Man does she finally refuse to see him.

Rob then turns to Karen, coaxing her into a rendezvous at the bunker where they had sex on their arrival. Having won Bunker Man's confidence and acted the pimp, telling Bunker Man he will procure a woman for him, he has Bunker Man waiting for Karen. Rob waits until Bunker Man has raped Karen before rushing in and killing him with a meat cleaver taken from the kitchen, but cannot hide his own excitement at watching his wife raped. The event arouses him to climax, enacting both his fears of her sexual activity with another man and his desire to see her disempowered and punished for making him feel inferior. At the same time, he re-establishes himself, in his own mind, as a masculine and powerful figure, coming to the rescue of his wife by killing her ravisher. Only such extreme measures, at great cost, allow Rob finally to feel secure.

A similar insecurity characterises *Rug Comes to Shuv*. As drunken Rug and Shuv argue about whether or not Rug will sleep with Shuv's unwilling wife, Lorraine, to facilitate Shuv's divorce plans, the conversation spirals through violence and violent sexual expressions. In turns Shuv calls his wife a 'slag' and then beats Rug when he suggests Lorraine is unattractive.[47] When Rug refuses to acquiesce, he insults Rug's sexual prowess, accusing him of being an 'arse bandit' or of over-masturbation rather than having an active heterosexual sex life.[48] 'Too much tugging, man, that's it', he tells Rug. 'You've rubbed and rubbed till you've rubbed it away.'[49] The men square off over sexual power, each boasting about his own potency and insulting the other's as a means of working themselves into enacting the plan Shuv has created. In turn, the men come to blows, establishing sexual power through fighting. Because Shuv emerges the winner, Rug acquiesces to his plan. In a prior version, *Singing Mrs Murphy*, Shuv forces Rug into a version of crying 'uncle', singing a sexually degrading song while Shuv, joining in, works himself into a frenzy and continues beating Rug, further establishing the link between physical and sexual prowess.

In addition, Shuv's worry that he will lose custody of his daughter to a woman with 'bad morals and that',[50] which prompts his scheme to drink his wife unconscious and then have Rug rape her, echoes Rob's idea that by setting up his wife's rape so he can kill Bunker Man, he is using the right means to achieve the proper ends. Yet Shuv so desires the security of having his daughter in his custody that he wants this plan to work, even though he has little, if anything, more to offer her than her mother does.

Such overt violence moves underground in stories such as 'Tongue', where the hints of violence work through characters' relationships but are not fully revealed. As Dugald struggles to learn his routine at the butcher's shop, he is harangued by Kenn, the butcher, who glares menacingly at him while slowly sharpening his knives. Only when he proves, by processing the raw beef tongue, that he is beginning to recognise and remember his tasks does he meet with Kenn's grudging approval. 'You ken it fine,' Kenn says. 'Good man.'[51]

Disconnections and isolations

Yet such approval comes rarely to McLean's characters. More often than not, they are plagued by loneliness and isolation, without meaningful connections to other individuals in their communities. For some of them, these disconnections and insecurities lead to, or stem from, paranoia and mental instability. In the third section of 'Three Nasty Stories', the insane narrator rants along the streets at the rush-hour crowds moving past him. From his first-person ravings, we see he is completely disconnected from the rest of the city by his delusions. Yet his greatest concern is that he seems invisible and inaudible to them. 'No cunt takes fuck all notice, no cunt looks or seems to listen', he says. 'Listen you fucking dirty bastards!'[52] The narrator resembles *Bunker Man*'s Rob, who cannot convince the people around him of the threats he sees.

'The Doubles' presents the same paranoia, as Peter, in the midst of a nervous breakdown, thinks first that an impostor has taken his wife's place, and then that everything in the house has been replaced by an exact replica, at once similar but horribly unfamiliar and threatening. Despite his wife's attempts to comfort him, he feels isolated and unsafe, shouting at the walls and staring fearfully out the window at the now-strange landscape. A similar emotional breakdown occurs in 'Dying and Being Alive', staged later as a monologue in *One Sure Thing* as Keith, obsessed with a fear of death and the aftermath, tells his young children that the 'one sure thing' in life is death. When his wife chastises him for scaring them, he becomes almost maniacal at the thought of being cremated or undergoing an autopsy, convinced that after death he will feel everything happening to his body as if he were still alive. Consumed by such fears, he is unable to do anything but watch the television for hours at a time, cut off from his family and from the outside social environment.

Such disconnective relationships appear in 'Doubled Up with Pain', too, as John regales his young son with amusing stories about how he met the boy's mother. Yet when the boy asks where she has gone, John's shrug and silence suggests she has left him because of his drinking. John's experience and story of his relationship to his son creates a situation in which the reader is asked to witness and assess the story John tells, recreating the relationship and inquiring about its demise. In this sense it resembles McLean's *I'd Rather Go Blind*, which consciously plays on the 'pseudo-therapeutic, genuinely-voyeuristic chat shows' on television,[53] revealing the tension McLean feels lies between art and reality. Such shows, criticised for staging the high drama that appears on them, are no different than Shakespearean dramas like *Macbeth*, he explains. 'Now we don't need soliloquies: you just sit your prince down in front of a TV camera, a baying audience, and a shamelessly probing host', he comments.[54]

Although these cathartic tell-alls purport to reconcile individuals who cannot connect, they do not solve anything, as the characters in *I'd Rather Go Blind* illustrate. Set with an arrangement of chairs lined up on stage, the play offers a young couple, Colin and Sally, Colin's mother Rene, and Sally's father Alec, discussing the problems in Colin's and Sally's marriage. As Sally reveals Colin's physical abuse of her and lambasts him for lying about it, Alec and Colin get into a physical tussle on stage, reminiscent of the *Jerry Springer Show*. When Rene tries to stand up for her son, she and Sally get into a similar fight, slapping at each other until separated. Like all good tell-all shows, additional secrets are revealed, such as Rene's and Alec's own affairs with each other. Yet, when Rene offers the reconciliation and apology that purport to be the goals of such conversation, the other characters turn on her for destroy-ing the melodrama, returning again to their name-calling, threats, and accusations.

Some of these personal alienations McLean offers not only involve a disconnection with individuals or existing social environments, but also reflect the changing communities that have characterised contemporary north-east Scotland. In 'After Guthrie's', for example, Carol and Ronny feel removed from the neighbourhood in which they used to live as they visit the newly gentrified local pub, now sleekly decorated and catering to a younger, more upscale clientele. Although Carol remembers feeling connected to the old square, 'happy not working, happy just sitting around smoking and talking, happy going out for a pint or two, in Guthrie's now and then',[55] she now feels as if the neighbourhood has passed her by, leaving her and Ronny in a worse position than they used to be. The old square is being renovated too, with 'scaffolding on most of the houses, and the noise of sandblasting'.[56] Their unfamiliarity with a neighbourhood they no longer recognise echoes their emotional estrangement from each other.

Revisiting rural Scotland

This renovation and gentrification of many areas in north-east Scotland stems from the economic impact of the North Sea oil industry. 'Everyone who lives within fifty miles of Aberdeen has their lives affected by the oil every day', McLean comments. 'I felt this particularly true of folk of my own age group … who have grown up alongside the industry, and whose notion of their identity is far less fixed and certain than that of their immediate ancestors.'[57] Douglas Gifford sees McLean as, in part, rejecting a 'vital and colourful interaction between Highland and Lowland histories' and instead noting the 'non-communities' that exist in present-day Scotland.[58] Yet McLean, for all of his lonely characters, offers glimmers of such communities in *Julie Allardyce* as characters wrestle with dual affiliations between the oil industry and rural agriculture.

In this sense, McLean sees a connection between his own work and that of Alan Warner because of the rural focus each of them uses in exploring contemporary Scottish life.[59] Like Warner, McLean aims at a 'kaleidoscope of experience' in *Julie Allardyce* to illustrate the 'bits of culture' that have come into north-east Scotland because of the oil. 'People born in all parts of the globe have settled there, and locals go off to work and live in the Middle East and Texas', he comments. 'Life in the north-east these days is fragmented'.[60] As a result, *Julie Allardyce* offers the audience different stage styles, ranging from 'naturalism, folktale-telling, stand-up comedy, Brechtian epic, *son-et-lumière*, bothy nicht',[61] to express the variety of experiences in the region due to the oil industry through the variety of theatrical mediums available to McLean as a writer.

In one scene, for example, all of the characters troop onstage beating on oil drums and petrol tins. During their beating, they provide Julie with a list of facts about north-east Scotland as farming country then switch sides and recite a list of facts supporting north-east Scotland as oil country. These litanies reveal the tension between the two at the same time that their cacophony displays the social upheaval, ill or good, that the oil industry has created. In another scene, Julie and her brother, Drew, sporadically fight as the scene progresses, becoming more and more serious with each fight, as Julie relates her experiences with her brother to David, who is entirely oblivious to the fight sequences.

Julie's own story offers a similar fracturing of experience as she both relishes her job on the offshore oil rigs, and longs to own and cultivate the family farm her brother now has. This split illustrates a larger social split between the rural agrarian and the rising technology and changing culture of Aberdeen and its surrounds due to the oil industry. Yet Julie's ultimate choice is not forced, as the final scene of the play explains. As Julie's best friend, Angela, marries Drew in front of all the characters, the characters split into their different factions, oil industry and agrarian. Yet Angela and Drew talk with each group, moving easily between them. Rather than a forced bifurcation, the oil industry appears to offer an additional choice to people who otherwise would have to choose agriculture or leave for one of the southern cities.

However, although Julie rejects the oil industry and moves back to the farmland, more often the movement *is* away from the rural areas into the cities. As the unnamed walker in 'Hours of Darkness' comes upon what he remembers as the large town of Haven o'Braidon, for instance, he notices only a small number of windows with lights on, much fewer than he remembered. As he walks through the streets, staring at the blackened windows, he realises that all of the buildings are boarded up and painted to look like windowpanes, concealing the vacancies within. One of the women he meets, Melanie, is anxious to leave the area. 'There's nothing here. It's a shitehole,' she says. 'I tell you, I'm just going to piss off from here completely, go to London or Glasgow or somewhere.'[62] David, in 'New Year', also wants to leave, remembering regretfully the town he and his parents have left to move to a small village. In town at New Year's, he recalls, all of the bells in the churches and clocktowers and all the ships in the harbour would sound to ring in the new year. In the village, however, there is only the lone church bell. He finds the village lonely and isolated, not like his life in town.

In *Blackden*, McLean most fully explores the permutations of rural life in north-east Scotland. *Blackden*'s central figure, eighteen-year-old Patrick, describes the village of Blackden as a motorcyclist's wall of death. 'If you didn't watch out you'd spend your whole life whizzing round and round the walls', he thinks. 'Going a hell of a speed, maybe, but never actually getting anywhere.'[63] From the theatrical rendition of *Blackden*, in which the various other characters from the story give monologues about their interactions with Patrick, it seems as if, by his mysterious disappearance, he might have gotten out of Blackden after all, as Stephen Dedalus flees Ireland in *A Portrait of the Artist as a Young Man*. McLean sees Patrick's story through the three-day course of the novel as very similar to Dedalus's experiences near the end of *A Portrait*, but also 'like an awful lot of people who grew up in the Scottish countryside'. Such people, McLean explains, 'fly off and try to make it somewhere else. Kids get fed up growing up in small places like that.'[64]

For Patrick, the small place offers only the same experiences – 'round and round to the same places, round and round with the same people'.[65] He is so eager to find new experiences that he half-believes Shona's tales about eavesdropping on a witch's ceremony at the old standing stones. Yet, as the theatrical version reveals, many of the other characters are satisfied with the life Blackden has to offer. Shona admits that Blackden is 'not New York. It's not even Aberfuckingdeen', but people can 'drink, shag, dance the Gay Gordons to your heart's content'. When she considers whether or not this is *living* rather than *existing*, 'a couple year ago I'd've said no, I would've been out of here!' she replies. 'Working at Altens, going to the parties, the raves ... But I don't ken: you get fed up of all that after a while. Well I did anyway.'[66] Brian, Patrick's childhood friend, feels the same way, rejecting the gentrification of the area by the influx of new oil money. He announces he would smash 'these incomer bastards' bungalows if I could. Coming in here, *changing* the place. Terrible.'[67] Even Patrick's employer, Bill, likes Blackden despite its drawbacks. 'Folks here think the cities are full of slums: I'll tell you, they've got nothing on the country around Blackden!' he exclaims. 'Up to your arse in mud and shite, rats running all over, sheep shaggers in the byre and New Age bastards shitting at the stone circle. Christ, I love the country life,'[68] he laughs.

Yet, despite Brian's disgust and Bill's laughing comments, Blackden has been changing, albeit painfully, in keeping with the increased oil money and commerce between north-east Scotland and the rest of the country. The transformation of the local pub into a more upscale restaurant and bar, for example, contrasts with the old bicycle, owned by first his grandfather and then his father, that Patrick rides around the town. The local bed and breakfast, offering a taste of country life, lives up to its promise when the proprietor shoots a rat scratching at the kitchen window, splattering its innards across the glass to the horror of the wealthy city woman inside who had been exclaiming happily, 'isn't nature wonderful?'[69] The Goodman croft, among the more ancient and backward that Bill describes, is purchased by a wealthy southern couple who plan to renovate it into a small country estate rather than a working farm.

Thus, McLean's vision of Blackden offers two versions of rural life. It appears to 'expose the dreary boredom of much of its life, and its evolution into the new ways of bar suppers, fast cars, television chat shows,'[70] and the gentrification of old crafting territories by wealthy Southerners. Yet, at the same time, it combines this 'social realism with hints of deeper and non-material possibilities' through the 'echoes of older ways of life' that arise in events such as the late-night curling match, Patrick's childhood relationship with his grandparents and their memories of an older, more traditional life, or the stovie dance.[71] At the curling match, for instance, teams made up of young and old players vie equally on the flooded and frozen tennis court as Patrick watches with his grandfather and listens to his stories about the techniques and the players. When Patrick brings dinner to his grandparents before going to the stovie dance, he settles down to listen to another of his grandfather's stories, even though it makes him late to meet his friends at the pub.

Gifford sees this combination of contemporary and traditional rural life as McLean's reinvention of Scottish traditions in a form that acknowledges social change but recognises their continuing relevance.[72] McLean considers *Blackden* a 'patchwork of stories, points of view, jokes, folktales, memories, family history, village history, to downright lies and shaggy dog stories'.[73] Even the spectre of the ancient Celts and Druids arise in Shona's story about seeing people cavorting in a paganistic cere-mony at the ancient standing stones in the woods. The novel offers an amalgam of experiences that reflects on the changing landscape of north-east Scotland, a combination of rural and modern, northern tradition and southern technological innovation and commercialism.

Texas travels

Despite McLean's focus on north-east Scottish life, however, his travelogue, *Lone Star Swing*, explores his search for western swing music and the legacy of Bob Wills and the Texas Playboys on a four-week tour through Texas. He offers pointedly humorous encounters with Texans who are ignorant of, or naïve about, his Scottishness, such as the woman and children to whom he recommends James Kelman as a writer to read when she offers him sympathy over the recent death of James Herriot, or the two black-leathered bikers who wish him a belated happy St Patrick's Day when they learn he is from Scotland. Yet his primary focus is the people and the music he encounters throughout the trip. He offers genealogies of various western swing bands as members peel off to join different groups, come back together, and peel off again into different combinations. His descriptions of the music illustrate his fascination with it, as he describes one performance in which 'the steel and sax riffed in unison before shooting off wildly in acute angles to the original melody, shattering the weel-kent tune into a thousand jagged fragmented notes ... before turning on a dime and – suddenly, casually, wondrously – bring all the pieces together again into a smooth seamless whole for the final unison chorus.'[74] The music lingers in his mind, as he takes 'an hour to walk the half-mile home' from the performance. 'I dawdled, I took detours, I danced with my shadow, and I stood motionless for minutes on end replaying all that wonderful music in my head one more time, before it started to fade.'[75]

Yet his travelogue offers links to his other works, despite the seemingly different subject of western swing music. Most of the areas through which McLean travels closely parallel the small rural communities that are the focus of his Scottish writing. He lists the population signs as he drives through: Turkey, 503; McLean, 849. As he passes through various small towns, he notices the ghost and near-ghost towns scattered around, many inhabited by older people. The young people 'all head off to the bright lights: Amarillo, Lubbock, Wichita Falls', one old woman tells him.[76]

The stories he collects from the various western swing old-timers in all their exaggeration, modesty, and revelation of secrets also reflect the sort of local lore he explores in *Blackden*, as Patrick collects stories from Shona and his grandparents during the three-day span of the novel. Cliff Kendrick reveals the time he and his brother, Bob Skyles, had to sue their father for a share of the proceeds from their concerts, for instance, and Walt Kleypas talks about playing the season at Sun Valley when Hemingway frequented the hunting resorts there.

Even the music McLean describes as western swing offers a kaleido-scopic spectrum, as do his depictions of contemporary north-east Scotland. The music is 'square dances, reels, and schottisches, stomps, rags and waltzes. It's strings, brass and lap steel guitars, jive-talking, yodelling and scatting', he says.[77] Such combinations break down what he sees as the atomisation of American culture. 'Music has become some-thing to separate people, to build walls between them', he says. 'I love the old stuff that brought people together, that knocked down the walls.'[78] To illustrate this musical collection, he rattles off a few of the recordings by Bob Skyles and his Skyrockets: 'The Arkansas Bazooka Swing', 'Sweet As Sugar Blues', 'Swat the Love Bug', 'The Fox Trot You Saved For Me', 'The Hill Billy Fiddler', 'Jive And Smile', 'Eskimo Nell', 'One More Drink And I'll Tell It All'.[79] The variety in western swing also allows him to defy the typing that he sees in classifications of Scottish identity. 'A lot of folk assume that, because I'm into western swing, I must be into all things western: they expect to find me down the local Cowboy Club in a tartan shirt, Doc Marten bootlace tie, and chaps my mum's run up from a pair of old curtains', he says. 'Liking James Kelman novels doesn't mean you have to like Harry Lauder and Walt Disney's *Greyfriar's Bobby* too, and liking Bob Wills doesn't mean I have to like *Rawhide* and George Bush, thank Christ.'[80] The process of discovering western swing illustrates the universality that resisting such identity typing offers, allowing the expansion of identity that McLean sees in contemporary north-east Scotland.

Notes

1 S. Redhead, 'Bunker man: Duncan McLean', in S. Redhead (ed.), *Repetitive Beat Generation* (Edinburgh, Rebel Inc., 2000), 102.
2 S. Redhead, 'Introduction: the repetitive beat generation – live', in S. Redhead (ed.), *Repetitive Beat Generation* (Edinburgh, Rebel Inc., 2000), xxiv.
3 *Ibid.*
4 Redhead, 'Bunker man', 108.
5 *Ibid.*, 103.
6 D. McLean, 'Introduction: getting an edge', in *Plays: I* (London, Methuen Publishing Limited, 1999), x.
7 *Ibid.*, ix–x.
8 Redhead, 'Bunker man', 104.

 9 *Ibid.*
10 A. Lawrence, 'Duncan McLean: Scottish writer', 11 July 2001, available at www.freewilliamsburg.com/still_fresh/mclean.htr
11 McLean, 'Getting an edge', xiv.
12 Lawrence, 'Duncan McLean: Scottish writer', n. pag.
13 *Ibid.*
14 *Ibid.*
15 *Ibid.*
16 *Ibid.*
17 *Ibid.*
18 D. McLean, 'Bod Is Dead', in *Bucket of Tongues* (London, W. W. Norton & Company Ltd., 1992), 80.
19 *Ibid.*, 85.
20 D. McLean, *Singing Mrs Murphy*, in H. Ritchie (ed.), *New Scottish Writing* (London, Bloomsbury Publishing PLC, 1996), 195.
21 D. McLean, 'Three Nasty Stories', in *Bucket of Tongues* (London, W. W. Norton & Company Ltd., 1992), 163.
22 *Ibid.*, 165.
23 D. McLean, 'The Druids Shite It, Fail to Show', in *Bucket of Tongues* (London, W. W. Norton & Company Ltd., 1992), 216.
24 D. McLean, 'A/deen Soccer Thugs Kill All Visiting Fans', in *Bucket of Tongues* (London, W. W. Norton & Company Ltd., 1992), 36.
25 *Ibid.*, 41.
26 In some ways, resembling Alex's decision at the end of the British publication of Anthony Burgess's *A Clockwork Orange*.
27 D. McLean, 'When God Comes and Gathers His Jewels', in *Bucket of Tongues* (London, W. W. Norton & Company Ltd., 1992), 14.
28 D. McLean, 'Loaves and Fishes, Nah', in *Bucket of Tongues* (London, W. W. Norton & Company Ltd., 1992), 193.
29 D. McLean, 'Lucky to be Alive', in *Bucket of Tongues* (London, W. W. Norton & Company Ltd., 1992), 244.
30 D. McLean, *Julie Allardyce*, in *Plays: I* (London, Methuen Publishing Limited, 1999), 8.
31 *Ibid.*, 21.
32 'Quine' means young woman and 'loon' means young man. *Ibid.*, 29.
33 McLean, *Julie Allardyce*, 45.
34 D. McLean, *Bunker Man* (London, W. W. Norton & Company, Inc. [Jonathan Cape Ltd., 1995], 1997), 38.
35 *Ibid.*, 183.
36 *Ibid.*, 246.
37 *Ibid.*, 128.
38 *Ibid.*, 91.
39 *Ibid.*, 146.
40 *Ibid.*, 152.
41 *Ibid.*, 247.

42 *Ibid.*, 248.

43 *Ibid.*, 247.

44 *Ibid.*, 245.

45 McLean explains that *Bunker Man* is 'essentially a 1990s reworking' of James Hogg's *Private Memoirs and Confessions of a Justified Sinner* where Rob, believing he is one of the 'saved' by his realisation of the evil the world tries to hide, feels vindicated in using whatever means necessary to achieve justice, even though it is clear to the reader and those around him that he is slipping into insanity. Redhead, 'Bunker man', 105.

46 McLean, *Bunker Man*, 281.

47 D. McLean, *Rug Comes to Shuv*, in *Plays: I* (London, Methuen Publishing Limited, 1999), 98.

48 *Ibid.*, 100.

49 *Ibid.*, 99.

50 *Ibid.*, 98.

51 D. McLean, 'Tongue', in *Bucket of Tongues* (London, W. W. Norton & Company Ltd., 1992), 237.

52 McLean, 'Three Nasty Stories', 172.

53 McLean, 'Getting an edge', xvii.

54 *Ibid.*, xviii.

55 McLean, 'After Guthrie's', in *Bucket of Tongues* (London, W. W. Norton & Company Ltd., 1992), 53.

56 *Ibid.*

57 McLean, 'Getting an edge', xii.

58 D. Gifford, 'Contemporary fiction I', in D. Gifford and D. McMillan (eds), *A History of Scottish Women's Writing* (Edinburgh, Edinburgh University Press, 1997), 595.

59 Redhead, 'Bunker man', 106.

60 McLean, 'Getting an edge', xiii.

61 *Ibid.*, xiii.

62 D. McLean, 'Hours of Darkness', in *Bucket of Tongues* (London, W. W. Norton & Company Ltd., 1992), 136.

63 D. McLean, *Blackden* (London, Martin Secker & Warburg Limited, 1994), 229.

64 Lawrence, 'Duncan McLean: Scottish writer', n. pag.

65 McLean, *Blackden*, 229.

66 McLean, *Blackden*, in *Plays: I* (London, Methuen Publishing Limited, 1999), 119.

67 *Ibid.*, 153.

68 *Ibid.*, 127.

69 *Ibid.*, 114.

70 D. Gifford, 'The return to mythology in modern Scottish fiction', in S. Hagemann (ed.), *Studies in Scottish Fiction: 1945 to Present* (Frankfurt am Main, Peter Lang GmbH, 1996), 48.

71 *Ibid.*
72 *Ibid.*, 49.
73   Lawrence, 'Duncan McLean: Scottish writer', n. pag.
74 D. McLean, *Lone Star Swing* (London, W. W. Norton & Company
     [Jonathan Cape, 1997], 1997), 255–6.
75 *Ibid.*, 256.
76 *Ibid.*, 304.
77 *Ibid.*, 3.
78 *Ibid.*, 177.
79 *Ibid.*, 99.
80 *Ibid.*, 138–9.

3

The Islands of
Alan Warner

Warner and counterculture

Alan Warner joined Irvine Welsh as one of the first writers to be involved with Kevin Williamson's Rebel Inc. When Rebel Inc. became an imprint of Canongate, more of his work appeared in Rebel Inc.'s first book project, *Children of Albion Rovers*, in 1996. The publication of *Morvern Callar*, Warner's first novel, associated him more closely with the 'youth culture' writers, described by Steven Redhead as the 'repetitive beat generation'.[1] *These Demented Lands* and *The Sopranos*, both of which join *Morvern Callar* in their use of music playlists and contemporary young adult issues, have consolidated this view of Warner as, like Welsh, a representative of a new pop culture/counterculture literary voice.

Yet Warner is wary of such classifications, particularly given his own writing background and the goals he has for his fiction. He does not see himself as a member of this counterculture movement, explaining that he is 'cautious about using myself as material' because he feels he is not an appropriate spokesperson for the movement.[2] However, Redhead notes, Warner's position, until the early 1990s, as a literary outsider, places him with other contemporary Scottish writers who similarly work against persisting notions of a literary canon. As Kevin Williamson explains in the imprint 'manifesto' for Rebel Inc., Warner has helped writers such as Welsh and Duncan McLean isolate the problems inherent in selecting British canonical works.[3] 'What does *Brideshead Revisited* mean to an unemployed single mother living in a damp run-down orbital housing estate south of Glasgow?' Warner asks. 'What does *Trainspotting* mean to a privately educated Hampshire man earning £180,000 per year?'[4] Warner recognises his own deep-seated feelings of externalisation as a young Scottish writer. 'The most contemporary Scottish book I'd read was Iain Crichton Smith's *Consider the Lilies*, which is a wonderful historical novel but it made my concept of a contemporary Scottish literature seem more distant', he confesses. 'What a sense of alienation! That has never left me. I can't express how completely I believed there was nobody alive in Scotland writing a book.'[5] Like Welsh, Warner exposes the lifestyle of figures rarely included in the literary canon, examining the impact of contemporary youth culture through characters such as Morvern and the five teenage girls in *The Sopranos*. In the process, he explores the implications of this culture for contemporary rural communities.

Rave and the pleasure principle

In *Morvern Callar*, Warner creates a character largely devoted to the party scene, both in the 'Port' in north-west Scotland and in the resort beaches of the Spanish Riviera. The inside jacket description of the novel calls Morvern a character who displays the 'vast internal emptiness of a generation' through the 'profound anomie of the rave scene'.[6] As the novel progresses, we see Morvern dispose of her suicidal boyfriend's body, submit and publish his book manuscript under her own name, and move to the Spanish Riviera with his inheritance. Although these actions, coolly and unregretfully committed, speak to the 'internal emptiness' the novel's dustjacket describes, the novel has gained most critical attention for its characterisation of the rave scene and its effects on youth culture.

Throughout the novel the twenty-one-year-old Morvern supplies us with a highly detailed, running commentary on her actions, including her beautification and clothing rituals, her sunbathing technique, and her party escapades. Her meticulousness in attending to and describing her daily routines while at the Spanish resort fill the hours until the nightly rave begins:

> I used the harder side of emery boards on my toenails and had to leave the cuticle remover on much longer. I fitted my toe-dividers in then applied basecoat, two coats colour and a top coat to protect. I used the same varnish as for fingernails: the bronze plum and fuschia.[7]

In addition, she provides us with a complete soundtrack for the Walkman she has semi-permanently attached to her ears, from the moment she receives the Walkman and leaves her boyfriend's body on the floor on her way to work, to her return five years later, walking penniless and pregnant along the snow-covered roads back to the Port.

The running soundtrack and Morvern's evident commitment to a music culture prepare the text for the rave life she pursues while living at the Spanish resort. For her, the recreational drug culture, so central to Welsh's characters in *The Acid House* and *Ecstasy*, is merely a peripheral contribution to her immersion in the raves. She dances for hours before buying a trip to sustain her through the remainder of the evening, concentrating instead on absorbing herself in the larger, animal organism of the rave party. 'You felt the side of a face lay against my bare back, between shoulder blades. It was still part of our dance', she explains. 'If the movement wasnt [sic] in rhythm it would have changed the meaning of the face sticking there in the sweat. You didnt [sic] really have your body as your own, it was part of the dance, the music, the rave.'[8] For Morvern, the rave experience fills her desires for a recreational lifestyle.

Rave culture figures similarly in Warner's sequel, *These Demented Lands*, which ends with Morvern's account of 'The Big One, DJ Cormorant's millennial' twenty-four hour rave party.[9] As Morvern moves through the crowd, she describes a cross-section of rave culture enthusiasts, including 'tribesters arriv[ing] in tents, stalls, caravans, portakabins',[10] and all of the characters she has met on her travels from one end of the island to the other. By the end of the novel her pregnancy comes full circle; conceived during the raves, her daughter is born just before millennium midnight.

Although Morvern loses her Walkman when the ferry sinks en route to the island, limiting her provision of a textual soundtrack, she includes potential music accompaniment in her narrative. When she first sees Aircrash Investigator crossing a hill ridge, for example, she suggests possible music selections. 'If you had to imagine the right music for the sight of him moving across the skylines it might be Stone Temple Pilots doing Big Empty offof [sic] The Crow soundtrack', she comments, 'or if you had to choose a Verve song you'd obviously go for something offof [sic] the first album, Slide Away would be best'.[11] For Morvern, the rave and music culture provides a socio-cultural structure lacking in her previously mundane life in the Port.[12]

The Sopranos, Warner's third novel, normalises this cultural phenomenon to a limited extent, presenting characters who do not abandon themselves to the rave culture in which Morvern immerses herself, but who do work within the 'pleasure' principle. Fionnula, Kayla, Chell, Orla, and Manda concern themselves with men, drinking, fashion, and music rather than with more long-term concerns such as employment, partnered relationships, and life goals. As in *Morvern Callar*, Warner provides the reader with detailed descriptions of characters' appearances and tastes. 'Remember', says Kylah,

Ah was going to bring the silver shirt, wear it three top buttons open and my light coloured stretch pants – those shiny ones that flare out at the feet, with the little pockets here and the side zips and with the black, strappyish sandals, tan toe-nail varnish, ma hair slicked back and glossed, with a parting, and tan eyeshadow, a totty wee sliver of silver cross top of the eyelids here, lighter on the bottom then a coat of black under that, mascara and dark colour lipliner, tan lipstick to go with ma nails an toes then a glisteny lipgloss on top?

Now, she continues, 'I'm no wearing that. I'm wearing ma hair down wi that Miss Selfridges denim skirt ah got fro the catalogue an the blue T-shirt, the one wi navy cuffs an collar the white sandally high heels, red lipstick, nail varnish.'[13] Such extensive details delineate many character-istics of the youth culture Warner presents. As Zoe Strachan notes, the details concerning characters from such writers as Welsh and Warner 'tend to be just right – they wear the right clothes, listen to the right music, go to the right clubs, take the right drugs, and so on – for people in their situations'.[14] In *The Sopranos*, the five girls take advantage of their trip to the city in order to indulge in the entertainment scene they feel is lacking in the Port, which does not even have the McDonalds they crave. In the process, Warner reveals the priorities of this youth culture, down to the bands Kylah favours with her 'adolescent ears, impatient ears'[15] and the clothing retail stores, such as French Connection and Schuh, that they prefer.

Yet Warner questions the validity of his novels as such easily categorised portraits of youth and rave culture or as 'guidebooks' to that culture. 'I think critics and some readers often confuse a reference to some aspects of "popular culture" as an endorsement of support for it; they assume it's being celebrated', Warner tells Redhead. '*Morvern Callar* came to be looked on by some people as a sort of lifestyle tract in nightlife culture', he continues, citing a woman who told a friend of his that she 'based her life on *Morvern Callar*'.[16] The problem with such assumptions, Warner explains, is the additional assumption that 'somehow the (politically reactionary or at best indifferent) clubculture' displayed in studies such as *Altered State* 'is *valid* history but everything else is not'. In reality, Warner claims, such a socio-cultural history represents only a 'small proportion of the British population' and 'is becoming as inward looking and self-referential as the worst bourgeois history of Great Men'.[17] As a result, he claims, 'popular music has become such a tool in the 1990s monopoly capitalism while an entire underground, experimental musical movement in orchestral and free

jazz is denied coverage'.[18] To illustrate his claim, Warner points to the
music he writes about in *Morvern Callar*. 'I wasn't just dropping a load of
fashionable song titles', he argues. 'The range of the music referred to
was very wide, dare I say "catholic"', ranging from Stravinsky, to Pablo
Casals, to James Blood. Yet nobody wanted to 'discuss that music, just
the "rave" connection'.[19]

In effect, Warner explains, the assumption that his work must be
'celebrating popular culture' stems from a disturbing 'critical faculty who
seem increasingly obsessed with that culture' when, in fact, his intent has
been to attack 'aspects of that culture'.[20] When reviewers create links
between, for example, *The Sopranos* and the Spice Girls or *Father Ted*
because *The Sopranos* involves five trend-conscious girls and a priest,
Warner announces, the result is a 'poverty-stricken' criticism that is
invested in telling 'the "people"' not to feel guilty about their pop culture
tastes.[21] 'It always seemed to me that my treatment of that so-called "rave
culture", especially in *These Demented Lands*, was pretty cynical', Warner
says. 'I think there is a clear mocking of the ephemerality of it.'[22] In
addition, the commitment to such a lifestyle results in a flattening of
experience – in the instant-gratification, soundbite, youth culture
Warner's novels present, characters such as Morvern move through life
events as though shellshocked, unable to register the lasting implications
of their situations. This flatness arises in Morvern's narrative when we
compare her technique for painting her toenails to her method for
disposing of her boyfriend's body.[23] 'What you do is divide the limbs and
wrap them in a good few layers of binliner and absorbent hessian sacking
bound again and again with strips of thick parcel tape', she informs us.
'You dont [sic] get difficulty with the head or limbs, it's the organs
pushing out from the torso sodden through with blood. The two torso
packages needed almost twice as much wrapping but I made a good job
of them.'[24] For Morvern, events cease to matter, including the foetus
with which she returns to the Port, and which, though she is pregnant
throughout, figures in the narrative only at the end of *These Demented
Lands*. For Warner, the import of the 'obsessive, prosaic catalogues' of
music he provides in *Morvern Callar* serve a '*dramatic* function', rather
than as cultural icons. Morvern listens 'not to *her* music but to the
favourite music of her dead boyfriend',[25] he explains. Her music choice
reveals the emotional insufficiency of rave culture as a substitute for 'real'
life – the depth of feeling lost in that 'vast internal emptiness' emerges
only in Morvern's music choices.

Gender typing

Although Warner has received acclaim as a male author writing through female characters, particularly the first-person narrative of *Morvern Callar*, his detailed accounts of material youth culture undermine some of this narrative progressiveness. Warner's depictions of these women reinforce many gender assumptions, such as the overwhelming concern with clothing and personal appearance. Morvern's obsessive finger- and toenail painting runs through *Movern Callar* and into *These Demented Lands*, in which one of her first acts is to scrounge nail varnish from the honeymooning wives at The Drome hotel so she can paint her toenails. In addition, her clothing choices reflect an intense concern with appearance – she dresses carefully to walk to work at the Superstore only to change immediately into uniform upon arrival. After work she changes yet again into club clothing that her friend Lanna supplies, the two of them changing and applying makeup in the wharf's unheated lavatory before appearing at the local bar. Such a concern about appearance places Morvern within a commonly perceived stereotype of female behaviour. Even at The Drome, she shortens the already mini-skirt the hotel's owner, Brotherhood, buys for her, despite the numerous warnings she has received about him on her travels across the island.

In *The Sopranos*, Warner takes this cosmetic concern to an extreme as the five girls pay an exhaustive amount of attention to their appearances during their day in the city. As soon as they escape from school choir rehearsals for the upcoming competition (their ostensible reason for being in the city at all), they head for McDonalds to change into more streetworthy clothing than their Catholic school uniforms.[26] Their devotion to this task assumes 'a businesslike, religious deliberation an sobriety', he writes. 'A ritual they each treated wi more reverence than ingestion of any transubstantial host; cause the vestiary metamorphosis was going bring [sic] about an immediate transformation that the body and blood of God's son never could'.[27] Such a fascination with clothing and personal appearance continues throughout the novel as the girls move from one escapade to another.

Warner taps into common stereotypes of Catholic schoolgirls, the assumption being that when let loose and given free reign, they run amok, engaging in all manner of illicit, and often lascivious, behaviour. Certainly the students of Our Lady of Perpetual Succour School for Girls conform to such expectations. While the other choir members shoplift at Woolworths and BHS, Orla, Fionnula, Kylah, Chell, and

Manda, in addition to the newcomer Kay, engage in more outrageous exploits. They all drink excessively, Kay so much so that she ends up in the hospital, and pick up a variety of men. At one point Chell and Manda return with two men to their flat, accompanied by another man they picked up, unbeknownst to them, in a brothel, while Kylah chaperones Orla's sexual exploits with another man at his flat.

Warner also accesses other common stereotypes in his development of these characters. In keeping with the concept of lascivious Catholic schoolgirls, we see the elevated pregnancy rates among the Our Lady of Perpetual Succour girls. While the town slang for the convent school is 'The Virgin Megastore', as Chell and Manda reveal to the men they pick up, there have been twenty-seven students pregnant 'since last September'.[28] In the development of these stereotypes, Warner limits his characters to proscribed social roles. The 'material girl', fun-loving, hair-brained characteristics the sopranos display offer little opportunity for personal growth or meaningful development. Instead, such roles seemingly reduce these women to a single common denominator, creating a conservative rather than a progressive narrative.

In the process, Warner reminds us of his own position as a male author writing through female bodies – a palimpsestic construction that only thinly veils the male gaze to which he subjects his characters and, as a result, his readers. As fellow writer Janice Galloway notes, male writers present 'male interpretations of women. Male visions … Alan Warner's women for example. Never done fiddling with their stockings'. While such a vision, she continues, does not 'invalidate what he's saying', it 'does remind you Alan's doing the observing'.[29] Galloway's comment illustrates a narrative construction that is as similarly binding as the female stereotypes Warner presents. The cinematic quality of his writing creates images of women as they often appear in film, subject, as Laura Mulvey explains, to the male gaze that dominates cinematic depictions of women. As a result, she says, the viewer/reader is also subject to this male gaze, seeing women as the male director/author sees them.[30] If in *These Demented Lands* Morvern's soundtrack suggestions for the first appearance of Aircrash Investigator create a cinematic image, then his depictions of her, when the narrative voice shifts from Morvern to him, create a similar impression. Yet the focus of each 'film' differs. Morvern's account presents characters and events, describing what occurs in detail reminiscent of *Morvern Callar*, but her vision, for example, gives us no sense of Brotherhood's or Aircrash Investigator's appearance. When Aircrash Investigator describes her arrival to dinner at The Drome, however, he focuses on her physical presence. 'Her arms were bare and tanned, she was wearing black Levi's but she disarmed that long-tight-jeans look by the neat battered boots she was wearing.'³¹ Later in the bar, he describes her in her mini-skirt as having legs that are 'like long splashes from a bucket'.³² Morvern's appearance becomes central to his account, giving us one of the few characters we can envision.

The interaction between Morvern and Lanna in *Morvern Callar* appears scripted as a soft-porn film. Lanna dresses and undresses Morvern, they shower together, bathe together, and engage in orgiastic sex with two male university students at a party. Such interaction leans toward the male girl-on-girl fantasy. In *The Sopranos*, Warner goes one step further and creates an overt lesbian relationship, which reaches its crisis point on the dance floor at the Mantrap when Kay and Fionnula dance together and kiss. In this 'scene', the two girls are surrounded by a predominantly male crowd, which moves in for a better view of the 'action'. As Strachan observes, 'in one sense Fionnula and Kay embody an exceptionally clichéd male fantasy – not only lesbian, but Catholic, and schoolgirls as well!'³³ Such representations confine these women to the same stereotyped roles that, as Chapter 6 explains, women writers such as Janice Galloway question.

Gender troubling

Yet in the process of creating these stereotypes, Warner posits subversive avenues for personal exploration that instead offer new pathways for gender construction. His presentation of women's sexuality, for example, while seemingly bound by the male gaze, provides new sexual options that evade the limited opportunities the Port offers. Although, as Strachan notes, the sensual/sexual encounters between Lanna and Morvern, Kay and Fionnula present male fantasy fulfilment, Warner moves in *The Sopranos* from such eroticised images to the potential of a relationship between Kay and Fionnula. Certainly Kay's previous lesbian experience is made safe by her participation in a male/female ménage à trois – her resulting pregnancy reassures the reader of her 'proper' sexual comport-ment during at least part of the experience (Morvern's ménage à quatre with Lanna and two male university students is even more reassuring, providing a proper boy/girl, boy/girl pairing that legitimises their orgiastic behaviour).³⁴ Yet Warner commits to an 'outing' of Fionnula and Kay that dissembles the male-oriented voyeuristic scene he creates between them on the dance floor. When the two girls reach Kay's room,

Fionnula replaces the male gawkers on the Mantrap dance floor as she watches a naked Kay playing the cello. The overt image of the two girls 'snogging' on the dance floor dissolves into the more sensually presented image of Kay embracing the cello. Warner subtly replaces a male viewer's gaze with Fionnula's through that image of Kay and the cello – the cello's hourglass (woman's) shape between Kay's legs both dispelling intimations of phallicism and prefiguring her impending sexual experience with Fionnula (who we assume will replace the cello between her legs). In addition, Warner's intensively detailed, descriptive narrative blurs when Fionnula and Kay eventually consummate their budding sexual relationship. Warner removes the male gaze entirely, refusing the pornographic fantasy by presenting their sexual experience in a sentence that speaks more to the *fact* of consummation than the *act* of it:

> Fionnula'd been disappointed then as they got ruder, way beyond the just snogging it got mentally good; you knew where it felt bestest till Kay had whispered, I'm aghosted and it's nice to do things in the morning too, and they'd laid near, fingers holding, all sodden with sweat from one atop the other, and close, sometimes murmuring things and halting sleepy sentences with kisses till Kay slept.[35]

At the same time that Warner re-visions the male sexual gaze, he reworks sexual categorisations. Kay's quickly uttered caveat to Catriona's (Manda's older sister) behaviour during the ménage à trois that 'Catriona isn't lesbian! Just that bit bi'[36] again makes her experience 'safe', and both Kay and Fionnula admit to liking sex with men as well (although Fionnula admits to liking women 'maybe more')[37] creates a bisexuality that is socially 'safer' than lesbianism. Yet Strachan sees Fionnula's lack of reference to herself with any sexual label, either bisexual or lesbian, as the potential in Warner's writing for disrupting convenient categories of sexuality that confine as much as the gender stereotypes he invokes. Strachan suggests such an elision could indicate a 'trend towards "sex without labels" which Andy Medhurst envisages or, [Roland Barthes's image of] "the arbitrary nature of sexual definition, the extent to which our sexualities are shaped by the larger social discourse"'.[38] Whether or not Warner intends such a sexual rewriting, his presentation of Fionnula's achieved sexual awareness presents alternatives to the restricted sexual roles the Port offers her. Given the options of tart or prude, Fionnula chooses neither.

Morvern Callar similarly overturns gender expectations, although Warner challenges the relationships available to Morvern rather than the sexual possibilities that face her. Initially, we see Morvern at the end of a six-year relationship after her live-in boyfriend has committed suicide.

When Morvern continually refers to him as 'He' and his possessions as 'His', Warner creates intimations of an uneven power relationship between the two characters (we never even learn 'His' name). And, as the novel progresses, we see that Morvern's actions suggest an escape from such a confining relationship structure. Instead of accepting the burden of unfulfilling relationships, such as she sees her friend Lanna and her stepfather, Red Hanna, do (and we assume she has done), Morvern chooses the anonymity of the rave culture after her relationship ends. At the resort, she can move from liaison to liaison, selecting and discarding partners. When she becomes pregnant, she maintains mobility – a break from a literary tradition that traps women in the household and within rigidly gendered family structures.

As the narrative continues in *These Demented Lands*, Morvern hides her pregnancy not from shame, but from a sense of autonomy as she challenges Brotherhood's sadistic chauvinism. By figuring herself as a sexually available woman, Morvern toys with Brotherhood and entices Aircrash Investigator, allowing herself a freedom she would be denied if she revealed her pregnancy too soon. When she does reveal her pregnancy, she realises the threat her body holds for Brotherhood, relying on his squeamishness to empower her. 'It's always fears about hygiene at the bottom of yous [men]', she announces scornfully, 'fear of the body'.[39] Morvern remains the only central woman character amidst a pantheon of men as the novel progresses – a men's club epitomised by 'Brotherhood', the owner of The Drome and the man of whom everyone else on the island is wary. Thus, when Morvern triumphs over Brotherhood, frustrating his lascivious intentions and blowing up his hotel, she asserts a rightful female presence on the island; a presence hinted at by her foster-mother's grave near The Drome and lent continuity by the birth of her daughter.

Emotionally attached to Aircrash Investigator, Morvern still avoids a traditional resolution to the relationship. Her story ends not with a marriage to legitimise both her and her daughter, but Aircrash Investigator's offer to 'hold your hair while you puke'.[40] Aircrash Investigator's intent, although crudely expressed, offers companionship and mutual support without the bonds of traditionally available female roles. She can be mother and lover and need not accept the role of mother and wife. Morvern represents a 'stark, unflinching' Scottish woman who breaks up gender expectations at the very moment that she seems to conform to comfortable stereotypes of feminine behaviour.

Remapping the Highlands and Islands

Through Morvern, Warner not only builds and razes gender constructs, but also provides the reader with a traveller who explores the new configuration of the Scottish Highlands and Islands. While the landscapes through which Morvern travels, particularly in *These Demented Lands*, echo the literary tradition that glorifies and rusticates the Highlands as a receptacle for traditional Scottish culture, they also present to the reader a 'weirding' of the landscape as socio-cultural and technological change infiltrate the environment. As Morvern travels across the island, she encounters a pantheon of characters that represent a 'new' cross-section of Highland and Island Scottishness.

Morvern's travels carry her through the traditional landscape of the Highlands and Islands – a strange and ruggedly beautiful collection of hills and rocky coastline. She moves from the harbour to the interior of the island, past the laird's castle and across the 'mysteriousness of mist banks, darkness, the lantern sky behind and gold embers of the islets strewn along the river with burn-out smoke rising in the cold dawning air, making the waterway look on fire'.[41] Yet the more recent trappings of contemporary technology and the spread of urban lifestyles into the previously isolated environment alter this traditional landscape as Morvern progresses. The roadway sign, pointing to the Outer Rim, the Inaccessible Point, and Far Places suggests that geographical and historical isolation; the scarcity of transportation prompts Morvern's three-day hike across the island. Yet the sign's arrow pointing to The Drome transplants an unfamiliar edifice to the island, balanced against the laird's castle. And, as Morvern begins her hike, we see that the castle itself has been transformed – fitted out with a miniature railroad, the Kongo Express, and an exotic animal zoo (from which animals occasionally escape, treating the island's residents to sights of grizzly bears and kangaroos being airlifted out of the hills and back to the zoo), belying the sign announcing 'historic castle'.

As she crosses The Interior, she finds the hills littered with Army rations dropped by the island's erratic helicopter pilot, causing the residents to dub the hills 'the land of milk and honey'.[42] Even Morvern's approach to the island indicates the changes she can expect in the landscape. As she swims ashore from the sinking ferry, she passes over The Phosphorous Beds, caused, the Harbour informs her, by 'hundreds of tons of phosphorous bombs' dumped there after World War II.[43] The changes in the landscape continue as Morvern crosses through such provocatively named places as the Hinterlands and the Mist Anvils. Her encounter with university students vainly trying to follow fifteenth-century Ordnance maps with a herd of cattle through the altered landscape further exemplifies the changes that have occurred.

The transformed landscape parallels the social changes that have occurred in the Highlands and Islands area. Morvern travels on the ferry with two television-aerial repairers, revealing that the island has been 'wired'. When she meets two men carrying their dead father's coffin to the shore for an illegal sea-burial, their conversation is repeatedly interrupted by the dead man's ringing cell phone. 'He asked to be buried with it ... he was very attached to it ... never out of his right hand', they tell her. The coffin itself is adorned with the matched license plates from the dead man's Jaguar, 'DAD 007'.[44] Later, Aircrash Investigator's foray to the Outer Rim Hotel and Bar reveals whelkers there for the Low Tide Festival, drinking, smoking marijuana, and dropping acid before using their 'DUCK amphibious vehicle ... purloined from the army' to continue collecting shellfish, 'so wasted they all think they're extras on Star Trek'.[45] All of this change culminates in DJ Cormorant's Millennium rave, for which all of the island's inhabitants and visitors from the mainland congregate at The Drome. In presenting Morvern's Highlands and Islands, Warner illustrates the reach of urban culture and its impact on areas of Scotland long considered reliquaries of traditional Scottish culture. The amalgam, he suggests, represents a hybrid of Scottish experiences.

Morvern's encounters with the inhabitants of the island also contribute to this impression. Douglas Gifford notes that the 'truth of Highland communities is that they are packed with absurdly and vividly nicknamed characters, often disillusioned refugees from cities and the south, and living grotesquely alternative lifestyles in curious conjunction – and even atonal harmony – with the relics of older and traditional Celtic civilisation.' The effect, he suggests, is a 'Mad Max post-modern nightmare to accentuate the reality of the New Highlands'.[46] Certainly the island's characters fit such a description. As the novel progresses we encounter such men as Devil's Advocate, a priest who assesses the canon-worthiness of would-be saints, Knifegrinder, a grizzled, misplaced Hell's Angel, Argonaut, a salvager and aspiring percussionist, and a cast of other unlikely named characters such as Superchicken, Nam the Dam, Halley's Comet, and High-Pheer-Eeon.

Such characters, and Morvern's interaction with them, illustrate Gifford's 'curious conjunction' not only in the events of the novel but also in the narrative itself. The combination of whelking and amphibious vehicles, or the 'historic castle' and its Kongo Express kiddie train, as well as the two men carrying their 'hip' father's coffin to the ocean, exemplify the cultural conflation Gifford suggests. In addition, Warner's narrative parallels such a conflation, the writing itself reflecting the cultural shift that has occurred. The naming of characters, for example, such as Aircrash Investigator, whom Morvern calls, on various occasions, 'The One Who Walked the Skylines of Dusk with Debris Held Aloft Above His Head', 'The Coated One Who Walked the Skylines', assumes a poetic quality – one that Morvern overturns when she eventually refers to Aircrash Investigator as 'The Debris Man', and 'The One Who ... etc ...', skipping attempts at lyricism and cutting to the chase. Morvern's language also plays between an archaic form and contemporary slang. When she meets Most Baldy and First Spoken carrying their father's coffin, she formally announces her intentions, stating, 'I cross the Interior to The Drome.'[47] Yet when asked questions she replies in the negative, 'nut'. This stylistic combination carries into the structure of the story as well.

Mythologising the Highlands and Islands experience

Warner circles around the events of the story, layering not only Celtic and Highland culture, but also Greek and Christian mythology. The names Argonaut and High-Pheer-Eeon (Hyperion) play on ancient Greek myths – the Argonauts being the group of heroes that accompanied Jason on his quest for the Golden Fleece and Hyperion being one of the Titans, sometimes thought to represent the sun. Yet the two characters in *These Demented Lands* are anything but heroic. Ironically, Argonaut is a narrative facilitator of Warner's Christian mythology. He transforms Aircrash Investigator into a Christ figure, lashing his arms across an airplane propeller and adding a jellyfish to represent the crown of thorns. He is also present at Morvern's delivery, one of the 'three wise kings' who 'follow[s] the light in the eastern sky, Nam the Dam hovering overhead'.[48] Finally, he implicates Morvern in the Catholic doctrine, telling her she is actually dead and in purgatory on the island.

Warner's use of Christian themes threads through the narrative. The presence of Devil's Advocate, for example, and the mutterings about Brotherhood being the 'Devil' play with larger issues of good and evil, while the birth of Morvern's child in a barn at the birth of the new millennium, accompanied by the three wise men, suggests a new Jesus Christ. Even subtle Christian references pervade the text. The ferry, for example, is named *Psalm 23*, and the burning phosphorous beds suggest hellfire and brimstone.

Yet Warner subverts this Christian tradition (a strong influence in traditional Highland life and literature) through his modernisation of the issues at stake. Devil's Advocate watches Brotherhood and The Drome not to assess miracles for sainthood, but to recover the pieces of spaceship Brotherhood has supposedly hidden on the grounds. Morvern's child, born in the back of a Volvo hatchback in the hayfilled garage, is a daughter, a female messiah of decidedly non-virgin birth (remember *Morvern Callar*), carried 'into Egypt'[49] from the island, the 'land of milk and honey', with her mother in a coffin used for serving chilli at the rave. Warner secularises common Christian themes, calling attention to the mutability of traditional concepts in the face of urbanisation.[50] By layering these narrative threads, Warner complicates easy assumptions about the Scottish Highlands, suggesting a constantly shifting socio-cultural landscape that adds to his blurring of traditional distinctions between urban and rural.[51]

Exploring socio-cultural conditions

In the process of travelling through these shifting Highlands and Islands, Morvern and the girls in *The Sopranos* experience and exhibit the socio-political conditions of north-western Scotland. Warner's characters illustrate the grim conditions that facilitate the self-indulgent youth culture's transport into narrowly scripted working-class lives – 'political realities, at least as far as I understand them in the Scottish Highlands', Warner says.[52] For instance, Morvern's job at the Superstore stocking shelves and Kaylah's life dream of working at the record counter of Woolworths offer the most opportunity for working-class women. In addition, the insular nature of small communities such as the Port mean more social constrictions, causing women to conform to social expectations with little opportunity for self-expression or alternative options. As Fionnula explains to the middle-class Kay, 'you have a bit of space' but 'someone would be sure an clipe on me' if she were discovered engaging in homosexual activity.

In *The Sopranos*, Warner illustrates the crippling effect working-class economic hardship has on the girls. When Kay suggests near the beginning of the novel that the pregnant Michelle might not want to come out with them for the evening, Fionnula reminds her of the difference between their economic situations. 'Staying in at night is just for folk who have nice, BIG houses that are comfortable to stay in, where ya can get a bit privacy', she snaps. 'In a wee house yer sat looked at the four walls or sat wi yer folks in the front room wi the telly blaring crap … it's a crippling feeling.'[53] Kay's inability to understand the cramped quarters not only of working-class housing but also of the working-class community characterises the rift between working-class and middle-class expectations. Kay, destined for university, moves in radically different social circles than the sopranos do.

This discrepancy between the haves and have-nots emerges in some of Warner's background vignettes of the sopranos, in which we see formative experiences or situations that define them. 'Manda Tassy. Can't afford heating on winter school mornings, she'd sleep in her shirt, a panty-liner keeping her knickers okay', Warner writes.[54] Manda and her father occupy the lowest working-class position, so financially strapped that they need to share the weekly bath, her father 'slip[ping] into his daughter's used bathwater, this poor Cleopatra, the creaminess created by two cups of powdered milk poured under the hot tap'.[55] Such experiences reinforce the social restrictions that chafe Warner's characters. We learn that Manda is becoming more disapproving of alternative behaviour, lashing out at Fionnula and her sister, Catriona, when she learns about their homosexual experimentation. Yet it is this same experimentation that Manda yearns for as well, and acquires only when she takes advantage of the opportunities for fun and excitement that so rarely appear.

As a result of such grim circumstances, Warner's characters retreat 'from hope into hedonism',[56] indulging when opportunities arise and refusing to consider the consequences that too closely parallel the grim lives they see before them regardless. Such an attitude toward freedom and capricious behaviour explains the numerous girls from Our Lady who leave pregnant, such as Michelle. The limited options available for the future colour their actions now, suggesting why the girls run amok when finally exposed to the liberal environment of the city. Such low expectations, personal and social, also reveal why potentially successful women such as Kylah cannot convert that potential into opportunity. When Kay asks Kylah how she can throw her talent away behind the record counter, Manda retorts, 'what good it is [sic] being talented in this dump? Who's interested in talent here?'[57] As a result of such reduced perspectives, Kylah spends her limited time in the city buying CDs and drinking in bars rather than pursuing a musical career and setting up auditions.

Morvern, too, realises the limitations her position in life imposes on her and breaks free at the first opportunity. At sixteen she chooses a long-term relationship with a thirty-four-year-old man in order to escape some of the consequences women such as Michelle suffer. Yet such a choice imposes its own restrictions. Morvern is doomed to 'a forty-hour week on slave wages for the rest of your life', her stepfather says. 'No big pleasures for the likes of us, eh?'[58] Thus, when her boyfriend commits suicide and leaves her some money, Morvern spends it all on a short resort trip for her and Lanna. A similar desire guides her when she learns that his father's inheritance has been signed over to her name. She ignores the possibility for future investments of the inheritance that will ensure a limited but comfortable income and instead uses it to fulfil desires she never thought possible to attain. 'At last, Time was the one thing I had been able to buy', she announces.[59] During her time at the resort (the end of the novel suggests four or five years), she goes sleepless for days, 'not wanting to miss a minute of the beautifulness of sunrises and sunsets'.[60] After a night of raving and swimming, she walks back to her apartment, thinking of how she 'hadnt [sic] slept for three days so I could know every minute of that happiness that I never even dared dream I had the right'.[61] For Morvern, the ability to indulge in what she thought would be unfulfilled dreams is worth returning to the Port penniless and pregnant. Such experiences reinforces Stephen's observation in *The Sopranos* that '*these chicks are damaged goods*' [empasis in original].[62] The combination of crippling socio-economic situations and elusive moments of small pleasure presents a picture of the contemporary Scottish Highlands in which, Fionnula argues, 'all gets swept under the carpet and politician folk can ignore it cause no one'll fight it'.[63]

Yet Warner offers images of redemption that counter such dire situations and propose means of bypassing the dourness that defines the Port and other similar locations. In the process, he suggests that the same spirit that encourages the instant gratification his characters seek also allows them to overcome the oppressive futures that face them. Morvern's defiant lighting of a Silk Cut at the end of *These Demented Lands*, reminiscent of her chain-smoking in *Morvern Callar*, announces to the reader her intention of continuing to follow the pleasure principle and to involve her daughter in such a life. Similarly, Orla, dying from a relapse of her cancer and telling no one until the very end of the novel, tries to enable her friends in their small pleasures, buying boots for Manda that she adores but cannot afford. She also recognises her opportunity to keep her friends from being expelled by using her illness as leverage. 'Imagine the scandal if they expelled me and I'll be gone in six month', she tells Fionnula.[64] Orla's recognition of her impending death allows her the sexual freedom previously denied her. She indulges much as Morvern does at the resort, recognising that the results of her actions will be inconsequential.

Finally, the image of Lord Bolivia in *The Sopranos* offers an unquenchable spirit to the reader. A foul-mouthed parrot brought back to Our Lady from a South American mission, Lord Bolivia escapes the convent only to be attacked by seagulls, stabbed and driven away, given up for dead. Yet he returns at the end of the novel, 'in red and emerald splendour', swooping down on the drug dealer's budgie cage in Stephen's care and flying away with it, 'across the bay towards the secret forest where all the escaped exotic birds dwell'.[65] With this image, Warner overturns the earlier defeat of Lord Bolivia's escape and transforms him into an agent of change. As a fairy tale symbol, he introduces the final chapter of the novel, in which the girls gather together again in an expression of undefeated solidarity, refusing to bow before the fate offered to them. For Warner, this sense of community that unites against socio-economic obstacles truly characterises the Highlands and Islands he describes. His youth culture is not the downtrodden city youth Welsh presents, but the ebullient resistance to such a position that characters such as Morvern exhibit.

Notes

1 S. Redhead, 'Introduction: the repetitive beat generation – live', in S. Redhead (ed.), *Repetitive Beat Generation* (Edinburgh, Rebel Inc., 2000), xvi.
2 *Ibid.*, xxvi.
3 K. Williamson, 'Introducing Rebel Inc.', 1 June 2000, available at www.canongate. net/rebel/rip.taf?_n=6.
4 K. Williamson, 'Kevin Williamson on the Classics', 1 June 2000, available at www.canongate.net/rebel/rip.taf?_n=7.
5 S. Redhead, 'Celtic trails: Alan Warner', in S. Redhead (ed.), *Repetitive Beat Generation* (Edinburgh, Rebel Inc., 2000), 130.
6 A. Warner, *Morvern Callar* (New York, Anchor Books, [1995] 1997).
7 *Ibid.*, 200.
8 *Ibid.*, 215.
9 A. Warner, *These Demented Lands* (London, Vintage, [1997] 1998), 202.
10 *Ibid.*, 202.
11 *Ibid.*, 56.
12 An issue this chapter will address.

13 A. Warner, *The Sopranos* (London, Jonathan Cape Ltd., 1998), 100–1.
14 Z. Strachan, 'Queerspotting', 1 June 2000, available at www.spikemagazine.
    com/0599queerspotting.htm.
15 Warner, *The Sopranos*, 58.
16 Redhead, 'Celtic trails', 131.
17 *Ibid.*, 128.
18 *Ibid.*, 129.
19 *Ibid.*, 132.
20 *Ibid.*
21 *Ibid.*
22 *Ibid.*, 131.
23 See the passage cited earlier in this chapter.
24 Warner, *Morvern Callar*, 86.
25 Redhead, 'Celtic trails', 132.
26 Although these uniforms have been shortened at the hem and
    embellished with coloured shoelaces for fashion suitability.
27 Warner, *The Sopranos*, 107.
28 *Ibid.*, 198.
29 C. March, 'Interview with Janice Galloway', *Edinburgh Review*, 101
    (1999), 94.
30 L. Mulvey, 'Visual pleasure and narrative cinema', *Screen* 16.3 (1975).
    Alasdair Gray also works with this concept of the male cinematic gaze
    in *1982, Janine*, invoking the masculine gaze then turning the construct
    upside down through his female characters' refusal to succumb to the
    sexual scenes he has scripted for them.
31 Warner, *These Demented Lands*, 103.
32 *Ibid.*, 113.
33 Strachan, 'Queerspotting', n. pag.
34 *Ibid.*, n. pag.
35 Warner, *The Sopranos*, 310–11. The image of Lord Boliva reflects
    Morvern's escape as well as Fionnula's intentions to leave the Port as
    soon as she leaves Our Lady.
36 *Ibid.*, 193.
37 *Ibid.*, 192.
38 Strachan, 'Queerspotting', n. pag.
39 Warner, *These Demented Lands*, 188.
40 *Ibid.*, 214.
41 *Ibid.*, 44.
42 *Ibid.*, 37.
43 *Ibid.*, 8.
44 *Ibid.*, 22–3.
45 *Ibid.*, 167.
46 D. Gifford, 'Ambiguities and ironies', *Books in Scotland* 62 (Summer
    1997), 4.
47 Warner, *These Demented Lands*, 20.

48 *Ibid.*, 212.
49 *Ibid.*, 215.
50 The catholic legitimisation of miracles receives similar treatment in *The Sopranos*. Father Ardlui conceives of a plan to bring economic prosperity to the Port by asking the sopranos (who refuse) to claim visions of the Virgin Mary and thus create a new pilgrimage site.
51 A theme in Duncan McLean's work as well.
52 Redhead, 'Celtic trails', 133.
53 Warner, *The Sopranos*, 67.
54 *Ibid.*, 91.
55 *Ibid.*, 90.
56 Redhead, 'Celtic trails', 133.
57 Warner, *The Sopranos*, 256.
58 Warner, *Morvern Callar*, 47.
59 *Ibid.*, 199.
60 *Ibid.*
61 *Ibid.*, 222.
62 Warner, *The Sopranos*, 309.
63 *Ibid.*, 273.
64 *Ibid.*, 317.
65 *Ibid.*, 312.

4

Iain Banks'
fiction factory

The science fiction writer(?)

Iain Banks, Robert Yates claims, occupies an 'unusual place in English letters. He is that elusive type – the hugely popular writer, working frequently in genre, who is also deemed serious'.[1] Banks' writing is, to some extent, schizoid – he writes 'mainstream' fiction under the name 'Iain Banks', but also writes science fiction (SF) under the name Iain M. Banks. While his work has become enormously popular, his position as a 'serious' writer often gives critics pause. 'Novels lacking that crucial middle initial are regularly lauded by the literary critics, novels with it are either ignored outside the SF field or curtly reviewed with grudging sufferance',[2] Stan Nicholls laments. Alan MacGillivray echoes this observation, noting wryly that critics of Banks' works follow the same patterns of commentary. 'The first decision ... has invariably been to ignore large areas of Iain Banks' science fiction and concentrate on what is rather dubiously called his "mainstream" fiction', he writes. 'The second decision has been to consider Banks primarily as the shock/horror writer of *The Wasp Factory* and to interpret later writing in the light of that sensational debut.'[3] While the enforced literary distinction between his mainstream and science fiction 'can be irksome at times',[4] Banks admits, it also offers assistance to his readers. 'Some people just don't like SciFi. And let's be clear, mine is SciFi with a capital S and a capital F, it's not Near Future', Banks says. 'It's got big space ships and everything.'[5]

Banks' science fiction ranges from creating planet-bound, seemingly medieval communities visited by more technologically advanced peoples travelling incognito, as in *Inversions*, to the self-described 'space operas' of the Culture novels, spanning galactic distances and focusing on the Culture – an effectively intermixed society of hedonistic, genetically enhanced, sex-changing people and the sentient, artificial intelligences (AIs) of drones and Minds (more powerful and quirky AIs who 'live' in and control the gigantic GSV ships and stationary Orbitals as well as military vessels). His mainstream fiction runs a gamut of topics: the post-apocalyptic, guerilla-controlled landscape of *A Song of Stone*; the financial connivings and investigations of high-level executives in *The Business*; the travels of young religious cult figurehead Isis through an unfamiliarly secular Britain in search of a wayward member in *Whit*; and the macabre musings of a sexually-disturbed adolescent in *The Wasp Factory*. Yet the bifurcation of these works at times appears artificial. 'Almost all of his 14 books, SF or not, share some degree of reliance on the fantastic', Oliver Morton notes. 'What divides the novels into two groups (besides the obvious M.) is not much more than the author's choice of literary reference points.'[6] In support, Morton cites American critic David E. Cortesi, who suggests that 'Banks uses the conventions of SF the way Robin Williams uses the voices and slogans of pop culture: you recognise his quotes and impressions, but they come so fast in such outrageous combinations that everything is new and fun again.'[7] Douglas Gifford affirms such an observation, calling Banks 'eclectic, protean, cross-generic'.[8]

Disrupting the genres and narrative manipulation

While Banks himself still feels 'like a SF writer who happens to write mainstream, rather than the other way around',[9] the distance between his SF and mainstream works is shorter than we might expect. Banks' writing in both genres blurs the distinctions between the two, creating the cross-generic works Gifford suggests.[10] Though Banks writes SF with 'big space ships and everything', he plays with the genre, changing commonly accepted forms to create those 'outrageous combinations'. In *Inversions*, for example, Banks overturns expected SF narrative models as the novel progresses. Although a Culture representative has acquired an influential position as the King's physician, protected by her AI (in the form of a dull and antiquated knife), the story concerns itself instead with the struggles for power on a technologically stilted planet within a recently de-Emperored Empire. The narrative itself shifts back and forth between two small Kingdoms carved out from the wreckage, illustrating the political tension between them and the bids for power that eventually collapse one of them. Similarly, in *Against a Dark Background*, Banks consciously constructs a world that has 'no real sense of a civilisation progressing in a lively way'. While there is 'a feeling that this society is gradually building up to something, something terrible', the outcome is not 'the usual "everything's going to completely change" scenario beloved of so many SF novels', Banks says. 'It will still be roughly the same society. By doing that, I was trying to act against what you normally expect to find in the genre."[11]

In many of Banks' SF novels, the outcome of the characters' actions has little, if any, impact on the direction of the local political system let alone the future of a society or a planet. 'I've read so many SF books where the action is terribly, terribly important to the fate of everyone and everything', Banks notes. 'Well, if you look at history, this is very unusual indeed. What usually happens is that people suffer and die and get involved in all sorts of mayhem and catastrophe and it doesn't make that much difference in the end."[12] As a result, the final scene of *Against A Dark Background* reveals merely that Sharrow, pursued by legally enabled religious assassins, escapes their attempts, holding the religious artefact she has been seeking and leaving behind a trail of dead bodies.

Such assertions work contrary to the idea of space opera, in which everything unravels on a grand scale. Instead, Banks constructs the backdrop for space operatic crises, but details characters' actions on a minor scale. Banks concedes this impetus behind *Consider Phlebas*, in which the main characters struggle with one another to find and claim a ship's Mind on a forbidden planet. Nearly all of the characters die, the Mind is collected and restored to the Culture, but the event, in the larger scope of a vast Culture-Idirian war, merits not even a footnote in the 'historical' annals of the war offered to the reader at the end of the novel. This disruption of expectations reveals, Alan Riach suggests, how Banks' novels 'frequently depend upon or obliquely comment on traditional genre fiction'.[13]

These narrative manipulations are not limited to his SF novels, however. Although Banks laments that 'there's far more freedom in science fiction' because 'with the mainstream stuff, there are fixed things you can't change, parameters that you're not allowed to step outside',[14] he does transfer some of the permissiveness of SF writing into his mainstream works, blurring the lines of fantasy and reality within a single cohesive narrative. This shading between his science fiction and his mainstream narratives allows him to edge past such parameters, playing with narrative form and linguistic convention in ways that slyly makes SF readers out of mainstream audiences.

Narrative form becomes a vehicle for this translation in his mainstream novel, *Walking on Glass*. Each of Parts One through Five contains three chapters; one chapter about Graham Park, an art student

passionately in love with sara ffitch, another chapter about Steven
Grout, a paranoiac who believes himself to be a prisoner in 'the final
confrontation of Good and Evil', watched and attacked by invisible laser
weaponry everywhere he goes, and a final chapter about Quiss and
Ajayi, two otherworld warriors banished to a crumbling tower, built
from books, to play interminable games of skill until they can answer
the riddle that will release them. Grout's conceptualisations of the
forces against him introduce the concept of alternate universes and
dimensions – a concept continued and broadened by Quiss and Ajayi,
whose wanderings through the tower reveal some of those alternate
dimensions.

In Part Five, Banks combines the narrative storylines, teasing the
reader by providing these alternatives as possibilities for interpreting the
events of the novel. Grout, involved in a near-fatal accident, is now
interred in a mental hospital, unable to remember his life before the
accident. As he sits outside at the asylum, we learn about the old man
and woman who sit in the hospital library and play games all day – very
much like Quiss and Ajayi. In addition, Grout finds a matchbook that
asks and answers the riddle question posed to Quiss and Ajayi. The
following chapter returns to the tower, where Quiss has destroyed the
game board in a fit of depression, leaving them with only one answer to
give for their escape. As he storms away, Ajayi returns to the books she
has been reading, starting one that begins with the phrase 'He walked
through the white corridors' – the opening sentence of *Walking on Glass*
itself. This narrative, layered much like the onion to which Banks
compares the Culture universe,[15] introduces fantastic elements that are as
much at home in his 'M' works as they are in his mainstream texts.
Although Banks 'can't take Fantasy seriously',[16] he does incorporate such
elements through manipulations of his characters' mental states. The
conflation of the realistic and the fantastic, Riach notes, 'fold[s] graphic
accounts of imaginary acts into vivid descriptions of a mundane world,
populated by trapped, lonely, or puzzled people'.[17] We can read Quiss,
Ajayi, and Grout as mentally impaired, allowing us entry into the fantasy
worlds they create.[18]

Linguistic manipulations and the realm of the fantastic

Banks also uses dream sequences as a means of developing such fantastic
or supernatural elements without requiring their presence in the 'real'
narrative itself. *The Bridge*, for example, another series of layered stories,

uses the construct of a comatose man in order to explore the alternate worlds of the Bridge itself. The layered accounts that Banks presents – the life story of middle-aged Alex, now in a car-accident induced coma, whose socio-economic rise parallels the social changes in Scotland from the 1960s through the 1990s; the life of a barbarian swordsman, cursed with a familiar perched on his shoulder, who blunders through and plunders various fortresses and the Underworld; and the search of an amnesiac patient, Orr, for clues to his past while living on a seemingly endless bridge – entangle one another, creating holes through which the reader can see the other incarnations of Alex's psyche as he struggles back to consciousness.

At various points on the bridge, for instance, Orr's television tunes into the grey image of a man in bed, attended by nurses and doctors. When he lifts his telephone receiver, he is greeted by the steady beep of a heart monitor. These slips in reality allow the reader to link him to his 'true-life' identity as Alex. Similarly, the barbarian's wanderings through the Underworld reflect Alex's comatose state (while the appearance of a Culture knife-missile, as in *Inversions*, breaks through from Banks' SF world). As the barbarian ages and is reborn, thanks to the familiar, in the body of a younger swordsman, Orr moves closer to recovering himself as Alex – the grey image on the screen suffuses with colour and he is left in a room that mirrors the one on the screen. 'My subconscious, I suspect, is trying to tell me something', he says as he dresses in a hospital gown and climbs into the bed provided. On awakening, he rejoins Alex, having fused the three identities into one.

The first person narrative of the barbarian swordsman in *The Bridge* also reveals Banks' play with language. The swordsman's dialogue is written in what some critics see as a crudely phonetic Scottish dialect:[19]

> I luv the ded, this old basturt sez to me when I wiz trying to get some innfurmashin out ov him. You fukin old pervirt I sez, getting a bit fed up by this time enyway, an slit his throate; ah asked you whare the fukin Sleepin Byootie woz, no whit kind a humpin you lyke. No, no, he sez, spluttering sumthin awfy and getting blud all ovir ma new curiearse, no he sez I sed Isle of the Dead; Isle of the Dead tahts whare yool find the Sleeping Beauty, but mind and watch out for the – then the basturt went and dyed on me. Fukin nerv, eh? Ah wiz ded upset but thare you go these things are scent to trie uz.[20]

The dialogue functions both as a piece of dark humour and as an illustration of the various levels of civilisation and social development Alex's comatose mind wanders through,[21] suggesting that the various

universes of Culture, fantasy, and 'reality' are internalised and inter-
changeable in the human mind.

Banks uses a similar linguistic play in *Feersum Endjinn*, another
tripartite novel in which one of the characters speaks in the same
phonetic Scottish dialect that Alex's barbarian does. In this novel, levels
of consciousness again become the focal point, although the construct
involves carefully and purposefully striated levels of consciousness rather
than the random personality splitting of a comatose state. Each person
exists both in the 'real' world and in The Crypt, a multi-layered storage
facility for all of the 'souls' of a future Earth's inhabitants. As Bascule
roams through The Crypt, we hear his frank and naïve dialogue much as
we hear the barbarian's in *The Bridge*. Bascule's mental simplicity allows
Banks to unravel events on a level that contrasts with the more intellect-
ually attuned narratives we read concurrent to Bascule's. In addition, as
in *The Bridge*, the phonetic narrative offers some comic relief as characters,
caught in situations beyond their understanding, struggle to make meaning of their shifting circumstances.

Banks offers similar linguistic play in *Excession*, another Culture
novel. Many short chapter segments involve dialogue only among the
Minds as they discuss ways to approach a potentially threatening space-
time phenomenon that has suddenly appeared in the galaxy. As the
drama unfolds, however, Mind names such as 'No More Mr Nice Guy',
'The Anticipation of a New Lover's Arrival', 'Serious Callers Only', 'No
Fixed Abode', and 'End in Tears' employ a humour similar to the use of
phonetic dialect in *Feersum Endjinn*. The twentieth-century phrases and
clichés (often from advertisements) illustrate the dichotomy between
such banalities and the immensely sophisticated technology that the
Minds display. Such names complement the casual 'talk' among the
Minds during their discussions, presented again in late twentieth-century
slang. When one of them asks if the Mind 'Wisdom Like Silence' should
be 'the agent of information release', another replies, 'Oh, witty. Well, if
it isn't in the huff'.[22] Such dialogue contrasts with the highly technical
and formal transmissions that also occur among Minds, such as the
initial message sent describing the excession (complete with parenthetical
code translations):

    xGCU Fate Amenable to Change
      oGSV *Ethics Gradient*
      & strictly as SC cleared:
    Excession notice @
    Constitutes formal All-ships Warning Level ø

[(in temporary sequestration) – textual note added by GSV *Wisdom Like Silence* @].

Excession.

Confirmed precedent-breach. Type K7^. True class nonestimal. Its status: Active. Aware. Contactiphile. Uninvasive sf {trans.: so far}. **LocStatre** {trans.: Locally Static with reference to}: **Esperi (star).**

First ComAtt {trans: CommunicationAttempt} **(its, following shear-by contact via my primary scanner @·) @· in M1-a16 & Galin II by tight beam, type 2A. PTA** {trans.: Permission to Approach) **& Handshake burst as appended, x@ 0.7Y** {trans.: (light) Year}. **Suspect signal gleaned from Z-E** {trans.: Setetic Elench} **/ laisaer ComBeam** {trans.: CommunicationBeam} **spread, 2nd Era. xContact callsigned "I." No other signals registered.**[23]

This dialogue illustrates the dichotomy between the two levels of communication. *Excession*, perhaps more so than Banks' other novels, explores in depth the technological dominance of the Culture Minds, describing the concept of hyperspace and the Minds' existence within it, and contrasting the decision-making autonomy of the Minds to the ignorance of the human population. As the narrative concerning the human participants unfolds, we see their relative unimportance to the larger concern at hand – their contribution to the investigation of the excession is negligible. Decisions occur at the Mind level, not the human.

Technological ambiguities

Banks often presents the ambiguous role of technology in both his SF and mainstream works. Technology offers power that can enable positive or negative results. At times, he indicates, such results become indistinguishable from one another. The Culture itself represents this ambiguity. It carefully protects its technology – limiting access to its citizens and preventing other civilisations from access, thereby preserving its technological superiority.[24] At the same time, it uses its superior technological presence to influence other civilisations it considers to have outdated governing systems, despite its professed dedication to autonomy and individualism. In *The Player of Games*, for instance, the Culture arranges the downfall of Azad's imperial structure, in which all governmental positions and social status are determined through gaming tournaments, by introducing its own player in the Game. The Culture, *Consider Phlebas* explains, employs the 'careful and benign use of "the technology of compassion"' in order to further its need to do 'good works to justify the relatively unworried, hedonistic life its population enjoyed'– relying on its Contact division to interfere with other cultures and 'overtly or covertly' guide their development along lines agreeable to the Culture.[25]

Horza, suspicious of the Culture's hypocrisy, sees the technological dependency of the Culture as a hegemonic threat. 'You want to know who the real representative of the Culture is on this planet?' he asks a government official of Sorpen. 'It's not her [the human Culture ambassador] … it's that powerful flesh-sliver she has following her everywhere, her knife missile. She might make the decisions, it might do what she tells it, but it's the real emissary. That's what the Culture's about: machines.'[26] Morton suggests that 'Banks' machines save us from ourselves. They remake society in their own perfectable image.' Yet a primary focus of his work is 'humanity's endurance in the context of such reality-transforming structures'[27] – humans remain an integral part of the Culture.

The power relations between man and technology play out not only in Banks' SF novels, but also in works such as *The Business* – one woman's account of her position in The Business, an ancient, world-wide conglomerate that acts nearly invisibly behind much of the world's commercial movement. As Kate Telman describes the history of The Business and takes us through the events of a few months, we see the way technology has both advanced and threatened the commercial structure of the conglomerate. It enables The Business to more quickly and easily share corporate files and collect/dispense information along the world-wide threads of its influence, but the complexity of the technology also means that individuals can create, use, and disassemble computer structures that allow corporate fraud as well as the accumulation of personal wealth and power beyond the boundaries allowed by the conglomerate. Kate, whose own contribution to the conglomerate has been her successful predictions about the booming information technology and Internet market, eventually rejects these technological accoutrements and opts instead to move to Thulahn, a small, impoverished, monarchic state in the Himalayas. While Kate turns her back on the high-speed world of Silicon Valley, she imagines bringing social improvements to Thulahn – hers is no retreat to the bucolic life. 'We can't escape what we are, which is a technological species', Banks argues. 'Technology is neither bad nor good, it's up to the user.'[28]

Religious disharmonies

This focus on the interactions between technology and humanity feeds into Banks' 'strong anti-religious attitude' – a sentiment evident in all of his works. 'Banks's scientific and technological leanings lead him to dismiss religion and beliefs in greater powers than the human and natural as superstition that can positively harm human health',[29] MacGillivray argues. Such a position appears in *The Business*, for example, when Kate explains that all executives 'must renounce all religious affiliations, the better to devote themselves to pursuing a life dedicated to Mammon'.[30] However, she notes, such a renunciation requires only that people be 'prepared to swear they've stopped believing' in order to 'weed out the real zealots' whose fervour might compromise their devotion to The Business.[31]

Religion becomes more of a contested issue in *The Crow Road*, a cross-generational story of Prentice McHoan's family. As we learn about Prentice's relationship with his father, we hear the bitter debates about religion that have separated them. An avowed atheist, Kenneth prides himself on having raised children who question their environment and make their own decisions. Yet, Prentice argues, his refusal to accept a belief in God or any sort of religious leanings makes him close-minded, although Kenneth claims that he does not want Prentice to have 'some doctrine thinking for you, even for comfort's sake'.[32] The rift between them remains irreconciled – Kenneth, in a drunken argument with his religious brother, Hamish, climbs the lightning-rod of the church during a thunderstorm and is struck by a wayward bolt, killing him.

Hamish's religious leanings have inspired him to create his own Christian 'heresy' based on afterlife punishment meted out according to the exact wrongs one has done to other people during his/her lifetime – what Prentice calls 'something dreamt up by a vindictive bureaucrat on acid while closely inspecting something Hieronymus Bosch painted on one of his bleak but imaginative days'.[33] When Kenneth dies, Hamish considers it to be God's punishment for his heresies, renouncing them for the strict scriptures of the church. Yet the novel has consistently presented Hamish as a ridiculous figure – Kenneth nicknames him The Tree – slow and deliberate, easily led, the opposite of Kenneth's own quick-witted mind. By offering the possibility of Kenneth having been punished for his atheism, and revealing that Hamish accepts such a reading of the event, Banks dissuades the reader, and Prentice, from thinking the same. On contemplating the series of deaths he has experienced,

Prentice realises that he does not believe in an afterlife. 'Death was change; it led to new chances, new vacancies, new niches and opportunities; it was not all loss', he says. 'It was only a sort of sad selfishness that demanded the continuation of the individual spirit in the vanity and frivolity of a heaven.' Such a belief would belie the value of human wisdom, which Prentice thinks of being 'beyond itself; in intelligence, knowledge and wit as concepts – wherever and by whoever expressed – not just in its own personal manifestation of those qualities'. Thus human wisdom is able to 'contemplate its own annihilation with equanimity, and suffer it with grace'.[34]

Banks also writes against proselytising, comparing it to imperial invasion in *Consider Phlebas*. The Culture chooses to fight against the Idirians, whose dogmatic religious beliefs lead them to conquer and forcibly convert other civilisations and races. He continues with this concept of dogmatism in *Against a Dark Background* in which Sharrow is legally hunted by a religious sect, the Huhsz, who need to sacrifice her in order for their Messiah to be born by the decamillennium. Other sects appear in the novel as well, as equally confining and overbearing as the Huhsz are. The Sea House, for example, acts as a dual prison/monastery. Scholars who use the House's library inappropriately, as Sharrow's half-sister does, are confined there until their relatives supply the necessary 'ransom', while the brothers, too, live in isolation. Banks suggests the mental imprisonment such religious institutions embody in his description of the House itself – a description at once grim and ludicrous. The dark and musty interiors of the house, extending multiple stories, are contained within rooms and corridors whose walls are engraved with a variety of grooved tracks. All denizens of the House are manacled and chained within these tracks – the closer to the inner workings of the sect, the nearer to the centre of the house one is tracked.

By using a literal confinement to suggest a mental one, Banks reveals his own feelings about the way religions and cults rise and prosper. 'The more sophisticated and complex society gets, the more choices you have to make and the more confused you can get', Banks suggests. 'Some people just throw up their hands in horror and escape, to a monastery or a nunnery or an army or whatever ... that's the appeal of cults.'[35] Certainly Sharrow's half-sister, Breyguhn, imprisoned in the House for stealing into the library to conduct research,[36] becomes susceptible to such influences, raving about the need for regaining universal supremacy as the decamillennium approaches.

Banks introduces the Solipsists, 'dedicated to self-fulfilment, union-

rate security provision, and – where possible – robbing the rich',[37] to illustrate the nonsensical reasoning he feels religion offers to its followers. Sharrow meets the Solipsists' leader, Elson Roa, who has 'realised that I always had been God. God in the monotheistic sense that I am all that really exists'. He explains the presence of all of his fellows as apparences who 'are the sign that my will is not yet strong enough to support my existence without extraneous help',[38] noting that they all call themselves 'God' as well except for one atheist apparence who calls himself 'me'. In effect, each Solipsist considers him- or herself God, explaining away the presence of the other members, and many elements of the outside world, as elements of their own creation present to test themselves or illustrate their progress. Roa considers Sharrow such an apparence. When she enquires if he is immortal, he asks, 'What do you think? I may have created you as a platform for part of just such an answer.'[39] Later in the novel, when Sharrow re-encounters him and asks after Keteo, a member of his team, he replies that Keteo 'appeared to become religious and join some decamillennialist faith. A section of my personality I am best rid of, I think.'[40]

This false reasoning and rationalisation allows the Huhsz to persist in their belief that Sharrow must be sacrificed. When others question the historical accuracy of the reason the sect gives for this conclusion, its leader announces, 'history is people and records and the human memory and therefore not infallible … *we* have divine guidance in this, which *is*.'[41] Banks presents these various sects to suggest the danger such blind-guided thinking offers both individually and socially. 'In a sense, *Against a Dark Background* uses weird faiths as symptomatic of the bigotry, calcification and imminent breakdown of our own society', he explains.[42]

Banks presents the harm an over-commitment to religion and mystic superstitions can cause in other novels as well. In *The Wasp Factory*, for example, the teenage Frank creates and relies on a complex spiritual system to protect himself and the island on which he and his father live. The system requires daily visits to the Sacrifice Poles, stakes planted along the perimeter of the island, dangling an assortment of small dead animals, in order to sprinkle them with urine, as well as visits to Old Saul, a dog's skull Frank has fashioned into a shrine to which he sacrifices other animal remains. Frank's self-perceived tenuous hold on the island can last only so long as he follows such important rituals. While some of his routines, such as the anointing of new slingshots with body fluids as a talisman, are relatively harmless, others of his duties achieve more alarming results. Frank firmly believes in retribution for past transgressions. He kills his cousin Blyth, for example, after Blyth has used a home-made flame-thrower on Frank's and his brother Eric's rabbit hutches, killing all of their pets. He murders his younger brother, Paul, for similar reasons. When his wayward mother returns to the island and goes into labour with Paul, Frank is left unattended with Old Saul, who mauls him and severs his genitals. Because Paul is the root cause for Agnes' and his fathers' carelessness, Frank must murder him as well.

Frank's world is fraught with Signs – every action and occurrence points to the future. In order to decipher these signs, he turns to the Wasp Factory, an old clock tower face transformed into a maze through which he puts live wasps, watching their paths in order to determine the future. As a result, Frank feels his balance on the island is precarious – a feeling that leaves him incapable of leaving the island for any length of time. Only within his carefully maintained spiritual territory does he feel safe.

This idea of religious exclusion extends to *Whit*, a novel that details the travels of teenage cult icon Isis Whit, leader-in-training of the Luskentyrians, an anti-technology, agrarian cult in rural Scotland. When she is sent to recover her cousin, Morag, who has renounced the faith, she discovers the false history of her grandfather's establishment of the religion and a conspiracy for religious dominance within the cult while she is gone. These machinations stem from Banks' own reservations about the formation of religious groups. 'I've got a sneaking suspicion that a lot of these people who claim to be religious leaders actually aren't religious at all; they just want copious amounts of sex, drugs and success', he explains. 'It's about manipulating people.'[43] Such is the impetus behind the Huhsz in *Against a Dark Background*. Robbed of the Lazy Gun, a powerful and ancient weapon, by one of Sharrow's ancestors, they conveniently receive a 'vision' that requires the sacrifice of one of her female heirs unless the Gun is recovered. Similarly, Isis discovers that her brother, Allan, and her Grandfather have been plotting to commercialise the sect, rewriting the holy book, the *Orthography*, to exclude her as anything but a figurehead, soliciting funds, tapping into the gourmet and organic foods market, and creating a cult franchise in other countries. Only by using the information about her grandfather's deceitful past and his false renditions of the cult's birth can she avert these attempts to disempower her and alter the religion's course. Although Isis at first considers abandoning her faith, given what she has learned about the 'outside' world and the dishonesty at home, she remains convinced the community's organisation is sound and useful. 'Essentially', Banks explains, 'Isis makes the recognition that the value of the Luskentyrian cult is in their community values rather than their religious ones'.[44] Her belief in the social values of her community enable her to continue as its leader.

Socio-political avenues and anti-conservatism

Such concern with the social and political implications of cultural structures characterises much of Banks' work. A rabidly anti-Tory/anti-conservative writer,[45] Banks incorporates his liberal view into most of his novels, SF and mainstream, to illustrate the negative aspects of imperial and capitalist juggernauts. The Culture itself is structured as a group of 'anarcho-libertarians', albeit 'very well-armed',[46] to counter a trend Banks notices in much SF writing. Seeing the 'imperialist American view of the future world that hard SF has tended to carry on with' since the 1940s and 1950s, he decided that there existed a 'moral, intellectual high-ground in space opera that had to be reclaimed for the left'. To his reasoning the imperialist trend in SF is infeasible. 'Once you have some form of reliable space travel it becomes difficult to imagine what we would regard as a state or an empire being able to hold together', he says. 'People would just leave. If you're self-sufficient and mobile you can do what you like.'[47] As a result, Morton argues, the Culture presents a 'use of technology to create a social space in which exploitation and oppression can't exist'.[48] 'I'd read so much SF which seemed just to assume that our current political-economic systems – and especially US-model capitalism – would just continue on almost unchanged into the stars and that just seemed blind, blinkered', Banks explains. Although some have suggested that the Culture might be based on the US, Banks finds that concept 'slightly bizarre ... I suppose the Culture might appear a bit like the US likes to pretend it is, or its own citizens especially – intervening on the side of good and justice and so on, but ...'[49]

Some of Banks' characters see the Culture in this light as well. Genar-Hofoen in *Excession* reads criticisms of the Culture's 'cozy proto-imperialist metahegemony',[50] and levies his own complaint that the Culture prefers to 'replace evolution with a kind of democratically agreed physiological stasis-plus-option-list while handing over the real control' to machines rather than rely on 'evolutionary pressures' for cultural development.[51] The Culture does manipulate the development of other societies, but Banks sees a radical difference between using that manipulation for one's own good, paying lip service to the 'greater good' being served, and interfering for less selfish reasons as the Culture assumedly does.

Certainly Banks creates a dramatic contrast between the Culture and other societies it encounters to illustrate the problematic design of imperialist and capitalist structures. The currency-free, pleasure-seeking Culture appears remarkably enlightened against what MacGillivray characterises as 'unflattering pictures of societies that ignore the plight of the weak and poor, that are prey to superstitious ideologies, that solve problems by violence and war'.[52] In *Consider Phlebas* and *Excession*, for example, the Culture clashes against single-minded, imperialist drives by the Idirians and the Affront – both set on conquering territory for their own needs and desires. Although the conflict with the Affront is finessed by a group of Culture Minds, who recognise the threat the Affront pose and entice them into declaring war to preserve the Culture's image, Banks suggests that such a political and social construct as the Culture offers far more personal freedom and sound moral ideology than other systems that exist.

This socio-political focus appears in his mainstream novels as well. In *The Bridge*, for example, Banks offers Alex's life to illustrate the changing social landscape from the 1960s through the 1990s. Alex, a working-class, socialist university student, eventually becomes a wealthy member of a prominent engineering firm and sheds his working-class roots, striving even to change his accent to blend more easily with his lover's society friends. As Alex's social condition changes, though, he tries to maintain his social awareness – an attempt that seems pale in comparison to his economic situation. Although he often feels forced to choose the lesser of two evils – buy a large house or give up the tax dollars to Thatcher's government, for instance – he does not deny all of the success he has achieved. He becomes increasingly willing to be led along that path, not resisting the directions his life has taken. His car accident on the bridge becomes a symbolic resistance to that lifestyle – an action that can prompt change in his life.

The bridge world in which he, as Orr, arrives, satirises the 'class and economic systems and structures' Alex has confronted in the 'real' world,[53] Gifford explains. The layered bridge offers a literally stratified culture – the powerful and wealthy live on the topmost layer while labour classes and the impoverished live on layers closer to sea level. Even language becomes stratified, such that Orr cannot understand working-class speakers (an inversion from Alex's working-class roots). Although

Orr begins on a higher level, a position that reflects Alex's present social stratum, he eventually spirals downward and leaves the bridge altogether, travelling to the mainland and becoming embroiled in the nightmarish world of civil wars, military coups, and other despotic activities. Only when he returns to the bridge is he offered the opportunity to reclaim his life as Alex, having witnessed the worst of the social structure he has benefited from in the 'real' world. Yet he returns to it aware of its illusory nature, on a par with the illusion of the bridge. His life has been part of 'our collective dream, our corporate imagery ... it was half-nightmare and I almost let it kill me, but it hasn't. Yet anyway.'[54] Although he recognises that the dream has not changed during his coma, he acknowledges that his own role in that process will, if not change, at least render him more aware of the choices available to him.

Like *The Bridge*, *The Crow Road* offers characters' perspectives on the socio-political situation, ranging from Kenneth's challenge to his children, nieces, and nephews when they race up a hill that 'last one there's a Tory!'[55] to Prentice's internalised and almost casual dislike of the Thatcher government. Yet Kenneth, despite his communist ideology, becomes financially successful as Alex has in *The Bridge*. Although he hides his wealth and investments from his children, on his death Prentice realises the amount of money he has earned writing. Kenneth leaves a good amount of money to 'right-on causes: CND, Amnesty International and Greenpeace',[56] but the bulk of his estate goes to his family. Prentice, upon learning of his inheritance, engages in a lifestyle similar to that of his Uncle Fergus, long considered a Tory stuffed-shirt by his more liberal relatives. He rents a large house in Glasgow, complete with antique furnishings and a palatial, tapestry-hung bedroom, and hires an expensive solicitor to get him off a shoplifting charge. These events do give him pause: 'it seems wrong I got off because I dressed in a suit and I could afford an expensive advocate', he tells Ashley. 'If I'd come from Maryhill and I wasn't reasonably articulate and didn't have any money, even if I *had* just forgotten I hadn't paid for the book, I bet everybody would have told me to plead guilty.'[57] Yet he finds the financial solvency reassuring, although he still rumbles about Tory government.

Both *The Bridge* and *The Crow Road* offer criticisms of conservatism and the Tory government through character dialogue, but novels such as *Canal Dreams* and *Complicity* incorporate political criticism more fully into the substance of the stories. In *Canal Dreams*, celebrated cellist Hisako Onoda, en route from Japan to New York via the Panama Canal (due to her fear of flying), becomes embroiled in a CIA plot to disrupt the reversion of the Canal to Panamanian control. The CIA introduces a terrorist element that will require the US to 'step in' and restore order, in the process solidifying the US's control of the canal. When she faces Dandridge and accuses him of shooting down a US plane of congressmen in order to escalate the situation and legitimately bring in US forces, he points to the efficacy of the plan, justifying the action by pointing to similar terrorist acts that have furthered countries' agendas.

Later in the novel, when Hisako is now in a position to destroy his terrorist group, he points to the common ground between Japan and the US, trying to justify their actions in the name of mercantilism. 'It's all about trade; yes, *trade*; trade and spheres of influence and ... and opportunities, the possibility of influence and power', he argues. He then tries to justify the force the US uses to maintain its position as a world power, saying, 'to stay great you have to stoop; no ways round that. You can try and distance yourself from the people who do the stooping; I mean distance yourself from the cutting edge, but it still remains your responsibility.' The result, he claims, is that 'you have to do bad things in a bad world, if you want to stay able to be good ... there's all these people think goodness and rightness is somehow indivisible, but it isn't; can't be, in fact. It's a razor's edge.'[58] Dandridge claims that atrocious methods are necessary and legitimised to create a greater ending, relying on what Banks considers an imperialist motive of self-determined righteousness. Yet Dandridge also notes the moral ambiguity that subscribing to or benefiting from a capitalist system implies. Although both Alex, in *The Bridge*, and Kenneth, in *The Crow Road*, have benefited from the capitalist system they deplore and speak against, they do not accept their complicity in that system – a complicity that Dandridge, for all his moral bankruptcy, recognises.

Banks addresses such issues more thoroughly in *Complicity*, a first-person narrative centred on Cameron Colley, a morally ambiguous journalist whose passions for drugs, alcohol, sadomasochism, and computer games make him an unlikely protagonist. He becomes implicated in a killing spree that has left a number of powerful men, primarily big businessmen and government officials, gruesomely murdered. Eventually, the culprit, his childhood friend Andy, reveals himself to be the killer, explaining that his motive for the killings stems from his participation in the Gulf War and Cameron's own ravings against Tory government and capitalist conservatism. 'All of them had all they could ask for in life, but they all wanted more', he tells Cameron. 'They all treated people like shit, literally like shit; something unpleasant to be disposed of.' The only recourse, he argues, is to 'make them feel frightened and vulnerable and *powerless*, the way they made other people feel all the time'.[59]

Andy, like Dandridge, accepts his own role in the process, telling Cameron that he, too, is a 'product of the system ... so I come along and I do what I can get away with, because it seems fit to me to do it, because I'm like a businessman, you see?'[60] While Cameron has also paid lip service to the sentiments Andy expresses through his murders – much of what Andy uses as his arguments is lifted, purposefully, from editorials Cameron has written – he is unwilling to accept his culpability for allowing such a system to continue and for participating in it himself. Andy may feel that responsibility and guilt, but Cameron denies it.

Yet Cameron also recognises the powerful emotions expressed by Andy through his murders. When he leads the police to the body of a male rapist who attacked the two of them as children – a rapist they beat unconscious then threw down an air shaft – he learns that the rapist survived the fall and crawled to an adjacent air shaft before dying. Although he regrets the pain caused, 'part of me rejoices, that is glad he paid the way he did, that for once the world worked the way it's supposed to, punishing the wrongdoer'.[61] The murders Andy commits involve a similar amount of punishment – in each case he creates an intense fear in his subjects, informing them of the reason for his actions and choosing lengthy and/or gruesome methods. When murdering a pornographer, for example, he injects him with semen collected from male prostitutes. A businessman is bound so that his limbs lose circulation and is then injected with HIV-infected blood, while a Parliament member is tied to his dog kennels, forced to witness their shooting, then is bled to death himself. In effect, Andy delivers a variety of horrific acts upon anchors of business and governmental conservatism. 'There's a moral point to that ghastliness, pain and anguish', Banks explains, 'which is why I would absolutely defend *Complicity*'s extreme violence, because it was supposed to be a metaphor for what the Tories have done to this country'.[62]

The theatre of the macabre

Most of Banks' works examine grim, often macabre events that affect his characters, leading some critics to label him a horror writer. In *Canal Dreams*, for example, Hisako Onoda experiences firsthand the actions of Dandridge's 'terrorists': she is gang-raped and forced to witness the gruesome deaths of her fellow passengers. Yet Onoda enacts her own horrors on the terrorists, stabbing one with her cello spike, and setting fire to others by igniting an oil slick surrounding the terrorists' ship. Banks' *The Wasp Factory*, which first earned him his reputation for the horrific, details Frank's activities on the island, ranging from the torture and death of wasps in the Wasp Factory, to the killing of small animals for his Sacrifice Poles and the torching of an entire rabbit colony, to the childhood murder of his cousins Blyth and Esmerelda, and his younger brother Paul. He conceals an adder in Blyth's prosthetic leg while he is sleeping, for example, and constructs a giant kite to which he lashes Esmerelda, releasing her over the North Sea. He also coaxes Paul into detonating an unexploded World War II bomb. In addition, we learn of Frank's mentally deranged brother, Eric, who torches and kills dogs, and at one point sets fire to a flock of sheep. Frank also provides us with the reason for Eric's insanity: his discovery, while working with vegetative children in a teaching hospital, that a child, fitted with a steel skull plate, has had its brain eaten by maggots.

Banks extends this concept of human suffering and brutality to *A Song of Stone*, a novel that occurs in an unidentified European country embroiled in military and political turmoil. Banks places his narrator, Abel, and his lover, Morgan, in the hands of a guerilla troop that holds them hostage in their castle. As the novel unfolds, Abel experiences the frank brutality of the soldiers, including their wanton destruction of the castle's antiquities during their post-battle celebration, and his imprisonment, bound and clasped within an iron helmet, in the castle's old well. At the end of the novel, he is forced to witness Morgan's gang-rape and slow death as they bind and drown her before they execute him.

Banks' SF works offer similar incidents in which characters experience traumatic events that fall beyond the pale of 'normal' violence. In *Consider Phlebas*, a captive Horza is forced to watch another captive being devoured alive by a cannibalistic group of religious zealots awaiting the apocalypse. He in turn loses the flesh of two fingers, stripped to the bone before he manages to escape. At the end of *Use of Weapons*, we learn that Cherardenine's cousin, Elethiomel, killed Cherardenine's sister, fashioning a chair from her bones and sending it to him. In *Excession*, Banks offers a species called the Affront, creatures who thrive on death and pain, and who have genetically manipulated their environment to create 'a kind of self-perpetuating, never-ending holocaust of pain and fear'.[318] Such manipulation extends from the creatures they hunt for sport, bred so that the scent of Affront sends them into frenzies, to the genital mutilation and culturally proscribed rape of female Affront.

Banks' detailed descriptions of the events that confront his characters contributes to his reputation as a writer immersed in grim and horrific depictions of the world, MacGillivray's 'heart of darkness'.[64] 'I don't pull punches. I think it has frightened off more women than it has men, which is a pity', Banks says. 'The fact that *The Wasp Factory* was seen a horror book, gory and all the rest of it, and because people have looked at the more grotesque aspects of the subsequent books, has had this effect.'[65] Certainly many writers, particularly SF writers, create violent scenes. Yet Banks offers scenes that stray from the normative violent events that readers anticipate and instead explores what Mac-Gillivray sees as 'the heart of darkness' that influences characters' actions. Banks' characters break numerous social taboos – Morgan and Abel in *A Song of Stone* are both lovers and siblings, for example, and Frank in *The Wasp Factory* discovers that his father has concealed Frank's true gender. 'I'm not Francis Leslie Cauldhame. I'm Frances Lesley Cauldhame', Frank reveals. 'When Old Saul savaged me, my father saw it as an ideal opportunity for a little experiment, and a way of lessening – perhaps removing entirely – the influence of the female around him as I grew up. So he started dosing me with male hormones, and has been ever since.'[66] Through such violent images, Banks questions the everyday 'civility' people take for granted, recognising that, however surreal his narrative events may be, they are too discomfortingly linked to the real horrors the world has to offer.

Violence and gender violations

Although Banks does not 'shrink from doing unpleasant things to people', he comments that such experiences happen 'almost always to men, it has to be said. There's so much violence against women in fiction, in real life, that if the plot demands it I try to be nasty to men as a rule.'[67] Certainly the rapes in his novels – Hisako in *Canal Dreams*, Morgan in *A Song of Stone*, the barbarian's victims in *The Bridge*, and Isis' grandfather's attempt in *Whit* – as well as Frank's hormonal manipulation in *The Wasp Factory* – establish women as victims. Yet more often than not Banks 'has a tendency toward creating strong female personalities',[68] Nicholls claims. These independently-minded women characters, like Banks, do not pull punches. Banks' creation of the Culture allows for a gender equanimity – people in the Culture can change gender through biological processes, and can choose to become pregnant, reabsorb or abort the foetus, or put the pregnancy in stasis through exercises of will rather than medical intervention. Such physiological flexibility stimulates and sustains social flexibility for the Culture, Banks explains. 'A society in which it is so easy to change sex will rapidly find out if it is treating one gender better than the other', he comments. 'Within the population, over time, there will gradually be greater and greater numbers of the sex it is more rewarding to be, and so pressure for change – within society rather than the individuals – will presumably build up until some sort of sexual equality and hence numerical parity is established.'[69]

Banks extends this sexual equanimity to his own writing, but notes the problems gender can cause in character creations. 'I find it fairly easy to write female characters', he admits, 'but I don't want them to act just like men, because that has the implication that only men can be strong central characters'. Yet Banks makes occasional reference to 'female' attributes so that his women do not 'seem too much like men', giving, as an example, his treatment of Sharrow in *Against a Dark Background*. When she returns a lover's slap with her fist, 'she's bested him in male terms', Banks notes. Such reconciliatory narrative gestures suggest the very gender typing Banks hopes to avoid. However, he says, 'normally I make very few concessions to my woman characters in the "traditional" sense'.[70] Instead, he offers characters such as Whit or Kate from *The Business*, as well as Hisako in *Canal Dreams* as strong and determined women who tackle, albeit not entirely unflappably, situations and decisions that would daunt many traditional heroines of fiction.[71]

But at the same time that Banks prefers to ignore gender pre-conceptions as 'some sort of prohibition' to his writing,[72] his novels often offer a gender play that challenges those very preconceptions. Many of Banks' female characters shift identities, slipping out of gender stereo-types to confound and complicate the narrative. For instance, Frank from *The Wasp Factory* overturns reader expectations by revealing him-self as a 'herself' at the end of the novel, forcing the reader to question assumptions of teenage male violence and instead to recognise the ways in which physiological sexing offers only a limited avenue for exploring gendered behaviour. Similarly, the seemingly simple bifurcation of strong woman/weak woman in *Inversions*, evident in the strong willed doctor and the pliable concubine, breaks down when the concubine is revealed to be a well-trained assassin, long ago planted to murder the presiding Protector General and disrupt his government.

Shifting identities and dysfunctional families

Ultimately this play with gender points to the slippery and shifting avenues of identity-making as characters struggle with the problems of defining self – a common theme in Banks' novels. But even more frequently, Banks' characters struggle to maintain a sense of identity in the face of familial pressure and complications, generally failing to disregard the impact their interactions with family members have. Such relationships plague Prentice in *The Crow Road*, for example, as he negotiates among the unresolved bitterness of his religious disagreements with his father, his suspicion and eventual implication of his uncle Fergus in his uncle Rory's mysterious disappearance and murder, and his feelings of alienation from the rest of his family. The family skeletons Prentice exhumes in *The Crow Road* become more macabre and dysfunctional for Frank in *The Wasp Factory* as he discovers the animosity between his parents has so embittered his father against women that he secretly manipulates Frank's hormonal balances to create the son he has lost out of the daughter he hates. As a result of this discovery, Frank must reconfigure his life as a teenage boy into life as a teenage girl – a difficult task given his indoctrination into the hatred of women. Women are 'weak and stupid and live in the shadow of men and are nothing compared to them', he has announced.[73] He does not even 'like having them on the island'.[74] Yet, with his newfound sexuality confronting him, he must come to terms with his gender anxieties and reconcile himself with his brother and father.

Banks brings these family betrayals into his SF novels as well, exploring the implications of childhood jealousies and alliances that spin out of control once children attain the power of adults but fail to reconcile family tensions and disputes. In *Use of Weapons*, for instance, the enmity between Elethiomel and Charardenine that early divides them generates gruesome consequences. As Charardenine and Elethiomel square off, Charardenine's sisters choose sides, Darckense supporting Elethiomel's endeavors and Livueta remaining loyal to Charardenine. In fact, when Elethiomel and Charardenine find themselves leading opposing sides in a civil war, Darckense's insistence on joining Elethiomel catalyses the events that lead to her murder and Charardenine's subsequent suicide. Although Elethiomel's subsequently assumes Charardenine's identity and devotes his life to dangerous missions for the Culture in atonement for his crimes – his gesture fails to sway the surviving Livueta, who refuses forgiveness even at his deathbed.

Similarly, Sharrow's half-sister Breyguhn in *Against a Dark Back-ground* betrays her in her search for the Lazy Gun, aligning instead with their cousin in his plans for corporate conquest. This willingness to sacrifice Sharrow to the Huhsz stems from Breyguhn's jealousy of Sharrow during their childhood and early teenage years. A young Breyguhn is so desperate to best Sharrow in any way possible that she seduces Sharrow's would-be lover, only to find him calling Sharrow's name as he climaxes. As a result, the long-standing grudge she bears Sharrow culminates in her attempts to eliminate her, only to be destroyed herself when Sharrow retaliates.

These family ties that bind, and often choke, reveal the sometimes crippling choices his characters make in determining the personal battles they fight. Similarly, Banks explores divergent life experiences that ask characters to reconcile internal conflicts in identity-making, often requiring a choice between life-desires. In *Espedair Street*, Daniel Weir chronicles his movement from a gawky working-class teenager to an international rock mega-star. Yet Weir, after his successes, retires at thirty-one to St Jutes, a mock-church-turned-house, conceals his identity, and tries to work through the memories he has of his career. At the same time, though, he ignores the possibility of returning to his life, and his almost-girlfriend, Jean, at the time before his band became so successful. Only after his suicide attempt does he realise the solution to his ennui and disenchantment with himself is to reclaim the more simple life he rejected in favour of fame and success. After redrawing his will to leave all his money and royalties to a friend, with plans to begin recording his own music from scratch, he tracks down Jean in the small northern town of Arisaig and appears on her doorstep, hoping she will accept him again, but expecting rejection after his long absence. When she invites him to stay with her, he realises that the simplicity of the life she has to offer him is what he has been lacking throughout all of his successes.

The disenchantment with the rock culture life Weir has carved out for himself arises in Banks' other works, as the youth culture he explores leads to disillusionment with high-paced lifestyles disconnected from characters' real desires and dreams. The elaborate diversions Weir and his bandmates find for themselves leave them searching for larger and more extreme activities on- and offstage – often resulting in disaster. Davey, for example, is electrocuted when the stage set's dry ice machine malfunctions, and Christine, pursuing another extreme stage setting that depicts her in the Crucifixion, earns the disapproval of right-wing conservatives and is eventually murdered by one of them. Weir, living in a world of wild parties, extensive drug use and conspicuous consumption, eventually reaches the brink of suicide before he realises the lifestyle he truly desires with Jean.

Such behaviour also appears in *The Bridge*, in which the highly idealistic, anti-capitalist Alex becomes successful and wealthy. In the process, he too discovers a 'jet-setting' lifestyle of drugs and fast cars, which eventually leads to his accident on the Bridge and his comatose state. Only after enduring the nightmarish world of the Bridge in his coma's alter ego does he realise what he has left behind in his pursuit of success. Upon recovery, he tries to reclaim the relationship he has lost and find purpose in his life again. Kate in *The Business* similarly rejects a high-flying lifestyle as an up-and-coming business executive to pursue rural development plans in Thulahn, seeing more purpose in such a life than, as she comes to realise, the corrupt and corrupting corporate world can offer her.

Modern traditions

These character identity-searches may have less to do with a concern for youth culture than they do with exploring the slick, cosmopolitan lifestyles such characters as Kate lead with the down-to-earth reality more rural existences appear to offer. Banks uses the geography of Scotland itself as a means of both delineating and connecting these two lifestyles. Often, as in Alan Warner's and Duncan McLean's work, the traditional divisions between rural and urban breaks down as characters move freely across the 'boundaries' from city to country. In *The Crow Road*, for instance, Banks depicts members of Prentice's family zipping along the narrow and winding roads north of the cities to reach their grandmother's village in BMWs and Mercedes from their successful careers in the city. In addition, the simple 'village' contains, in fact, the various family mansions. Prentice's Uncle Fergus, for example, has transformed a ruined ancient monastery into an elaborate house complete with its own telescopic observatory. The 'simple' life Prentice returns to when he fails out of university is the wealth of the family business, which he comes to inherit. A similar scene plays out in *Espedair Street* when Weir refers to his short ownership of an 'inner Hebridean island I picked up ridiculously cheap at an auction in London'.[75]

Similarly, in *The Wasp Factory*, Frank's life on the small coastal island offers some isolation from the prying eyes of outsiders and thus is well-suited for his father's goal of maintaining the fiction of Frank's

masculinity, but Frank is not entirely divorced from contemporary goings-
on. He goes to the mainland village often (separated from the island by a
mere footbridge) to visit his friend, Jamie, go to the pub to listen to
heavy rock bands that tour the area, and to purchase the materials
necessary for his bombs and other 'improvements' to the island. Banks
offers a strange geographic hybrid as Frank builds his bombs amidst
pastures of rabbits and sheep, illustrating the disruption of traditional
views of a rural, idyllic Scottish Highlands. Weir's acquisition of his
island in the Inner Hebrides in *Espedair Street* also points to the disruption of rural lifestyles not always welcome. 'The crofters resented me
even though I meant well', he notes. 'Who did this lowlander, this
Glesga Keelie, this youth of a "pop" star think he was? Why, I didn't
even have the Gaelic.'[76]

At the same time, though, the rural spaces of Scotland do offer relief
to some of Banks' characters eager to escape their own life complications. Weir's journey to visit Jean, for example, illustrates his departure
from the disappointing life he thought he wanted to the life he desires
now. The train he takes from Glasgow moves north, 'past housing
schemes and old factories and stagnant canals',[77] crossing snowy Loch
Lomond, 'startl[ing] a herd of forty or more deer, brown-black shapes
leaping and running across the white',[78] approaching Ben Nevis and the
other mountains on the West Coast, near Fort William before reaching
the small village of Arisaig where Jean lives.[79] This movement to the
Highlands, complete with the herd of deer, invokes the traditional
depictions of the Highlands as unspoiled wilderness and local tradition.
In fact, as the novel ends, Weir sits in the local banquet hall as Jean
decorates for a village dance, watching a small boy ride his tricycle to the
'simple, tootling, jigging music'[80] of Northumbrian Pipes – a far cry from
the electric rock music around which his career had centred. The scene is
idyllic and offers Weir the hope he has lacked, providing a vision for a
future within a community, rather than as an isolated figure in the
international sphere.

In effect, novels such as *Espedair Street* and *The Crow Road* offer a
vision of Scotland as a very small space, mapped by at once conflicting
and symbiotic urban and rural geographies that characterise the people
who live there. These small spaces contrast with the Culture space opera
novels, operating on a grand scale within the enormity of space, and the
massive collections of individuals the Culture supports. Yet, as Banks'
characters develop, such grand-scale stories pale in comparison to the
small tragedies and triumphs all of his characters, SF or traditional,

experience as they struggle through the complexity of political, social, and interpersonal conflicts that he creates.

Notes

1 R. Yates, 'A wee hard kernel of cynicism', *The Observer*, 20 Aug. 1995, 16.
2 S. Nicholls, 'Man of the Culture', *Starlog*, (December 1994), 11 July 2000, available at www.phlebas.com/text/banksinto3.html.
3 A. MacGillivray, 'The worlds of Iain Banks', *Laverock* (1996), 22.
4 Nicholls, 'Man of the Culture', n. pag.
5 Yates, 'A wee hard kernel', 16.
6 O. Morton, 'Iain Banks spoke with Oliver Morton', *Wired*, (June 1996), 11 July 2000, available at www.phlebas.com/text/banksintr3.html.
7 *Ibid.*
8 D. Gifford, 'Imagining Scotlands: the return to mythology in modern Scottish fiction', in S. Hagemann (ed.), *Studies in Scottish Fiction: 1945 to Present* (Frankfurt am Main, Peter Lang GmbH, 1996), 40.
9 S. McKenzie, 'Scottish writer Iain Banks spoke with Simon McKenzie', *Time Off*, (May 1995), 11 July 2000, available at www.phlebas.com/text/banksint10.html.
10 Although for narrative ease I will continue to refer to Banks' SF and mainstream novels as distinct categories.
11 Nicholls, 'Man of the Culture', n. pag.
12 Nicholls, 'Man of the Culture', n. pag.
13 A. Riach, 'Nobody's children: orphans and their ancestors in popular Scottish fiction', in S. Hagemann (ed.), *Studies in Scottish Fiction: 1945 to Present* (Frankfurt am Main, Peter Lang GmbH, 1996), 66.
14 K. Barry, 'Happy being grim', *The Irish Times* (18 Feb. 1997), 11 July 2000, available at www.phlebas.com/text/banksint20.html.
15 I. M. Banks, 'A few notes on the Culture' [posted www.rec.arts.sf 10 August 1994], 11 July 2000, available at www.soft.net.uk/theziggy/books/ibanks/culture. html.
16 McKenzie, 'Scottish writer Iain Banks', n. pag.
17 Riach, 'Nobody's children', 68.
18 As Riach notes, the main character of each of the three stories 'seems trapped and struggling to break out from the limits of his world'. 'Nobody's children', 67.
19 Gifford, 'Imagining Scotlands', 40.
20 I. Banks, *The Bridge* (London, Abacus [Macmillan Limited, 1986], 1999), 159.
21 Douglas Gifford suggests that Alex's comatose mind filters out the Freudian mind-layers so that the barbarian explores and enacts his id-fantasies. 'Imagining Scotlands', 40.
22 I. M. Banks, *Excession* (London, Bantam Books [Orbit, 1996], 1998), 135.

23 *Ibid.*, 123.

24 Despite the wayward knife-missiles that appear in other contexts.

25 I. M. Banks, *Consider Phlebas* (London, Orbit [MacMillan, 1987], 1999), 451–2.

26 *Ibid.*, 13.

27 Morton, 'Iain Banks spoke', n. pag.

28 C. Mitchell, 'Getting used to being God', 11 July 2000, available at www.spikemagazine.com/0996bank.htm.

29 MacGillivray, 'The worlds of Iain Banks', 26.

30 I. Banks, *The Business* (London, Abacus [Little, Brown and Company, 1999], 2000), 51.

31 *Ibid.*, 88.

32 I. Banks, *The Crow Road* (London, Abacus [Scribners, 1993], 1998), 146.

33 *Ibid.*, 176.

34 *Ibid.*, 484.

35 L. Fay, 'Depraved heart', *Hotpress* (May 1996), 11 July 2000, available at www.phlebas.com/text/banksinto5.html.

36 Banks suggests the hypocrisy of religious organisations in this event. The House does not allow women, so the brothers imprison Breyguhn in the House for her illicit entry to and presence on the grounds.

37 I. M. Banks, *Against a Dark Background* (London, Orbit [1995], 1998), 112.

38 *Ibid.*, 114.

39 *Ibid.*, 115.

40 *Ibid.*, 362.

41 *Ibid.*, 66.

42 Nicholls, 'Man of the Culture', n. pag.

43 'Great Uncle Iain', *Edinburgh Student Newspaper* (6 February 1997), 11 July 2000, available at www.phlebas.com/text.banksint19.html.

44 Mitchell, 'Getting used to God', n. pag.

45 'Banks' distaste for all things Tory crackles through his work like a static current', Fay notes. 'Depraved heart', n. pag.

46 S. A. Melia, 'Very likely impossible, but oh, the elegance…', *Science Fiction Chronicle* (October 1994), 11 July 2000, available at www. phlebas.com/text/banksinto2.html. For a detailed account of the Culture by Banks himself, explaining many of its attributes and his thoughts on their creation, see I. M. Banks, 'A few notes on the Culture'.

47 Morton, 'Iain Banks spoke', n. pag.

48 *Ibid.*

49 Melia, 'Very likely impossible', n. pag.

50 Banks, *Excession*, 188.

51 *Ibid.*, 187. For this reason Genar-Hofoen admires the Affront, a warlike civilisation with whom the Culture is at polite odds. In Banks' short story, 'The State of the Art', Linter, part of the Culture expedition

visiting Earth, becomes fascinated with Earth's social development, choosing to surrender his Culture heritage and live as a human.

52 MacGillivray, 'The worlds of Iain Banks', 23.

53 Gifford, 'Imagining Scotlands', 40.

54 Banks, *The Bridge*, 283.

55 Banks, *The Crow Road*, 27.

56 *Ibid.*, 344.

57 *Ibid.*, 377.

58 I. Banks, *Canal Dreams* (London, Abacus [Macmillan Limited, 1989], 1996), 166.

59 I. Banks, *Complicity* (London, Abacus [Little, Brown and Company, 1993] 1998), 297.

60 *Ibid.*, 300.

61 *Ibid.*, 249.

62 Mitchell, 'Getting used to being God', n. pag.

63 Banks, *Excession*, 185.

64 MacGillivray, 'The worlds of Iain Banks', 26.

65 J. Robertson, 'Bridging styles: a conversation with Iain Banks', *Radical Scotland* 42 (Dec. 1989/Jan. 1990), 11 July 2000, available at www.phlebas.cpm/text/interv4.html.

66 I. Banks, *The Wasp Factory* (London, Simon & Schuster, 1984), 181.

67 Morton, 'Iain Banks spoke', n. pag.

68 Nicholls, 'Man of the Culture', n. pag.

69 Banks, 'A few notes on the Culture', n. pag.

70 Nicholls, n. pag.

71 Although the fact that Kate turns her back on a successful business career in order to marry the Prince of Thulahn might be read as a movement back into traditional gender norms rather than a plan to bring development to the nation.

72 Mitchell, 'Getting used to being God', n. pag.

73 Banks, *The Wasp Factory*, 43.

74 *Ibid.*

75 I. Banks, *Espedair Street* (London, Abacus [Macmillan Limited, 1987], 1998), 117.

76 *Ibid.*

77 *Ibid.*, 238.

78 *Ibid.*, 239.

79 This journey is reminiscent of Duncan Thaw's journey to visit his father in the Highlands in Alasdair Gray's *Lanark*. Yet Thaw, unlike Weir, feels isolated rather than welcome as he peers into the window of the hiking lodge where his father, laughing and happy, is sitting. Where Weir receives the welcome he needs from Jean, having resisted his impulse towards suicide, Thaw instead turns to suicide and drowns himself in the nearby loch.

80 Banks, *Espedair Street*, 249.

5

Janice Galloway's
newly gendered vision

Writing on the edge

The new directions in Scottish writing created by Alasdair Gray suggested possibilities to Janice Galloway. 'Alasdair Gray's was a voice that offered me something freeing', she explains. 'It wasn't distant or assumptive. It knew words, syntax, and places I also knew yet used them without any tang of apology.'[1] *Lanark* offered a vision of Scotland not as a 'toty wee place with no political clout, a joke heritage, dour people, and writers who were all male and dead',[2] but as a viable, literary nation.

Yet within these possibilities for Scottish writing Galloway sees a deeply rooted misogyny – the elision of the female authorial voice and the female narrative experience. While Gray's voice 'knew the whole truth didn't belong to one sex' and was '*a man's voice that knew that's all it was – a man's* [emphasis in original]',[3] the Scotland Galloway experiences, as a woman and as a woman writer, belies the literary freedom *Lanark* proposes. In 'Objective truth and the grinding machine', Galloway describes the process by which she struggled to learn and become a writer, explaining the intense social pressure to *not* write that she has endured. Throughout the essay, Galloway provides a litany of obstacles to her writing, including an older sister who 'hit me (literally) if I brought back books by women authors. *Women canny write*, she'd say: *Women canny write*', and a secondary school curriculum that included no women writers, 'not even safely dead ones like Jane Austen or the Brontes'.[4] The 'symbolic' presence of women in male-authored books, Galloway notes, 'reinforce[d] the notion that women were not interesting in themselves and that ART did not concern itself with them. It took a bit longer to compute that *them* was *us*. *Me*.' While the crushing disappointment of a university education that only emphasised her secondary school experience nearly drove her from her degree, she credits her tutor's patronising statement that '*Girls often give up, it's nothing to be ashamed of* [emphasis in original]' as a galvanising force for her to finish.[5]

Galloway describes how such experiences hampered not only her sense of self-worth as a woman, but also her entitlement to literature and literary creation. 'Enjoying words was an occupation fraught with pain, full of traps, bombs and codes', she explains. 'At ten, I accidentally wrote a novel in blue biro and pencil … My mother found it but didn't tell my sister. She lit the fire with it.' Only after graduating university, embarking on a teaching career, and 'ten years and lots of reading I tracked down by myself', Galloway 'melted down all the bloody nonsense I'd been led to believe about AUTHORSHIP, WOMEN, SCOTLAND, CLASS and ART'.[6] The ensuing freedom finally allowed her to begin writing.

Galloway's work during the late 1980s and early 1990s locates her as one of the few Scottish women writers, along with Liz Lochhead and A. L. Kennedy, who gained authorial acclaim for her reimagination of Scotland. She is, Ian A. Bell notes, one of the writers who responded to *Lanark*'s dare to 'reclaim the right to represent Scottish culture on their own terms' by 'envisaging it from within and from below in ways far removed from the prevailing sentimental, romantic or "realistic" paradigms'.[7] For Galloway, gender provides a means by which to break open the contemporary Scottish experience and reveal what previous decades of Scottish writing had elided. This concern works through not only her fiction, but also her other writing. In 'Balancing the books', an editorial written for the *Scotsman*, she levies a pointed criticism at the financial support allotted to Scottish writers in general and women writers in particular. In the process, she reiterates a problem she notes not only in Scottish literature but also in many literatures – the validity of women's writing and its critical reception. 'Women writers are in the worst position', she claims. 'They do less well with publishers' advances. They are shortlisted for and win fewer prizes – not because they're less talented, but because of entrenched patterns of how to see and read literature, what subjects may be considered "serious".'[8] This critical reception colours the success women have in writing narrative alternatives to predominantly masculinist literary traditions. 'So-called women's issues are still regarded as deviant, add-on, extra. Not the Big Picture',[9] Galloway says. She expected such a reaction from Peter Kravitz, who eventually published *The Trick Is to Keep Breathing*. Kravitz was 'hugely encouraging, particularly as he saw my perspective was female and that interested him … whereas the kind of response I'd expected was "oh that's interesting dear, but did I realise it was about a woman?"'[10]

As her work has gained attention and acclaim, scholars such as Ali

Smith have hailed Galloway for creating 'an important voice in our fiction, a questioning and fearful and outraged woman's voice'. Such a voice, Smith continues, 'states a terrible dilemma of identity'[11] within Scottish literature – the need to accommodate the female voices within Scottish culture and the imposition of a masculinist literary tradition that has always excluded that voice. Yet while Galloway embraces alternative methods of reading and analysis that encompass women's writing, such as feminist analysis, she warily approaches the idea of herself as a feminist writer.[12] The difficulty with such a label lies in the expectations it creates, she explains. The feminist publisher Women's Press told her 'one of my characters wasn't a strong enough role model for women'. The assumption that 'ideological reasons' should guide the writing, she argues, detracts from the real experiences she is trying to create in her fiction.[13] 'My work is to ask, "What is it like to be an intelligent woman coping with the late twentieth century?" That's it', she declares.[14] Such a narrative agenda requires failures as well as successes, weaknesses that often triumph over strengths in her characters.

In her writing, Galloway identifies the problems of applying theoretical feminism too stringently to a text. As Glenda Norquay explains, Galloway's work illustrates Maralou Joannou's concern that theoretical feminism 'bludgeons literature out of its specificity and materiality and may easily lose sight of how the representation of woman is linked to historical facts and to historically contextualised situations'.[15] Galloway's work, Norquay claims, deconstructs such 'gendered subjectivities' by 'tak[ing] into account the materiality of people's lives' and making them central to the gender constructs she questions. By writing women who are often lost, often trapped within those situations, Galloway 'doesn't write about, but through, feminism',[16] revealing textual women who know the societal traps, see the potential lives they feel they ought to have, but are unable to break free from cultural confines.

Women on the edge

Many of Galloway's women characters are struggling, like Joy Stone in *The Trick Is to Keep Breathing*, 'in a male-dominated West of Scotland to re-assert her sense of self'.[17] Galloway's central character, Burgess explains, 'is frequently a woman alone, sometimes by choice, sometimes not. Her women live in a man's world but resist its assumptions'.[18] The isolation these characters endure is not necessarily a physical one – many are women within relationships who nevertheless feel externalised or alienated by the very structure of the relationship that should be nurturing them. They struggle to fulfil the role expected of them by their families or partners, but they cultivate a growing resentment, an unwillingness to completely toe the line, or a sense of bewilderment at the problems that arise.

Often these women try to work within domestic boundaries and fail. Like Joy, they try to be 'good',

> Where good = productive/hardworking/wouldn't say boo
> Where good = value for money
> Where good = not putting anyone out by feeling too much, blank, unobtrusive
> Where good = neat, acting in a credit-worthy manner
> Patient, thoughtful, uncomplaining

in order to 'reap the reward',[19] but they find that a reward rarely comes. In many cases the characters, and the readers, realise the extent to which women have been alienated by social expectations and condemnations. In 'Frostbite', for example, the narrator encounters an elderly drunk man while waiting for a late-night bus and tries to help him, missing her own bus in the process. She steadies him, helps him wipe away blood from a small head wound, and listens patiently as he tells her about the 'bad woman', a 'bad, bad bitchahell'[20] who hit him and broke his glasses, causing him to miss the bus. Throughout the experience she suffers through his patronising 'hen' and the realisation that he will tell her his story 'as though she weren't a woman herself, as if she shared his terms. As though his were the only terms.' She also knows that she 'wouldn't be expected to argue – just stand and listen'.[21] Yet despite her patient ministrations and well wishes to him after guiding him to the correct bus, she earns only a poorly aimed punch as the drunk man lumps her together with the 'bad woman' – with, in fact, all women, 'dirty whooers and filth the lot of them'[22] – and lashes out at her.

In 'Need for Restraint' Alice similarly becomes the scapegoat for male frustration after she witnesses a fight between two men in a shopping mall and voices a protest about their behaviour. Her refusal to stay uninvolved, to acknowledge that it is 'NOTHING TO DO WITH YOU',[23] angers her boyfriend, Charles, who on a previous occasion prevented her from interfering in a street fight. His public anger at her memory of the event, and his own feelings of shame for not acting himself, prompt her to allow him an 'out' – by touching his sleeve and thereby admitting guilt, she releases and absolves him, allowing him to leave her in the mall. In addition, Alice, like the unnamed narrator in 'Frostbite', recognises the details of daily interactions with men that erase her as a socially significant being or endow her with a contaminating presence. Her attempts to talk the men out of fighting do not dissuade them; only when a male voice tells them to 'break it up eh'[24] do they part, leaving Alice to feel 'clumsy, inept. Female.'[25] Even her touch becomes outcast as one of the men cringes when she reaches out to him, much as Charles moves away when she touches his jacket.

On some occasions, women try to break free of these behavioural expectations only to be forced back into submission by men who figure centrally in their lives. 'A Proper Respect' reveals a pregnant teenage Alice trapped by her doctor's notions of proper behaviour. When she dispels his first assumption that she should have the child, he then decides to contact her school to verify that her record warrants her continuing school and thereby justifies an abortion. He also refuses to allow her to keep the pregnancy and abortion a secret from her mother, insisting that she must sign consent forms even though he knows Alice is of age and need not do so.

In 'The Bridge', Fiona tries to fight against Charlie's assumptions about domesticity and women's roles in the art world, but she runs up against a similar entrenched sense of male superiority and patronisation that confronts Alice in 'A Proper Respect'. Charlie counters her claim that art needs to reflect the everyday nature of life by belittling the way women approach artistic careers, particularly women who postpone their careers to raise families. 'What you lot need to do is realign your priorities', he informs her. 'That's where women always fuck up, you know? Sentimentality.'[26] Charlie's smug lecture rests on the double standard Galloway sees persisting in gender structures – that women often choose between a career and a family while men are not expected to make such choices. Fiona, in fact, remembers vague rumours of Charlie having a wife and child in the US during art school; a family that he has now ostensibly abandoned to pursue his artistic goals. By warning Fiona about her career, Charlie reinforces his intention not to become involved with her[27] and elucidates the either/or future that she can expect, regardless of her considerations of her own talent or future plans.

While these cultural expectations of male superiority and flexibility at times confine her female characters, Galloway does offer women who refuse to submit to entrenched social codes. In 'Fearless', for example, the narrator recalls defying social norms and lashing out against an unfair social code during her childhood – a defiance that, as an adult, she feels is the necessary fight for women. She remembers one event concerning the town drunk, Fearless, a small filthy man who harangues women and children. Fearless's license for behaviour, the narrator tells us, stems from the fact that he does not harass the men, and that women, or rather a woman, have been the source of his anger. The men 'let him get on with what he did as his business', and smile 'for boys being boys or something like that'. The women are forced to endure Fearless's attacks and tantrums because 'you had to remember his wife left him. It was our fault really'. With an adult's hindsight the narrator sees this required endurance as another example of 'the way we put up with everything else that didn't make sense or wasn't fair; the hard, volatile maleness of the whole West Coast Legend'.[28] Like the narrator in 'Frostbite', this woman is subjected to a tirade against women one day when Fearless singles out her mother for his abuse. Unlike 'Frostbite''s narrator, however, the child, unwilling to conform to feminine social standards, lashes out at her abuser. She stares directly at Fearless, rather than averting her gaze, and kicks him in the shin. The adult narrator recalls this incident every time a 'Fearless' appears – 'blustering at bus stops where I have to wait alone'.[29] The problem is twofold, she claims. Women who, although they are 'less ready to comply, look away and know our place', still minimise themselves in the face of blustering male abuse and men who 'smil[e] and ignor[e]' because they 'don't need to. It's not their battle' combine to perpetuate a misogynistic social structure. Yet the narrator refuses to submit – 'I kick like a mule' she tells us.[30]

Feminist and domestic expectations

'Fearless' presents the conflict between domestic expectations of women and feminist expectations of self-empowerment. For many of Galloway's characters, the two identities conflict, leaving her women characters bewildered, searching for a formula to happiness in relationships and feelings of self-worth. These women scrutinise their every interaction with the men in their lives, struggling to balance personal needs with the role they are expected to play. Again, many of these women try to be 'good' and receive no reward, but also learn that being self-sufficient delivers only a mixed reward at best. These characters are trapped between contrary expectations – the dominant masculinist cultural expectation that they will fill carefully delineated roles, and the feminist expectation that they will fight against such typing. But, Galloway reveals, to negotiate successfully between the two extremes becomes impossible. Her women characters interpret and reinterpret the world around them according to different social maps and find themselves lost every time.

Galloway's first novel, *The Trick Is to Keep Breathing*, introduces Joy Stone, a Glaswegian woman in her late twenties who is struggling to stay emotionally afloat after her lover, Michael, has drowned while on holiday. As Joy moves painfully through each day, the reader sees her identity uncertainty as she tries, and fails, to define herself through the various daily routines and roles available to her. Her position as a drama teacher at a local school offers her an identity during her time in the classroom – 'it tells me what I am', she announces[31] – but as the novel progresses her ability to maintain the illusion of confidence and authority deteriorates, prompting increased absenteeism until finally she enters a convalescence hospital and takes a leave of absence. She also tries to fill a daughterly role for Ellen, the mother of her best friend, Marianne, who has taken a year-long teaching position in the US. Yet she cannot respond to Ellen's kind advice, motherly concern, and offerings of food-as-solace – a role that at once requires too much docility and too much effort.

Similarly, her position as a bookkeeper in a betting hall on Saturdays offers a routine that proves unable to support her. The married owner, Tony, insistently makes sexual advances, finally succeeding by getting her tipsy at dinner. To Tony, Joy matters only as a sexual conquest. Yet Joy puts herself in this role with David, a first-year student at university, who spends the night with her once a week. She prepares for his Sunday visit with an elaborate beautification routine intended to mask her distress and provide physical closeness as a substitute for emotional sustenance. For each of these men, Joy exists only on a sexual level, denying her a mental and an emotional presence, so these half-existences offer no support structure on which to rebuild her life. She is even denied a 'legitimate' mourner's role for Michael – a role occupied at the funeral and memorial service by his wife, even though the two were awaiting a divorce.

As a result, Joy turns inward, looking to the house she shared with Michael for solace and support. She centres herself in the kitchen, baking and cooking, creating food gifts for friends, 'a good wife going to waste'.[32] She polishes the glass jars of ingredients, stocking her cabinets with various flours, chutneys, and preserves, and she sews clothing, matching patterns and fabrics. Yet the domestic landscape also reveals beneath the surface a decay and instability that reflects, not counteracts, Joy's own shattered identity. 'The cleaning is just a sham', she tells us. 'Superficially everything looks fine but underneath is another story.' The cooker hides 'dried up breadcrumb and frozen peas, flakes of onion skin' and concealed grease. 'Broken glass crunches on the floor like sugar. I shove unidentifiable debris under the rug and hope it stays put.'[33] The barely concealed filth in the kitchen matches the unconcealed disarray in the bedroom: blood stains on the bed, broken glass on the floor, heaps of unwashed clothing, and cobwebs obscuring the windows.

For Joy, this domestic space, a space that should be nurturing, instead becomes threatening. The house lashes back at her, inflicting 'domestic wounds' – 'needles punctured pincushions into my finger ends and left little scratches on my wrists alongside the bruises from shifting furniture, sears from the oven and tears in my nails from cleaning'.[34] Sleepless nights lead to broken bedside water glasses, leaving long cuts on her arms and fragments ground underfoot in a trail to the similarly dishevelled bathroom. The house provides an additional threat, rather than a refuge. Joy cannot find solace in her house because it, too, requires her to engage in now meaningless role-play. The cooking and sewing, small domestic chores, dysfunction as healing activities, reminding her that she is a housewife going to waste because she no longer acts within a domestic partnership.

Joy tries to escape within the confines of her house through the various women's magazines she buys in the supermarket. The novel's text proclaims article headlines, claims and promises for self-improvement and self-fulfilment, at the same time that it reveals how ineffective, and personally damaging, such guidelines for living are. Bylines such as 'Kiss me Quick Lips – we show you how!' and 'Make this your BEST EVER CHRISTMAS!' share space with Joy's quiet desperation. She tries to make sense of these magazine dictates that at once describe ways of capturing men through sexy makeup and clothing and 'best ever' recipes, and also tell women to be more self-sufficient and independent, to be 'Young, Dynamic, Today's Woman',[35] and listen to 'Tough Talking from Women Who've Made It'[36] but cannot apply either of the two extremes to her own situation.

The magazines that occupy her time and frustrate her path to recovery also convey expectations from the hostile world she tries to escape. By allowing the magazines into her home, Joy violates the safe space of the house, reminding her of the dangers that await her 'outside'. And, in fact, these dangers – Tony, David, the Health Visitor sent by her doctor, Ellen bearing gifts of food, and her older, estranged sister Myra – all descend on Joy. At times, like Myra and Tony, they literally invade the house, causing additional damage to Joy's emotional health by demanding that she fill the role of some-time mistress or loyal younger sister when she is least able to defend herself. The house becomes a prison rather than a refuge; at one point she literally flees the house in order to escape Myra's enquiries and sisterly claims. Instead of protecting Joy and providing a retreat, her domestic space gives way time and again to this threatening external environment that demands she toe the social line at the same time that it alienates her from a meaningful sense of self. In addition, the domestic environment itself ceases to be a woman's domain and becomes hostile.

Galloway addresses this domestic 'betrayal' in a number of works. While in 'Last Thing' she explores the dangers that await women on city streets, as the narrator is attacked while walking a friend home, in 'Someone Had To' she explores the abuse of a young girl by the male narrator. The narrator becomes increasingly unsettled by Kimberly's refusal to conform to his behavioural expectations – she watches the household quietly, so that the narrator feels she is judging him. When he punishes her, standing her in the corner, for example, her eyes still follow him, prompting him to increase the levels of punishment in order to break her resistance and resilience. During this process the accoutrements of daily living – the cupboard in which he locks her and the bathtub he fills with boiling water and in which he immerses her body – take on the attributes of torturous instruments.

Yet in Galloway's stories, the more insidious tortures involve women who witness not only the larger injuries and injustices, but also the smaller, pervasive, day-to-day gender exclusions that leave them as lost as Joy is in a hostile environment. In 'Not Flu', for example, Rachel slowly becomes a stranger in her own flat as Peter and Marc, her partner and his visiting friend, exclude her from their relationship. At first Peter and Marc tease her for being too 'fussy and overprotective', making light of her domestic concerns and going to the pub without her, claiming she wouldn't enjoy it. But soon Rachel notices that they exist on a schedule meant to exclude her, arranging separate meals, working on blueprints together behind closed doors, and eventually speaking entirely in Dutch so that she cannot participate at all. When she changes the sheets naked one night after Peter has night sweats, his exasperated sigh at the evidence of her body and his request that she not be so 'obvious' reveal her to be superfluous. Peter wants her to be invisible in the household, preferring his relationship with Marc to Rachel's presence. In effect, Peter and Marc seek to erase her from her own house[37] – seeding the domestic environment with masculine prerogative despite Rachel's attempts to minister to their needs. The hints Rachel uncovers multiply like the mushrooms in Joy's cottage that slowly break down the infrastructure and reveal themselves only after spreading spores throughout.

Fairy tales dispelled

Threats to domestic stability and happiness for women hide beneath the surface of Galloway's stories. She exposes a harsh reality lurking in the fairy tale ending, revealing her women characters to be more like Cinderella's sisters, abandoned at the end despite their attempts at emotional self-mutilation,[38] than like Cinderella herself. When Galloway's characters conduct a constant enquiry into how best to arrange their lives, they inevitably sink into the guilt spiral that society offers them, blaming themselves for failings in their relationships, families, households, jobs, and themselves. In addition, Joy tells us, society trains women to spend their time waiting for 'fantasy future[s]' that suck away the present day and render them powerless. Women 'think things will be better if they wait longer', she says.

> ie [sic] when
> – I get away from my mother
> – when I live with the man-I-love
> – when I get away from the man-I-love
> – when my mother loves me more
> . – when anyone loves me more
> – when I finish the diet/buy new clothes/get a haircut/buy new make-up/learn to be nicer/sexier/more tolerant/turn into someone else[39]

The prevailing social sentiment promotes passivity, being 'good' while waiting for the reward while at the same time ensuring that women never feel 'good' enough. This need for self-acceptance *in spite of* the social models available for self-interpretation offers Galloway's women the only avenue for meaning-making – an avenue many of her women do not find. In effect, characters such as Joy must accept that their lives, like most women's, will not result in the 'new you!'[40] that her magazines claim.

The disruption of happily-ever-after formulae in Galloway's works allow women to question gender assumptions as her characters realise conformity to social norms does not deliver happiness or fulfilment. As Josiane Paccaud Huguet suggests, these stories speak 'to those who are no longer seduced by the Victorian Hearts and Flowers'[41] – romanticising women's virtues and rewards – including the characters themselves. Eventually, some of these women feel the stirrings of resentment at the behavioural assumptions they are expected to meet, although only rarely do they act against them.

In 'Fair Ellen and the Wanderer Returned', for example, the female character learns that the romantic notion of unrequited love serves only men, never women. After an absence of ten years, the Wanderer finds Ellen and expects that she will now marry him. Yet, as Ellen explains, the years of necessity, of first 'waiting' on her dying father, then her dying mother, and now her elderly and dying husband, married out of financial necessity, have crushed Ellen's hopes for her future. 'If he dies I will be free for the first time', she announces. 'Do you think now I want to wait again, to fetch and carry for you when your time is come after all these years of nothing?'[42] Ellen's life presents her with only two choices – a life of compromise and self-sacrifice with a partner, or a life alone.

In 'Sonata Form', Mona chooses the life of self-sacrifice – a choice that becomes evident as we follow her through the post-concert reception for her music virtuoso lover. She tidies his tuxedo, organises his bag, and arranges food for him at the reception while groups of women chatter at him. As one woman notes, 'somebody needs to be the practical one, able to do the organising and things',[43] the assumption being that Mona should fill that role. Accustomed to being secondary, she is rendered speechless when two musician friends offer her congratulatory roses for her pregnancy. Yet despite the genuine love she expresses for Danny, the end of the story reveals a distance between them – a distance also evident in the ways Charles and Alice react to the fight in 'Need for Restraint'. When Mona demands that Danny tell her their child will not be a musician he does not understand her need to feel that she and the child will be a consciously central part of his life. Instead, he refuses this reassurance, 'getting fed up with this, whatever it was'.[44]

This dysfunctional communication between the sexes becomes a central theme in Galloway's work. Her women struggle to communicate feelings and emotions but are met with hostility and incomprehension from the men with whom they need to connect. In turn, they absorb anger and blame, feeling guilty for being too demanding or, as the narrator of 'Valentine' suggests, 'hard bitch[es]'[45] – echoing the accusation the Wanderer levies at Ellen as he leaves her again. In 'Valentine', Norma accepts the saccharine verses from her lover's Valentine's Day card in place of his verbalisation of emotions. She tries to 'get below the surface' of the lines, 'which parts of it are closest to what he would say himself if he ever said things like that out loud. Only he doesn't', she continues. 'People don't, he says. That's what cards are for.'[46] Not only do cards replace the emotions she wishes to express, but also sexual caresses under the dinner table replace intimate conversation at the restaurant. Yet even the physical contact denies her the companionship she desires. After sex in the car on the way home, 'further touch is unlikely'.[47] Instead, as she walks into the sitting room, she hears his 'solution. Dirk Bogarde being earnest about something in a late-night movie. We always have the tv.'[48]

Disrupted communication also plagues Irene and Callum in 'Proposal'. When she realises during a visit to his parents' house that he had not yet told them about their upcoming holiday to Belfast and questions him about it, he lies insistently, refusing to address the larger issue she wants to discuss. To Irene, the lie represents a personal withholding – an 'evasion'[49] of the larger issue of emotional separation that lies between them. When Callum again evades the problem, bringing up his rejected marriage proposal to her and again asking her to marry him, we see the different levels of communication each occupies. Callum's refusal to address Irene's concern and insistence on binding her to the relationship, and Irene's inability to explain her own feelings and the importance of sharing information, reveal the emotional disconnection Galloway sees between men and women.

This disconnection provides insight into Cassie's relationships in Galloway's second novel, *Foreign Parts*. As a thirty-nine-year-old Cassie and Rona drive through Normandy on their holidays, Galloway inter-jects Cassie's recollections of past relationships into the story through a series of snapshots detailing past holidays, creating an image of former lovers that explains Cassie's single, and lonely, state. As the snapshots progress through the novel, we see that the ineffective communication between Cassie and her partners in turn guarantees a dysfunctional relationship. For each snapshot, Cassie associates the image with larger concerns and issues the photograph suggests, slowly revealing her fears about her own inadequacies as well as the assumptions her partners have made about her role in the relationship.

Photographs of Chris, her boyfriend of thirteen years, dominate the holiday snaps she shows us. From the beginning of the series we see the restrictions that Chris, and Cassie in turn, impose upon her. On their visit to Edinburgh, for example, Chris refuses to allow her to drive – 'fair enough. His car', Cassie tells us.[50] On holiday in Turkey, thirteen years later, Chris refuses to let Cassie buy decorative brass plates. 'It's my flat',[51] he announces, despite their having shared that flat for years. Chris displays a singularity that creates a void in his relationship with Cassie throughout the vignettes, warning her in Naxos to behave demurely so that he will not be 'left with the consequences'[52] and abandoning her in Turkey with a 'YOU'RE ON YOUR OWN' when a crowd of men follow them down the street, enraged by the short skirt Chris has encouraged her to wear.[53]

Yet Cassie accepts and even encourages this emotional separation and Chris's self-centeredness. When Chris insists on Greek beach holidays, sighing that he gets only two weeks of vacation and does not want to visit museums or ruins, Cassie thinks it 'seem[s] reasonable at the time. I didn't say two weeks was all I got too.'[54] She also feels the need to humour Chris in his own sense of importance, letting him get lost along Greek streets and pretending he had meant to take a 'diversion' all along, following at a 'respectful distance',[55] and not objecting when he pretends to be English rather than Scottish and talks 'in a drawl about the Houses of Parliament and London Our Capital'[56] so as not to be considered unimportant. Instead, Cassie makes 'tender allowances'[57] and acts 'supportive',[58] even though she constantly modifies her behaviour to coincide with what he wants. The short skirt that causes problems in Turkey, for example, is part of an outfit she has 'learned to wear on holiday' – what Chris expects of her.[59] When Chris stares 'regretfully' at his dirty travel washing, Cassie is 'meant to come to the rescue', washing clothing along Greek roadsides.[60] Eventually, Cassie takes solace in her sexual routine with Chris, 'still tr[ying] to get enough out of that'[61] even though all other aspects of the relationship alienate her – 'no trust at all', she comments.[62]

Yet despite her realisation that Chris is 'not Mr. Right after all',[63] Cassie continues to pursue relationships with men who are similarly self-absorbed, falling into the same complicit and 'supportive' role that she occupied with Chris. With Tom, she goes to the same resort beaches, watching him eye the near-naked women and ignoring her when other Scottish men are around to 'talk shop'. As in her relationship with Chris, she allows physical closeness to replace emotional closeness. 'I don't know what made me go anywhere with him at all', she muses, then remembers 'what he could do with his mouth'.[64] In effect, Cassie has moved to yet another Mr Wrong – she cannot break away from the need to please and to belong to a partnership, even when that partnership offers only distance rather than closeness. With Barry, her last relationship, Cassie tries not to beg for that closeness, settling for the physical and 'forc[ing] me to keep my emotions to myself'.[65] Yet when Barry reveals that he is returning to a relationship with his boyfriend, Cassie realises that 'even asking for that little from someone had proved too much'.[66]

As a result, Cassie begins to question the 'fairy tales and bride dolls',[67] the 'child in there pining for happy ever after'.[68] She speaks with Rona a number of times during their Normandy holiday about the alienation of women within heterosexual relationships, finally exclaiming, 'the knight on a white charger is never going to come, Rona. You know why? Because he's down the pub with the other knights, that's why.'[69] At the same time that Cassie struggles with these memories of defunct relationships, trying to determine where the fault lies, Rona has chosen to forsake relationships in favour of pursuing her own goals. 'You only get the one shot at things and men use up too much energy. It's just too easy to miss out on what your own life might be about',[70] she argues. 'Dependencies build up, then the power games … Trying to make him take on his fair share of the work involved, and I mean the emotional work as well as the cleaning the toilet stuff … The idea can be fine. But that's all it is. I'd rather keep it that way.'[71]

Rona's observation and choice illustrate a common quandary in Galloway's works. Many of her characters feel forced to choose between participation in a restricted relationship or the freedom to follow their own desires. Yet few characters are satisfied with the either/or position they occupy. Galloway, Burgess explains, creates women who 'want[] and need[] some other person; a continuing tension in women's lives'.[72] Women who are left on their own find managing their own lives, as opposed to being held responsible for someone else's happiness, a difficult task. Cassie 'wants closeness, desperately',[73] and her emotional openness creates a constant self-enquiry about how to interact. In turn, her feelings of self-doubt drive her from lover to lover after her first long-term relationship ends, seeking acceptance and trying desperately to fathom other people's desires.

This need in turn drives her relationship with Rona. As their holiday continues, Cassie attempts repeatedly to understand Rona, but cannot, until the end of the novel, recognise Rona's inscrutability as complimentary to her own self-awareness. Cassie's struggle to decipher and accommodate Rona's needs repeats the cycle of co-dependence she exhibits in her other relationships and results in equal frustration. But when Cassie suggests that the two of them share a flat and create a permanent companionship, then returns to that thought at the end of the novel, she realises the possibility of a relationship devoid of the caretaking responsibilities she has assumed with men. Rona offers a relationship of self-sufficiency and companionship, not dependence and guilt. The deepening relationship between Rona and Cassie, prompted by Cassie's acceptance of a new role divorced from sex or gender, offers a 'reinterpretation' or 'rough repair'[74] of self-identity that releases Cassie from co-dependency and instead offers 'a glimpse of new possibilities, of a way of living which might not be determined by all the old discourses' of gendered roles.[75] *Foreign Parts* at times presents Rona as a sensual physical figure through Cassie's eyes – a presentation that, paired with Cassie's consideration of Rona as a live-in companion, has led some critics to consider the possibility of a homosexual relationship budding between the two characters. Certainly the potential exists, although, as Galloway explains, even if Cassie is thinking "'I've been screwed enough by men, is it worth a go?'" sexuality 'doesn't work like that. Plenty of gay people would be largely heterosexual by now if it did.'[76]

Exploring the body

Despite such possibilities for companions who offer alternative emotional routes and potentially equal partnerships, Galloway's female characters remain body conscious, feeling the absence of both the sensuality and sexuality of male bodies. Cassie's physical desires figure prominently in her failed relationships. And when Rona asks why she misses men, Cassie remembers 'the silk of his belly … his pubic hair scouring the tip of my nose like a hat veil, like net … the bolt of hard softness stretched out next to where I am'.[77]

A number of Galloway's short stories rhapsodise about male bodies as well. In 'Where You Find It', for example, the narrator describes Derek's kisses as 'bringing something up from somewhere deep',[78] this 'root of this other tongue with taste buds bristling, studding up like braille [sic] saying I AM KISSING YOU NOW'.[79] In 'Six Horses' Eve gazes at a man's body hair, 'thick twine over his sternum and belly widens out into black ferns'.[80] The narrator of 'Bisex' envisions her lover's sexual contact with another man, 'falling blond, the fringe lapping the closed lids as his fist accelerates and your mouth opens, that catch in your breath … your hands lace, sticky'.[81] Some stories emphasise the sensuality of sexual contact. In 'David', for example, the narrator describes an impromptu liaison with David in the bathroom at a party, 'the pile of carpet pushing through the thin stuff of my blouse and I was arching like a bridge … the slip of a single vertebra. And he entered sudden and hard not like a man but guileless, his hair falling into my eyes'.[82]

Generally Galloway's male bodies do not frighten or intimidate – they become objets d'art that women characters capture within the story's photographic lens – snapshots of body parts, close-ups of skin and hair, emphasising sensuality. Yet when women's bodies enter these snapshots, the camera can turn cruel and ugly. In 'The Meat', for example, the reader learns that the carcass hanging in the butcher's shop, turning away uneasy customers, is the butcher's own wife, flayed and dressed, and ultimately thrown to the dogs in an alley. Women's bodies are often segmented and disconnected, and the fluidity of the body shifts from the moving body to the movement underneath the skin. Women's bodies break open and bleed, and, like the schoolgirl in 'Blood', whose bloody mouth frightens and drives away the male music student, are both fragile and threatening. These women overflow body boundaries, becoming dangerous both socially and textually.

Yet these women's bodies initially appear frail, sensitive skin breaking easily under external pressures. In 'David', for example, the sexually vulnerable narrator's lip splits under a kiss, prefiguring the impending sexual penetration, while in 'A Week with Uncle Felix', Senga receives a wasp sting on her hand that at once punishes her for acquiring sexual awareness.[83] 'Bisex''s narrator cuts her lip on the rim of a broken teacup as she envisions her lover's homosexual liaisons, while 'Blood''s narrator experiences the humiliating conflation of the blood flowing from the cavity in her mouth and the onset of her menstrual period – emphasised by the dentist's application of a sanitary pad to her mouth to slow the bleeding.

Similarly, Joy in *The Trick Is to Keep Breathing* suffers not only the 'domestic wounds' of keeping house but also the effects of anorexia. Her decision to stop eating, when she cuts her hand on a can of soup while plunging it into the can's 'flattened jelly … semi-solid mush seeth[ing] and slump[ing] over the sides',[84] stems from the social pressure following Michael's death. Joy's body succumbs to this pressure,[85] acknowledging the male culture that requires her to look sexually desirable despite her emotional emptiness, as her beautification ritual for David's visits illustrates. As Susan Bordo explains, Joy has bowed to a 'threatening masculine look' that 'materially inscribes its power onto women's bodies by constituting feminine subjects through an intense self-awareness about being seen and about taking up space'.[86] Her experience at Michael's memorial service, during which the Reverend Dogsbody socially 'erases' her existence by announcing the bereavement of Michael's wife without mentioning Joy, acts on Joy as a physical erasure, emphasising her physical unimportance. Joy tells us:

1. The Rev. Dogsbody had chosen this service to perform a miracle.
2. He'd run time backwards, cleansed, absolved and got rid of the ground-in stain.
3. And the stain was me.
I didn't exist. The miracle had wiped me out.[87]

Joy's physical erasure and her attempts to assist that erasure through her anorexic behaviour leave her feeling increasingly vulnerable and fragile – physically displaced. 'I have lost the ease of being inside my own skin', she announces.[88]

This physical dis-ease similarly affects the schoolgirl in 'Blood', who finds the yawning hole in her mouth, filled with blood, an uncomfortable reminder of the blood beginning to flow from her menstrual cycle. The dual bleeding, accompanied by the sight of the gnarled tooth that the dentist pulled, makes her uncomfortable in her own body, prompting her to escape to the 'fresh and clean' white music room. The music room contrasts with the girls' lavatory, the message that 'GIRLS ARE A BUNCH OF CUNTS'[89] carved into the door reminding the girl of her bodily discomfort in a way similar to Joy's estrangement from her own body.

Yet the embarrassment of the schoolgirl's body offers a power that transforms the claim that 'girls are a bunch of cunts' into a physical presence threatening men and masculinity. When she encounters the male music student who is, her instructor explains, 'afraid of girls and who could blame him haha',[90] the blood pours from her accidentally opened mouth, driving him from the room. The conflation of her bleeding mouth and her menstruating body displays the physicality of the 'cunt' the bathroom door denounces. In effect, Huguet argues, Galloway reveals the female body 'as the locus of projection for male fears',[91] imbuing it with a power that can overcome the social restrictions imposed upon it.

Smith suggests that in *The Trick* ... Galloway offers a similarly 'frightening, inescapable nihilism lurking beneath the acceptable construction of female identity'.[92] Such a nihilism functions, Margaret Elphinstone explains, as a 'subversive female vision through the text of a patriarchal world'.[93] Elphinstone ties this subversive woman to a new 'Scottish heritage for women writers' that involves the 'figure of the dangerous woman'. Such a woman, she continues, 'may sometimes seem to align herself with a feminist perspective, but she refuses to become quite ideologically sound' – a refusal that 'may be related to her psychological alienation from the patriarchal model'.[94] Joy's reaction to her environment reflects this psychological alienation. Much as the narrator in *Blood*'s 'Plastering the Cracks' has allowed language to slip away from her, such that 'when people spoke, their words became simply noise, disembodied from sense',[95] so Joy has become disassociated with the language of daily life, allowing her routines to slip over her without internalising the events. As Burgess explains, Joy's world 'is becoming less and less real to her',[96] but unlike the narrator in 'Plastering the Cracks', Joy cannot pull back and recentre herself. She no longer internalises the system. As a result, she threatens the status quo from outside the system, discomfiting doctors who try to fit her into the prescribed female complaints of the health service[97] and puzzling men who try to understand her in purely sexual terms. As a woman who offers potential chaos to easy definitions of womanly behaviour, Joy resists attempts at categorisation, becoming a physical threat at the same time that she physically wastes away.

This dilemma counters Ali Smith's criticism of Galloway's work as embodying a 'paradox of the woman writing fiercely and bleakly at once about how gender silences you, takes away your language'.[98] Often, her characters speak through the body, exploring, as Huguet explains, 'the underlying experience of fragmentation' as a means of 'restor[ing] the reality of the female body with its holes and losses'.[99] By writing through this reality, Galloway presents women who both garner strength and expose weakness through their bodily presence.

The body fantastic

Yet this realism or, as Smith identifies it, a 'gruff and bleak New Naturalism'[100] that runs through much of Galloway's work often cedes her 'alignment in critics' minds with urban realistic writers like James Kelman' for 'an element of the surreal and fantastic'[101] that opens another avenue for expressing her concerns about the way women interact with the often hostile world around them. At times, this element of the surreal allows her to 'question whether this world even perceives women as real'.[102] Burgess refers specifically to 'Scenes from the Life No. 27: Living In', a 'playscript' in which the audience focuses on the morning and evening preparations of Tony, a seemingly single man, in his 'bachelor pad'. Yet at the end of the one-act play, in which the audience's focus has been on the flat the entire time, a woman emerges, ghostly, from the bed after Tony has gone to sleep. The naked woman steps in front of a mirror in the room and strokes her body, the stage directions demanding that the 'audience must never be sure whether she is substantial or not'.[103]

By creating this ethereal woman, Galloway illustrates the marginalised social and domestic position of women. The woman lies concealed by the duvet throughout the scene until the final minutes and reveals herself only when Tony is asleep – her naked body indicates her sexual role, and she is isolated in the flat with no apparent social recourse. At the same time, the firm yet gentle stroking of her body belies her ghost-liness; it is as if she is literally stroking herself into being, a physical body that comes to life only when Tony cannot witness her. By incorporating this element of the fantastic, Galloway can more succinctly illustrate issues that realist fiction may obscure in day-to-day details.

Others of Galloway's stories address gender and social issues through her use of the fantastic. In 'Into the Roots', for example, Alice's wild, untamed, lushly growing hair assumes otherworldly properties as she resists prevailing social codes throughout her childhood and young adulthood. She enjoys the heavy fringe of hair that hides her eyes and makes people suspicious, empowering her with unpredictability so unappealing in a girl. At the end of the story, Alice reaches into a split tree trunk, alone on a rainy street, to find it filled with hair – the losses of past years returned. In this story Galloway invokes both body imagery – hair rather than blood overflowing bodily boundaries – and the fantasy of a tree filled with the hair of Alice's early years to illustrate the unfulfilled power Alice possesses; a power ignored while she lived in Charles' flat where she 'smoothed sheets, sewed neat cushions and learned to cook'.[104] The camera she carries at the end of the story speaks to ambition mislaid, a potential career sidetracked by her adult conformity, the scandal of living with Charles rather than marrying him notwith-standing, to social rules. Alice's fear of moving forward alone translates into her fearfully plunging her hand into the tree bole.

Stories such as 'It Was' and 'Breaking Through' also play with fantastic elements that fill characters' emotional gaps by recreating absent families or communities. The woman in 'It Was' finds her uncle George buried in clay and excavates him, restoring him to a life he does not realise he has left. Rather than revealing the truth, the narrator pretends he is alive as well, enjoying the presence of family and the memories of childhood. 'Breaking Through' also addresses this issue of family and community. When Blackie, the elderly Bessie's cat, voluntarily cremates himself in the fireplace, Bessie chooses to follow, assisted by the young Janet. The event acts as a bond between Bessie and Janet, bridging generations and restoring a sense of female community lost in the urban landscape of which Janet is a part.

Galloway's use of the fantastic also extends to the macabre, like

Welsh's and Banks' works do, illustrating larger social problems through her conflation of unruly bodies and threatening landscapes. In 'After the Rains', the sudden heatwave that dries out a city after nine months of rain initially brings the community together, celebrating the fine weather and rejoicing in the dryness. Yet those nine months, the hint of gestation implicit in the number itself, births a curious transformation. The florist begins to sprout buds and flowers, tendrils curling up her arms, and the grocer grows cabbages and peas. Down the block the narrator sees the supermarket check-out boy sprouting a grocery carriage and the Co-op manager growing a washing machine chamber in his torso. As the narrator watches, though, the transformations become more hideous, as each person assumes the physical attributes of their occupations. Council office members become huge white grubs and eyeless creatures, and screaming emerges from the butcher shop. The narrator herself transforms as the story ends, becoming, we can assume, a sheet of paper. The story elaborates on the lack of community and personal closeness expressed in other stories, using fantasy to illustrate the negative effects of community breakdown and the reliance on occupation and social position to determine relationships. The very environment that appears welcome enacts the horrible transformation.

Endangered spaces

Galloway's use of the environment in her work informs the issues she chooses to present. Like Alan Warner and Duncan McLean, Galloway infuses her work with a sense of place, although her sparsely described urban spaces provide a more subtle infiltration of narrative events than the landscapes McLean and Warner present. Galloway's landscapes become hostile and dangerous for men and women on a domestic, cityscape, and even a national level. In 'Love in a Changing Environment' the young couple's tranquil and contented existence in the flat above a bakery turns acrimonious and tense when a butcher's shop moves in. This domestic tension transforms into domestic menace in 'Babysitting', when we realise that Tommy and Allan are isolated in the flat with their dead father. Tommy barricades the two of them in, making only the most necessary forays for fish and chips because he realises that the invasion of the external world will disrupt the illusion of normalcy he has created, but the domestic environment begins to injure the two children as well. Tommy kneels on crushed sugarcubes that leave pockmarks in his skin, amidst the blood bruises and cigarette burn scars as the odour of

his slowly decaying father fills the flat. For Tommy and Allan, all environments have become dangerous.

'Peeping Tom' also addresses the conflation of internal and external
environments as the narrator, initially comfortable in her flat, becomes
aware of the tenuous, even illusory, safety it offers – the safety of her
domestic space is easily penetrated by undesirable peering eyes, rendering
the city and the flat perilous. Galloway extends this alienating peril to
'Tourists from the South Arrive in the Independent State', recreating
Scotland as a strange new nation in others' eyes, presenting the social
and cultural decay of contemporary urban Scotland through the decrepit
cityscape, 'long stretches of wasteground ... graffiti under the bridges',[105]
dependent on a patronising tourist trade for economic livelihood. In this
story Galloway exposes the political, economic, and cultural connections
that create such a hostile environment for her characters, illustrating
James Charles Roy's claim that 'landscape affects personality, culture,
and heritage. It shapes outlook, perception, and definition. At its lowest
denominator, it creates mood and disposition, an influence as basic as
how a person gets through his day.'[106] The urban and domestic landscapes Galloway creates underlie the daily injustices her often bewildered
characters suffer.

Scottish departures

Douglas Gifford sees such 'strong urban regionalism' as a 'retreat to
home territory in order to reassess identity; a process perhaps involving
stepping back to examine first principles in order to decide on future
development'.[107] Such an observation of Galloway's short stories and
novels illustrates the development of her writing and the direction of
future projects. Galloway's projects in the mid-to-late 1990s increasingly
moved away from an exclusively Scottish context to a more international
focus (*Foreign Parts* is set in France, for example), and her concerns with
gender, particularly women creatively involved in the arts, have moved
her to a historiographic interest in women composers and musicians. In
1995, for instance, the Chamber Group of Scotland commissioned her to
write a framing text to be spoken through a concert of four women's
compositions: Clara Wieck Schumann's Trio in G minor, Janet Beat's
Five Projects for Joan, Lili Boulager's Nocturne and Cortege, and Fanny
Mendelssohn Hensel's Trio in D minor. The text Galloway created
draws on journal and diary entries from, biographical material about, and
letters by, the composers and their peers, woven together by Galloway's

own commentary on the socio-cultural inequities involved for women who write or compose. Her focus on the external influences that suppress women's creativity reflects the experiences of her own struggles to write. In the text, she repeats an all-too-familiar list of disclaimers for women's success within the creative arts:

> She didn't write it.
> She wrote it but she shouldn't have.
> She wrote it but what she wrote about doesn't count.
> She wrote it but she only wrote one of it.
> She wrote it but she isn't really an artist and it isn't really art.
> She wrote it but somebody must have helped her.
> She wrote it but she's an anomaly.
> She wrote it BUT...[108]

These complaints, Galloway claims, are paired with the nineteenth-century 'critical fallacy that Art is not Life. Art is Truth, Beauty, an Eternal Flame. But it is not Life. Life is what ordinary people have. Artists are not ordinary people.' The problem, she continues, is that the fallacy 'has left a remarkably pervasive legacy'[109] that continues to colour women writers' struggles.

This focus on the widesweeping inequities for women writers has influenced Galloway's shift from writing about Scottish women attempting to come to terms with a familiarly hostile social structure to writing about larger social concerns for women. One of Galloway's reasons for moving out of a Scottish milieu, much as Duncan McLean's *Lone Star Swing* departs from the Scottish landscapes of his earlier works, concerns a pursuit of interests apart from the need to write through self-experience. But, Galloway explains, a more pressing concern is the increasing popularity of Scottish writing during the 1990s, which creates for her the 'danger of being contained, gift-wrapped. We were all "urban and gritty", even those of us who weren't.' The effect, she points out, is a conceptualisation of 'the chaps and their priorities' as the '"culture", according to the *New Yorker*. I kept wanting to write and say *Excuse me, there are women over here as well, taking only prescribed drugs if any.*' The problem becomes twofold, Galloway explains. 'The word "Scottish" started to mean this media-thing rather than anything else', and 'the most visible of it seems to be about being blokey – adolescent blokey at that.' In addition, her desire to *'make visible*'[110] the marginalised lives of Scottish women has, to some extent, been achieved, creating a desire to move on to other unexplored or under-appreciated areas for literary creativity. As a result, Galloway's writing is opening up new avenues for exploration, quieting claims, such as Ali Smith's, that her work is too heavily rooted in the bleak writing of the 1980s to offer a valid perspective of present-day Scottish literature.

Notes

1   J. Galloway, 'Different oracles: me and Alasdair Gray', *Review of Contemporary Fiction*, 15.2 (1995), 195.
2   *Ibid.*, 193.
3   *Ibid.* 195.
4   J. Galloway, 'Objective truth and the grinding machine', 6 June 2000, available at www.galloway.1to1.org/objective.html.
5   *Ibid.*
6   *Ibid.*
7   I. A. Bell, 'Imagine living there: form and ideology in contemporary Scottish fiction', in S. Hagemann (ed.), *Studies in Scottish Fiction: 1945 to Present* (Frankfurt am Main, Peter Lang GmbH, 1996), 220.
8   J. Galloway, 'Balancing the books', 6 June 2000, available at www. galloway.1to1.org/books.html.
9   C. March, 'Interview with Janice Galloway', *Edinburgh Review* 101 (1999), 85.
10 S. Coombe, 'Stella Coombe interviews Janice Galloway', *Harpies and Quines* 1 (May/June 1992), 27.
11 A. Smith, 'Four success stories', *Chapman* 74–5 (Autumn/Winter 1993), 192.
12 Galloway, 'Different oracles', 194.
13 Coombe, 'Stella Coombe interviews', 29.
14 March, 'Interview with Janice Galloway', 85.
15 G. Norquay, 'The fictions of Janice Galloway: "weaving a route through chaos"', in G. Norquay and G. Smyth (eds), *Space and Place* (Liverpool, John Moores University Press, 1997), 325.
16 Coombe, 'Stella Coombe interviews', 27.
17 D. Gifford, 'Imagining Scotlands: the return to mythology in modern Scottish fiction', in S. Hagemann (ed.), *Studies in Scottish Fiction: 1945 to Present* (Frankfurt am Main, Peter Lang GmbH, 1996), 30.
18 M. Burgess, 'Disturbing words: Rose, Galloway, and Kennedy', in H. Kidd (ed.), *Calemadonnas: Women and Scotland* (Gairfish, 1994), 98.
19 J. Galloway, *The Trick Is to Keep Breathing* (Normal, IL, Dalkey Archive Press [1989], 1995), 81–2.
20 J. Galloway, 'Frostbite', in *Blood* (London, Minerva [Martin Secker & Warburg Limited, 1991], 1992), 25.
21 *Ibid.*
22 *Ibid.*, 28.
23 J. Galloway, 'Need for Restraint', in *Blood* (London, Minerva [Martin Secker & Warburg Limited, 1991], 1992), 82.

24 *Ibid.*, 83.
25 *Ibid.*, 84.
26 J. Galloway, 'The Bridge', in *Where You Find It* (London, Vintage [Jonathan Cape Ltd., 1996], 1997), 153.
27 He even refuses her a kiss, denying her the physical contact that for her has replaced emotional contact.
28 J. Galloway, 'Fearless', in *Blood* (London, Minerva [Martin Secker & Warburg Limited, 1991], 1992), 113.
29 *Ibid.*, 115.
30 *Ibid.*
31 J. Galloway, *The Trick Is to Keep Breathing* (Normal, IL, Dalkey Archive Press [Polygon, 1989], 1995), 12.
32 *Ibid.*, 41.
33 *Ibid.*, 92.
34 *Ibid.*, 38.
35 *Ibid.*, 193.
36 *Ibid.*, 158.
37 We learn early in the story that Rachel has asked Peter to move in with her – a significant arrangement given the progress of the story, particularly when Galloway's works more usually entail a woman moving into her boyfriend's apartment and experiencing a subsequent lack of domestic entitlement.
38 And, as I will explain later in the chapter, physical self-mutilation.
39 Galloway, *The Trick*, 193.
40 *Ibid.*, 27.
41 J. Huguet, 'Breaking through cracked mirrors: the short stories of Janice Galloway', 6 June 2000, available at www.galloway.1to1.org/Josiane.html. Strikingly, Galloway's second volume of short stories, *Where You Find It*, has such an image on the cover – two sandwiches cut into heart shapes bordered by yellow roses. That one of the sandwiches has a bite taken out of it, an incomplete heart, indicates the dispelling of such a romantic myth – the hearts are edible, impermanent.
42 J. Galloway, 'Fair Ellen and the Wanderer Returned', in *Blood* (London, Minerva [Martin Secker & Warburg Limited, 1991], 1992), 75.
43 J. Galloway, 'Sonata Form', in *Where You Find It* (London, Vintage [Jonathan Cape Ltd., 1996], 1997), 27.
44 *Ibid.*, 34.
45 J. Galloway, 'Valentine', in *Where You Find It* (London, Vintage [Jonathan Cape Ltd., 1996], 1997), 12.
46 *Ibid.*, 3.
47 *Ibid.*, 13.
48 *Ibid.*
49 J. Galloway, 'Proposal', in *Where You Find It* (London, Vintage [Jonathan Cape Ltd., 1996], 1997), 208.

50 J. Galloway, *Foreign Parts* (Normal, IL, Dalkey Archive Press [Jonathan Cape Ltd., 1994], 1995), 31.

51 *Ibid.*, 155.

52 *Ibid.*, 80.

53 *Ibid.*, 142.

54 *Ibid.*, 90.

55 *Ibid.*, 80.

56 *Ibid.*, 179.

57 *Ibid.*, 68.

58 *Ibid.*, 179.

59 *Ibid.*, 136.

60 *Ibid.*, 111.

61 *Ibid.*, 144.

62 *Ibid.*, 85.

63 *Ibid.*, 189. When she finally enjoys herself on holiday, for the first time that we notice, on a long bus trip through the Turkish hills that Chris sulks through.

64 *Ibid.*, 206–7.

65 *Ibid.*, 212.

66 *Ibid.*, 222.

67 *Ibid.*, 249.

68 *Ibid.*, 250.

69 *Ibid.*

70 *Ibid.*, 246.

71 *Ibid.*, 247.

72 Burgess, 'Disturbing words', 100.

73 March, 'Interview with Janice Galloway', 95.

74 Norquay, 'The fictions of Janice Galloway', 328.

75 *Ibid.*, 329.

76 March, 'Interview with Janice Galloway', 95.

77 Galloway, *Foreign Parts*, 248.

78 Galloway, 'Where You Find It', in *Where You Find It* (London, Vintage [Jonathan Cape Ltd., 1996], 1997), 17.

79 *Ibid.*, 18.

80 J. Galloway, 'Six Horses', in *Where You Find It* (London, Vintage [Jonathan Cape Ltd., 1996], 1997), 221.

81 J. Galloway, 'Bisex', in *Where You Find It* (London, Vintage [Jonathan Cape Ltd., 1996], 1997), 90.

82 J. Galloway, 'David', in *Where You Find It* (London, Vintage [Jonathan Cape Ltd., 1996], 1997), 39.

83 Huguet, 'Breaking through', n. pag.

84 Galloway, *The Trick*, 38.

85 The cover photo to the Dalkey Archive Press paperback edition, Auguste Rodin's 'The Fallen Caryatid Carrying Her Stone' additionally illustrates this crushing pressure.

86 G. Rose, *Feminism and Geography: The Limits of Geographical Knowledge* (Minneapolis, University of Minnesota Press, 1993), 146.

87 Galloway, *The Trick*, 79.

88 *Ibid.*, 165.

89 J. Galloway, 'Blood', in *Blood* (London, Minerva [Martin Secker & Warburg Limited, 1991], 1992), 5.

90 *Ibid.*, 7.

91 Huguet, 'Breaking through', n. pag.

92 Smith, 'Four success stories', 178.

93 M. Elphinstone, 'Contemporary feminist fantasy in the Scottish literary tradition', in C. Gonda (ed.), *Tea and Leg-Irons* (London, Open Letters, 1992), 48.

94 *Ibid.*, 47.

95 J. Galloway, 'Plastering the Cracks', in *Blood* (London, Minerva [Martin Secker & Warburg Limited, 1991], 1992), 95.

96 Burgess, 'Disturbing words', 99.

97 'Dr Stead wanted to handle things his way … He is a proud man and takes it hard', Joy tells us. Galloway, *The Trick*, 95.

98 Smith, 'Four success stories', 191.

99 Huguet, 'Breaking through', n. pag. Huguet's essay argues for consideration of Galloway's volume of short stories, *Blood*, as a Modernist work, creating a relationship between James Joyce's literary and linguistic techniques and Galloway's writing.

100 Smith, 'Four success stories', 191.

101 Burgess, 'Disturbing words', 96.

102 *Ibid.*, 98.

103 J. Galloway, 'Scenes from the Life No. 27: Living In', in *Blood* (London, Minerva [Martin Secker & Warburg Limited, 1991], 1992), 123.

104 J. Galloway, 'Into the Roots', in *Blood* (London, Minerva [Martin Secker & Warburg Limited, 1991], 1992), 61.

105 Galloway, 'Tourists from the South Arrive in the Independent State', in *Where You Find It* (London, Vintage [Jonathan Cape Ltd., 1996], 1997), 161.

106 J. C. Roy, 'Landscape and the Celtic soul', *Eire-Ireland* 31:3–4 (Autumn–Winter 1996), 229–30.

107 Gifford, 'Imagining Scotlands', 35–6.

108 J. Galloway, 'Singing outside heaven', 6 June 2000, available at www.galloway.1to1.org/Singing.html.

109 *Ibid.*, n. pag.

110 March, 'Interview with Janice Galloway', 92.

6

A. L. Kennedy's introspections

Questioning feminisms

Like Janice Galloway, A. L. Kennedy has often been pigeonholed as a feminist writer, a label she too views warily. 'I've certainly had feminists come to my readings and walk out … I think they came expecting me to be someone who conforms to their agenda', she notes. 'No guy ever does a reading and has a whole load of guys at the back standing up and saying, "why aren't you redefining maleness?"' The assumption, she continues, is that 'to be a female writer you must be something else too'.[1] Such assumptions about Kennedy's work ignore the focus of her writing – that her 'female characters are always individuals before they are women',[2] as Ali Smith claims. 'Gender doesn't seem to be a barrier', Smith argues. 'She explores it and is not dictated to by it'.[3] Kennedy also sees this distinction in her work as compared to Galloway's. 'She started at a time when it was a very male environment because basically there was Jim [Kelman] and there was Alasdair Gray and there was Tom Leonard. And there's a very bloke-y kind of air', Kennedy explains. Probably Galloway 'suffered the most from having to be there and be by herself and be female. I know she's got an agenda about that', she continues, 'but it may be at least in part because she was kind of out on a limb a wee bit. But now it's easier'.[4] As a result, Kennedy's work addresses problems of interpersonal connections rather than of gendered issues.[5]

Yet at times Kennedy's female characters fall victim to confining and damaging circumstances that stem from the gender inequity Galloway's work explores. In 'The Moving House', for example, the adolescent Grace is reunited with her mother, after having spent an enjoyable childhood living with her great-aunt, but finds her mother's house an unsafe place. Her mother's boyfriend, Chick, molests her, making it clear at the end of the story that he will continue to do so during her time there. Similarly, the teenage girl in 'Friday Payday' relies

on prostitution to support herself and her boyfriend in London, seemingly resigned to such a lifestyle yet recalling the chilling details of her
relationship with her first pimp, who arranges a gang rape as final
'payment' when she leaves him. In 'The Poor Souls' Kennedy explores
the emotional pressure that women bear through the first-person narrative of a woman driven mad by her position as one man's mistress.
Spurred by jealousy, she pushes him down the stairs and claims to be his
widow, although the hospital tells her she is neither his wife nor has she
killed him. When she sees him with a woman and child at the end of the
story, we are uncertain whether the 'accident' occurred at all, or whether
instead she was abandoned and subsequently became mentally unbalanced.
Such grim tales of women's oppression within a masculinist society
parallel some of Galloway's observations in, for example, *The Trick Is to
Keep Breathing* as well as a number of her short stories.

   Galloway's and Kennedy's positions as two of the most prominent
women writers of contemporary Scottish fiction have led numerous
critics to pair them in literary discussions – a pairing both writers see as
somewhat artificially created. 'Because we're [women writers] fewer,
there's a strange expectation we'll somehow bounce off each other – you
know, because you're both women and you're creative', Galloway notes,[6]
despite their dissimilar focus on contemporary issues such as gender,
urban Scotland, and working-class lives. Smith, for example, argues that
while Kennedy, like Galloway, 'examines the hard times and lost lives of
people', Kennedy 'emphasises the determination to survive, even possible
routes of survival'[7] over the degraded conditions of her characters. A
number of her short stories entail women who leave family situations or
relationships in order to reclaim their own lives or to find personal
fulfilment without compromising their own identities.

   Such release can be bittersweet for her characters. They learn self-
sufficiency, yet often internalise isolation for self-protection too. In
'Sweet Memory Will Die', for example, the narrator suggests a childhood
of domestic violence and then outlines her own marriage – also fraught
with violence and, finally, separation and the loss of her son to foster care
and adoption. She returns to confront her father – 'Elmer made me hate
and now I am tired of hating and now I am here to see him and put that
right,' she tells us[8] – but learns that she no longer cares enough to see him.
She has found release but it offers no recompense for the life she has lost.

   'Armaggedon Blue' offers its character more emotional liberty.
Rather than feeling constrained by past relationships, the unnamed
character sees her trip to the Continent as a way to regroup and reassess

her own potential after her 'psycho' boyfriend, whose role as a 'mani-pulator' has kept her from being the 'excellent person' she is without him.[9] Unlike the character in 'Sweet Memory Will Die', she recognises her life as 'a fucking heroic struggle'[10] but refuses to allow herself to 'slide over the edge'.[11] Instead, she envisions a European holiday from which she will return having 'discovered something she was very good at and became a magnificent success'.[12] While her vision is desperately bright and influenced by the pills she has stolen from her boyfriend, her resolution to refuse such men in the future and rely instead on her own abilities suggests an awareness of selfhood hitherto hidden by her depen-dence on abusive and psychotic relationships.

Kennedy's short story 'The High Walk' actualises these hints of self-sufficiency as the male narrator realises that his long-term girlfriend, Anne, estranged by his affair with their female roommate, Marie, no longer considers him necessary. When he invites her on a weekend in the mountains, he expects her acquiescence means a reconciliation. Yet at the end of the story she refuses him, making it clear that she will not see him again. Anne's departure speech upon discovering his affair with Marie marks the beginnings of her self-sufficiency, as she abandons dreams of marriage and children with the narrator to erase the horrible experience of her own childhood. Instead, she finds fulfilment on her own and rejects him again, biting him when he tries to kiss her in the car. While we do not know what changes Anne has made in her life, we see her new-found strength through the eyes of the confused narrator.

In 'Cap O'Rushes', Kennedy presents us with a character who escapes an imprisoning and oppressive family life to pursue her own goals. Increasingly dissatisfied with her role in relation to her husband and two sons, she begins to call them 'the goblins', realising when they are away for five days that she begins to read, sleeps better, and 'every day the house grew cleaner and more fragrant along with her'.[13] When they return, she views them with an objective eye that illustrates how much she hates them, noting that the sitting room 'now smelt like a cave as she walked in'.[14] Finally she leaves, finding a job and a new apartment, buying shelves full of books she loves and adding a baby clothes business on the side. Accustomed to devoting her time and attention to the Goblin King and his goblin sons, she relishes the time spent to herself, doing her secretarial job in the small office efficiently and indispensably, but at an emotional distance. 'They didn't know her. She made sure of that. It was a strength'.[15] When a co-worker, Ben, makes advances, she politely refuses them, noting 'how relaxing it was for an apparently single woman to finally know that she didn't have to care'. The enjoyment she feels knowing that 'she was enough in herself' makes her wish 'it hadn't taken her so many years to be strong'.[16] This empowerment, while solitary, allows her to break out of her conventional and stifling role as wife and mother and instead become 'capable of as much as wanted [sic] to be'.[17] Whereas the narrator in 'Sweet Memory Will Die' suffers when released from her family, the main character here thrives on being alone, regardless of public opinion. 'People could think she was gay or frigid, or mad, or whatever they wanted, it didn't matter', she thinks.[18] She has shed the cultural baggage that urged her initially to marry the Goblin King.

In other stories, though, Kennedy addresses the need some of these women have for emotional release after discarding unrewarding relationships. In 'The Cupid Stunt', the main character craves physical touch rather than the 'flats and houses choked full with the husbandly, wifely comforts, including useful kitchen utensils, muffled children and bleakly smiling photographs'.[19] She rejects the available men offered to her by friends, disinterested in the companionship they have to offer and recognising their lack of the sensuality she desires. Instead, she hires a 'genuine and ethical' masseur to satisfy her physical cravings, calming her 'too demanding' body.[20] As her regular sessions continue, relieving her physical demands, she recognises that she is simply 'making do by arranging something which is better than nothing',[21] hoping for the opportunity to again pair the emotional and the physical within a fulfilling relationship.

Emotional fulfilments and isolations

Some of Kennedy's characters do attain these fulfilling relationships. In 'The Last', for example, Kath has left her husband, Bobby, for Martin. While Bobby's voice haunts her when she is alone in her apartment, trying to exact guilt for her abandonment, Martin's presence offers physical and emotional wholeness. With Martin she feels able to make plans for the future, to consider buying a house rather than renting flats. 'You only ever had the length of your life to get things done', she thinks. 'You should hurry, anyway, and not settle for second best'.[22] In this story Kennedy presents no history of domestic violence or evidence of spousal abuse. Rather, Kath, wanting to leave her unsatisfying marriage, initially uses Martin as an impetus to do so and falls in love with him instead. The emotional gratification she feels replaces the emptiness of her marriage and her single life afterwards, allowing her to plan for the future rather than remain static in the present.

The main character in 'Groucho's Moustache' also seeks relief from binding and unfulfilling relationships, wary of becoming quickly and easily involved with the men she tends to attract, the 'men who presented themselves under completely false identities'.[23] As she experiences men such as Matthew, a body sculptor who installs wall-length mirrors in their bedroom, she wonders if 'as I gradually discovered an incompatible stranger in my life, some other bemused woman was probably waking up … with a man steadily revealing himself to be just the chap for me'.[24] When she meets Ian, her wariness again surfaces, only to be engulfed again by her gullibility and curiosity. Yet Ian, who initially worries her by not revealing his occupation, reflects her own interest in truthful relationships when he announces that he is an embalmer, admitting, 'I have to be honest. I can't help it.' Ian's admission creates the opportunity for a real relationship, as the narrator's mind 'surf[s] ahead of me and think[s] of having children that would be more of the same as us, only double. An ocean-load of honest little people.'[25] Like Kath, she inadvertently finds the potential for fulfilment and trust when she least expects it, allowing her to envision a meaningful future.

Such empowering stories have, to some extent, drawn Kennedy's work along gender lines in critics' minds. Yet Kennedy challenges readers' assumptions about her as a woman writer, playing with conjectures on the necessity of applying gendered voices to her characters. 'There are some stories with no gender attached', she points out. 'It's quite interesting to see what sex the reader assumes the protagonist is.'[26] In 'A Perfect Possession', for instance, the narrator details in chilling and calm self-righteousness the disciplinary methods used to 'purify' their son and 'watch him cultivate his gratitude, piece by piece', for his parents' hard work and care. 'When we are finished, he will be a good boy entirely', the narrator affirms.[27] As the accounts of withheld toys, midnight searches and punishments for soiling the bedclothes, and even the removal of a bed pillow 'because he would sleep alongside of it, in spite of what we told him, and that was dirty'[28] unfold, the narrator remains genderless, leaving the reader to speculate on whether we hear the boy's father or mother speaking. While, as Kennedy suggests, the reader may assign the narrator a 'he' or 'she', the lack of any specified gender illustrates the relative unimportance of gender to the story and instead forces the reader to consider the troubled family structure as a whole. In Kennedy's works, gender often occupies a de-prioritised place. Instead, she focuses on the interconnections among characters as they struggle to succeed or, more often, simply to endure. 'It's about humanity … looking out of someone else's eyes, and planning them as human, whoever they are', Kennedy says. 'So you understand that there are no monsters.'[29] In 'A Perfect Possession', we see everyday people committing monstrous acts, illustrating both their humanity and their fallibility.

Kennedy's characters concern themselves with the personal connections and disconnections that channel their emotional well-being. Embedded in relationships or disengaged from them, these characters seek ways of creating proper emotional unions that will sustain them. In the process, Kennedy explores the integration of the physical and the emotional facets of her characters. In many of her works the body becomes an extension of the emotional self, not an object in and of itself. Sex and sexuality begin as central to the ways in which characters attempt to relate, but emerge as almost inconsequential when characters do or do not manage to connect.

Despite such attempts, though, many of her characters remain isolated, unable to understand lovers and spouses (or potential ones). In 'Rockaway and the Draw', for instance, Suzanne sees the way her husband, Ben, draws literal flocks of admiring people, but she cannot herself create a meaningful emotional relationship with him. While he cheerfully caters to her every need, remembering all of her likes and dislikes, being carefully considerate, she considers him emotionally distant. Their sexual activity, for example, reduces her to a machine, at least in her own mind. Ben will 'systematically take her apart, shake out the beat he wanted and then bolt her back into sleep'. Although she finds his 'technical spot-checks' physically satisfying, she finds him 'little more than mechanical'[30] and is unable to feel emotionally satisfied by the marriage.

The narrator of 'Failing to Fall' also feels an emotional disconnection as she tries to attain fulfilment through her pursuit of hasty and clandestine rendez-vous with a string of lovers. The travel to meet them, the process of anticipation, becomes her obsession, far outshining the actual engagement. During the taxi rides she feels the potential for happiness – one that dissipates when she reaches her destination. As a result, she engages in such 'falls' time and again, until she encounters another traveller with the same 'vocation'.[31] He gives her the 'fix' she needs, arranging no-show appointments so that she can feel 'so much more special again'.[32] Eventually, though, he ceases to call, reminding her that such thrilling and secretive events cannot substitute for real relationships. Her inability to maintain such relationships, or even to begin them, leads her to physical encounters that can stave off her emotional hunger, much as the unnamed character in 'The Cupid Stunt' substitutes physical gratification for emotional fulfilment.

'Animal', too, suggests an inability to appropriately express emotional need as Mark, leaving his successful role in a popular soap opera, relinquishes his last chance to approach Sally. As he and Sally rummage through the prop room, picking out some memorabilia for him to take, he becomes increasingly aware of her presence and the rapidly receding opportunity to express his interest in her. His role in the soap opera, dramatically emotive, has disabled him, making it impossible for him to speak. He makes small talk, trying to avoid the final leave-taking. 'As soon as he touched her fingers, they would be over', he realises. 'His last chance for not too much that he could put specifically into words would have expired before its definitions could be framed.'[33] Nervous about his own feelings, dissuaded by Sally's matter-of-fact conversation and efficient manner, he leaves the studio without revealing his desires.

Both Mark and the narrator of 'Failing to Fall' attempt to escape their emotional uncertainty, tricking themselves into veiling personal insecurities through 'thrill rides' or dissuading themselves from action. In 'Far Gone', McFee similarly deceives himself, denying Bonnie's marriage and arranging a frenetic series of flights to 'rescue' her from Ithaca, New York. Throughout his journey, he continually reassures himself of her unhappiness, her need for him, and the bright possibilities for their future together. He clings to phrases from her letters, isolating and misinterpreting them to fulfil his own emotional desires. For example, he sees her comment that 'Henry and I are as happy as we could ever expect to be' as a 'cry for help',[34] requiring his assistance to escape and return to him. While he may realise the futility of his actions – he refuses to call and announce his arrival, which might destroy his fantasies – he doggedly continues, consoling himself with frantic reassurances of his happy future. As the shuttle leaves for Ithaca, 'Both his arms were beginning to shiver although he knew that everything was fine now and that today his ending would be happy. Oh, yes.'[35] McFee cannot face his life bereft of Bonnie. His emotional emptiness requires such desperate and ultimately unsuccessful measures.

Personal betrayals and emotional injuries

Kennedy's stories often focus on such emotional disruptions or betrayals, the personal catastrophes of everyday, usually working-class, people struggling to stay afloat. At times such betrayals can be a misunderstanding of changing social roles. In 'The High Walk', for example, the male narrator cannot understand Anne's choice to see him once but not renew their relationship. She does not conform to 'type', refusing to assume the role of forgiving lover and source of comfort. Instead, she threatens him – as he sees it – with a possible pregnancy, lashes out when he tries to kiss her, and refuses to see him again after their weekend in the mountains. More common, though, are stories that explore the ramifications of betrayal, as characters become circumstantial victims of relationships that escape their ken.

In 'Bix', the male narrator, a recovering alcoholic confronted with a failing marriage and a disinterested wife, chooses to fabricate an affair in order to induce Maggie to leave him. While he feels the marriage must end, he cannot stop thinking about the happiness of their lives together before things turned sour. 'She had carried her joy and love for him like a baby', he remembers. 'The nursing of it had made her a second Mary, beautiful and serene and making the flesh and blood children they couldn't have, superfluous. Or so it seemed.'[36] Yet the catastrophic moment for him comes when Maggie surreptitiously returns and breaks his painstakingly acquired jazz record collection, carefully snapping each record and replacing it in its sleeve. This betrayal, retribution for the artificially constructed release from marriage he has engineered, finally drives him back to drinking. Maggie's anger and cruelty during the last years of their marriage and her final revenge destroy the safety of the narrator's happy memories, stripping him of his confidence.

A similarly underhanded betrayal occurs in 'A Short Conversation Concerning the Rain in America' when Chris meets Dorothy, another ex-girlfriend of her ex-boyfriend, in Copenhagen. As she speaks with Dorothy, noting the bitterness with which Dorothy, after all of the years that have lapsed, still speaks of his multiple girlfriends and the discussions she has had with many of them, she begins to distance herself from the relationship, discovering how she could easily become like Dorothy, obsessed with a long-absent lover. Yet when Dorothy mentions a story from his background concerning the death of his mother, Chris recognises her own childhood experience. He has commandeered her trauma of witnessing her mother's sudden and violent death from a ruptured ulcer and used it as a device for charming and luring women. The realisation of his betrayal of her painful memories, shared in intimate confidence, strips her of her self-confidence, leaving her awake that night feeling 'the new pain of unanticipated theft' and examining the 'particular network of betrayal'.[37] Like the narrator of 'Bix', Chris feels the cruelty of intimacy used against her – the danger of committing too much of one's self.

The narrator of 'Tea and Biscuits' experiences a more insidious betrayal at the hands of her much older lover, Michael, her former mentor and professor at university. Initially the relationship seems a storybook romance – the narrator waits until Michael has divorced his wife before committing to the relationship, saving her virginity until he is free. Yet the story becomes sinister when she reveals her recent trip to give blood, from which she has received a letter announcing that she has contracted HIV. While she has been committed to Michael, her contraction of the disease from him has literally destroyed her life, enacting physically what occurs emotionally in 'Bix'.

Such betrayals leave Kennedy's characters either numb with anguish, such as the narrators of 'Bix' and 'Tea and Biscuits', or angry at the injustices of loved ones heaped onto the already difficult struggle to survive. Such anger characterises the narrator of 'Night Geometry and the Garscadden Trains' who learns, at length, the treachery embedded in her marriage. While she has moved quietly and calmly through the years, her husband, Duncan, has assigned her various roles to legitimise his philandering and returns (of which she has been unaware) – 'wicked wife, wounded wife, the one he would always come back to, the one he had to leave and I never even noticed', she says.[38] 'It seems I was either a victim, an obstacle or a safety net. I wasn't me. He took away me.'[39] When she finally realises his true feelings, she notices the erasure of self that her marriage has enacted. 'It wasn't easy, crumpling up a marriage and throwing it away, looking for achievements I'd made that weren't to do with being a wife', she notes.[40] The result, she announces, is her recognition that 'we have small lives, easily lost in foreign droughts, or famines; the occasional incendiary incident'. Yet, she affirms, 'this is not enough'.[41] The narrator refuses the role to which personal catastrophe relegates her; she demands more from her life.

Fleeting connections

Generally, however, Kennedy's characters rarely occupy a position that allows them to make such demands. Instead, they grasp at the infrequent gestures made to them by others, realising closeness only sporadically, or cling to the relationships they establish despite external pressures. The narrator of 'Star Dust' reveals memories of a love affair from her youth with Archie, the man for whom she intends to leave her loveless marriage.

Yet Tam, her husband, refuses her attempts for personal happiness, threatening to bar her from seeing her daughter again should she abandon him. While she succumbs to his demands, refusing Archie and committing herself to her daughter, she remembers the brief relationship as if it were a piece of cinema, to be played repeatedly in her mind as the only happiness she has known. Similarly, the narrator of 'The Role of Notable Silences in Scottish History' has had only a brief glimpse of happiness. A historical researcher, she occupies her spare time by following, investigating, and writing mock obituaries of strangers. At one point, though, she meets and falls in love with a similarly-minded researcher, who is eventually murdered. Bereft and emotionally injured by her loss, the narrator struggles to express her feelings. 'My house is full of the roaring of us together, like the silence after loud music has been stopped', she says. She finally resorts to the technical and formal language of her occupation to qualify his absence, wanting to validate his existence by writing their experience. None of the newspaper clippings about the murder mention 'what we were together',[42] she explains, and 'the obituary I wrote for him before we first met' is 'inaccurate'.[43] Unaccustomed to emotional closeness, she cannot cope when that closeness disappears.

In 'Breaking Sugar', the main character experiences a less fleeting closeness with her elderly lodger, Mr Haskard, that she cannot share with her husband, Nick. While the two converse carefully and politely, a distance remains between them until one evening, when she comes upon Mr Haskard breaking sugarcubes to create violet sparks. The two of them share a connection, a realisation of similarity that she resolves to keep from Nick. 'He wouldn't understand', she comments. 'He would fail to see her point'.[44] Committed to a peaceful marriage by keeping differences of thought and perspective silent, she wants to hold the experience without having to justify herself to Nick. The relationship she shares with Mr Haskard offers her an emotional outlet her marriage cannot provide, even though she values the marriage too much to end it.

Sam and Helen, in 'Like a City in the Sea', share an intimate marriage whose delicacy and balance appears fragile in the face of the filmmakers shooting a documentary on the famous and elderly Helen's dancing career. Sam, thirty years younger, experiences the pain of potential loss as the event dispels illusions about the longevity of their marriage and exposes the limited amount of time remaining for the ageing Helen. Helen's age has precluded their having children, so Sam recognises the loneliness that awaits him and resents Twyford, the documentary's director, for prying into their tenuous future. 'Every day I think of Helen dying and of what I will do when she does and that makes it possible to stay here without being frightened',[45] Sam declares. Both Sam and Helen recognise her impending death as a central focus of their lives, but Sam finds Twyford's macabre interest in the dynamics behind their relationship invasive and unbalancing.

Precarious emotions and the walking wounded

Such bittersweet relationships define many of Kennedy's relationships. Characters' silent suffering is soothed only by the precarious ties they form and maintain. In 'The Snowbird', for example, the nameless father struggles with his ex-wife over his two daughters, clinging to their childish confidence in and love for him as a way to survive his life insecurities. They provide a balance for him as he worries about his job, doing research in a hazardous chemical plant, and his ex-wife. Their patience and indulgence, preparing medicine for his headache and carefully negotiating between him and their mother concerning the Christmas holidays, allow him a respite from his worries, creating the emotional support he desperately needs.

In the longer short story, 'Original Bliss', Kennedy more deeply explores the implications of these qualified relationships. Alienated from her abrupt and sometimes abusive husband, Helen, a middle-class housewife, gradually becomes involved with Edward, a world-famous psychologist. Each comes to the other with their psychic wounds uncured by other relationships. Helen, insomniac and consumed with the guilt of having abandoned her religious beliefs, and Edward, debilitatingly addicted to violent pornography, carry with them the burdens of their emotional isolation. Eventually, though, the two manage to create a relationship, although that creation suffers from various setbacks due to their respective conditions. Edward tries to work through his addiction, embracing aversion therapies and using Helen's presence as a means to resist temptation, but relapses time and again, particularly when Helen leaves him for a final encounter with her husband. Helen, too, fails in her attempts to reclaim her sense of self and assuage her feelings of religious and sexual guilt. She refuses to see Edward initially, moving in with him only after her husband discovers his letters to her and subsequently beats and rapes her. Yet, unable to erase her guilt, she returns to her husband and offers herself in an almost sacrificial manner, tempting him to beat her again. He does beat her, fracturing her skull, but then he commits suicide.

Only after both Edward and Helen suffer through such purgatorial struggles to reclaim themselves can they begin to relate to one another in ways that point to a future for their relationship, rather than as steps in each other's rehabilitative processes. At the end of the story they make love, Edward having battled against his pornography addiction and Helen having pushed away her guilt. While both characters remain injured, bearing the scars of their struggles, they have healed sufficiently to create a lasting relationship – one that can nurture and sustain them in the future.

In struggling to establish such connections with similarly 'damaged' individuals, Kennedy's characters also attempt to think about and understand larger events that affect their lives. At times, characters, like Helen and Jennifer, become the 'walking wounded', carrying familial and social histories that cannot be lost or rejected. Such characters ghost these histories on their day-to-day lives, illustrating the quiet catastrophes that occur all too often. 'The impetus for her writing', Smith argues, 'is the giving of voice and articulacy to ordinary people who have been silenced by their ordinariness, the calling for due recognition of the complexities of their lives'.[46] Kennedy herself sees this as a focus for her characters. 'Most of my people are in situations outside their control', she explains. 'So many people, if you actually get to know them at any level, are enormous inside and their life doesn't actually permit them to express what they want to.'[47]

Such emotional enormity at times translates into a search for spirituality as a way for characters to overcome familial scars. In 'Original Bliss', Helen initially seeks out Edward because of her real and tangible bereavement at losing faith in God. He 'had been always, absolutely, perpetually *there* … Infinitely accessible and a comfort in her flesh. He'd been her best kind of love. He'd willingly been a companion, a parent, a friend and He'd given her something she discovered other people rarely had: an utterly confident soul.'[48] The loss of that presence, she explains to Edward, makes her feel completely empty. 'He was that size of love. Can you imagine what might happen if a love so large simply left you for no reason you ever knew?' she asks him. 'It's like dying. Except it can't be, because dying ends up being what you want, but haven't got.'[49] As Helen struggles with this loss, she realises the importance of giving herself up completely, relinquishing control until she can feel God's presence in her life again. She leaves Edward and returns to Mr Brindle, accepting his abuse and his attempt to kill her as a means of testing her faith. When she emerges from the experience and rejoins Edward, she feels alive again, once more part of the 'confident soul' God offers to her.

In *Everything You Need*, Kennedy again explores the necessity of surrendering entirely to the concept of risk and death in order to attain a spiritual understanding of oneself and to attain the completeness Helen gains. Nathan, a writer in retreat on a small writer's island, works within the island's credo – that they must attempt suicide without committing, one way or another, to death or survival. As the novel begins, Nathan makes one such attempt, failing and exalting in the thrill of being alive. Yet he cannot sustain the experience and make it a significant part of his being, as Helen does. Instead, he returns time and again to the anguish he feels about his separation from a wife, Maura, he continues to long for and the daughter who thinks he is dead. Only when he manages to bring his daughter, unbeknownst to her, to the island and mentor her developing writing career can he begin to reconcile himself to his past and find peace in his relationship with her. His last act,[50] the one that finally completes him, is to write out his story for Mary to read, revealing at once their true relationship and the healing she has provided him.

In the process of Nathan's struggles, though, he turns away from the mystic spiritualism the island's founder, Joe, embraces and instead relies on writing through his family history and reclaiming familial connections with Mary. The novel he writes for her details the life he has lost with her and Maura, explaining the person he has become and illustrating both the love he feels for her and the emotional vulnerability this writing has created. Yet Nathan's experience is by no means unique. The glimpses he has of the other writers on the island reveal lives fraught by the 'quiet catastrophes' of their lives, revealing ancient scars that hint at family traumas as affecting as Nathan's story. Such family structures surface often in Kennedy's works, as she explores the relationships that inform and dis-form her characters. Dorothy McMillan suggests that Kennedy's narratives parallel those of Iain Banks in their engagement of problematic histories, particularly the convolution of personal and cultural histories. 'Like Banks, Kennedy employs time shift and fragmentation to indicate the tangled relationship of the past with contemporary experience', she comments. 'Linear history of the individual and the country is impossible, but they may just be caught in the gaps of time'.[51] Moira Burgess makes a similar observation, noting that Kennedy's works 'move about in time, cutting to and fro between present and past, and between different periods of the past. Sometimes we glimpse the future'.[52] In the process of exploring these temporal interactions, Kennedy allows us to examine the experiential layering that produce her characters.

Familial scars and the ties that bind

At times such familial attachments provide solace rather than pain. In 'Now That You're Back', brothers Tom, Phil, and Billy gather in Billy's camper in the Highlands to help Tom after his recent recovery from alcoholism. As the story progresses, Tom reveals the usual tension among brothers, chafing at what he imagines to be Billy's oldest brother proprietorship in drinking a lager and asking Tom if he wants coffee. 'It had been meant as a question', he knows, 'but he felt the words as an order'.[53] In addition, we glean from hints dropped during Tom's brief memories of his childhood the history of his father's alcoholism and domestic violence. He remembers his mother 'begging and harrying all of them into bed and safe out of the way' for his father's late-night returns home, and himself 'hoping for no noises, no crying, no footsteps suddenly storming to turn on their light'.[54] Such memories illuminate the problems Tom faces now – problems his brothers, having shared that childhood, understand all too well. Struggling to calm his fears, Tom is joined by Phil and Billy as they place their sleeping bags on either side of his to protect him against the memories that threaten to engulf him.

Like Tom, other characters face potentially crippling family memories, wounded and scarred by events Kennedy exposes to us. John, in 'Bracing Up', is haunted by the memory of his authoritarian grandfather, hearing his voice 'fumbling about in the back of your mind' even now.[55] As he moves through his day, he feels his 'Tad-cu still watching'[56] and imagines his grandfather's gruff and scornful responses. Although he claims invulnerability to his grandfather's presence, thinking that 'he couldn't reach you now. He'd pushed you so far inside – done it himself – that he couldn't get you and now it was safe to come out and take what you'd always been waiting for',[57] we see by his emotional isolation and solitary habits that his grandfather still shadows him. John has attempted to purge himself of that ghost, confronting his grandfather in his nursing home and enacting a final revenge by having him buried in England rather than Wales, but he is too greatly moulded by the experience, unable to feel safe in himself and unable to relate effectively and meaningfully with anyone he meets.

Such an attempt to excise childhood influences occurs in *So I Am Glad* when Jennifer explains her lack of emotion and detached demeanour – what 'I choose to call my calmness. Other people have called it coldness'[58] – to the reader. She foresees and tries to forestall our assumptions that her parents are the root of this emotional distance, announcing that she 'will tell you soon about my parents and the original ways they could have, but when I do, you'll already know they played no part in making me how I am ... for most of the years I spent near them, I was faking it.'[59] Yet her disclaimer breaks down as she reveals her relationship with her parents, the forced observer of their self-absorbed performances. 'At home we had nothing hidden'[60] she announces, soon illustrating that her statement is meant literally. Her parents bicker at one another in a way that eludes the young Jennifer. 'The way my parents were together was always very like a game', she tells us. Yet her parents go one step further, making her witness to their sexual interaction, demanding her presence as voyeur. 'They made my house unsafe', she tells us. 'Their gritted teeth, their damp faces, inquisitive eyes – there they would be, in ambush.'[61] Recognising their need for her reaction, she carefully cultivates disinterest and suppresses emotion, resolving not to allow them access. Finally, they cross the boundaries of the household and make the external environment unsafe too, driving maniacally home from Glasgow one evening with Jennifer and having sex as they speed around snow-covered corners. 'I would have been their unfortunate bystander, a chance casualty', Jennifer claims. By extending their actions to the 'innocent world beyond our house',[62] they encourage Jennifer to suppress her emotions entirely, building walls of defence that exclude all she meets.

While Jennifer insists that 'any after-effects have been minimal',[63] the details of her relationship with Steven and the vicious unravelling of the carefully controlled sadomasochistic boundaries they have woven reveal the self-delusion of her claims. The sight of Steven enjoying the pain she inflicts on his bound body enrages her because it relegates her to the role of voyeur much as her parents' sexual involvement required her to fulfil a similar function. 'There he is, alone with his pleasure, and it seems I can do no more than push him even further beyond my reach', she confesses. 'I feel all alone'.[64] As a result, she chooses to punish him, in the process lashing out at her parents who forced her into this emotional isolation. 'I unwind the belt from my hand ... then take a good hold on the leather again, this time with the buckle end free. I want to be nothing but angry and I am. Because dreams do come true if you want them to.'[65] Jennifer cannot appropriately express herself emotionally and so is left with no outlet save the illusory positions of power sadomasochism offers. Only when she breaks the sadomasochistic control frame can she vent her emotional anguish.

Yet such an outlet proves short-lived and ineffective. The anger Jennifer feels cannot sustain her emotional health for the future. The event leaves her more isolated than before, distanced from Steven as well as from herself. When she takes the final steps toward a fulfilling relationship with Savinien, however, she begins to feel emotionally enabled. Savinien offers her a similarly tainted personal history. The restored-to-life Savinien de Cyrano de Bergerac, he appears in her house, appearance altered and with little memory of his previous life. As he slowly regains those memories, he reveals a life of death and damage that strikes a chord with the taciturn Jennifer. 'There was a tenderness in him I'd never managed to find', she says. 'Then again, he also had a pain about him I didn't want to feel. Tenderness is dangerous, softly cataclysmic and never in the places you'd expect.'[66] While she begins to open up to the possibility of a meaningful relationship with him, she cannot fully express herself in ways that will complete that relationship.

Only when Savinien disappears and then returns, having experienced the darker side of the Glaswegian drug culture, does she see him as the same sort of 'damaged goods' that she is herself. While wandering the city he has come under the control of James, a drug dealer who dictates his actions by supplying or withholding the drugs to which he becomes addicted. James uses Savinien's duelling skill to challenge his enemies, rewarding him with drug fixes each time he wins. Like Jennifer, Savinien plumbs the depths of his degradation, at one point battling, killing, and eating an opponent's fighting dog. 'When I knelt by its shoulder, I gave it hope', he tells her. 'Trusting, it tried to move towards me and whimpered and then tried to move and then I cut through its throat and into its spine'.[67] Savinien betrays that trust much as Jennifer has betrayed Steven's – allowing her to recognise in Savinien both the rage and the calm that characterise her own emotional history. With such a recognition, she realises that she can emotionally engage him in ways heretofore unthinkable for her. She begins the process of true emotional healing.

Not all of Kennedy's characters are bound or restricted by negative family histories. Some, such as Margaret in *Looking for the Possible Dance*, are bound by comfortable memories that also isolate them emotionally from their adult lives. Margaret's closeness to her father, displayed in the many remembrances she has of their time together, carries through her daily life after his death. In the process, she becomes isolated from her lover, Colin. This distance becomes physically evident in the gash that develops in Margaret's vagina at one point when she and Colin are having sex. The literal rift, which prevents them from having sex for a time, represents the emotional rift between them. While Margaret cannot 'replace' her father with Colin, she also cannot move from her role as daughter into a role as wife. She must explore her own emotions and exhume her family history before being able to commit emotionally.[68]

Although she recognises the need to move forward, she feels confined by the memories that recur to her daily. She speaks to her dead father, accusing him of not preparing her for the world she must face without his protection. 'You said I should live Dad. Everything else is a waste of time', she says. 'But all I do is waste my time. How am I supposed to do anything else?'[69] Margaret, Gifford reminds us, 'is trapped emotionally in a dependence on her father … he is a powerful symbol of traditional family and community', and one in which she takes solace. Yet, Gifford continues, 'he prevents her from fulfilling her relationship with Colin in the present, a frustrating world of social work'.[70] Colin realises her hesitation, demanding that she commit to the future rather than remain tied to the past. 'Either we live together, we both commit ourselves, the whole thing, or we call it a day',[71] he tells her. As a result of this conflict, Gifford explains, Margaret seeks 'a way of carrying past into future, a way of accepting the disjunctions of present Scotland and Glasgow'.[72] Only by reconciling the past and the future and recognising the changing social landscape can she return from her reflective journey to London and commit to a life with Colin in Glasgow.

Social structures and the urban environment

Through stories such as Margaret's, Kennedy presents some of the larger social and political concerns of contemporary Scotland, illustrating flaws in both the systems created to help the urban working class and in the national ideology. Margaret enters social work as a way of contributing to community improvement, but learns that organisations such as the Community Link Centre are fragile structures, easily razed by individual conflict. While communal efforts can create a safe and liveable atmosphere such as occurs at the Community Link Centre's Grand Unstoppable Fisherman's Ceilidh, during which all the attendees of the Centre contribute to the festivities and create performances for the audience, such efforts falter when individual agendas interfere with the greater community good. Gus, eager to advance himself with Mr Lawrence, falsely tells him that Margaret provided them with marijuana. Gus's self-promoting action enables Mr Lawrence, already angry at Margaret for spurning his advances, to fire her.[73] His action begins his larger plans for closing down the Centre and ridding it of 'undesirables' (the more vocal members of the Centre) before reopening it as 'something professional'.[74]

Yet the order of events in *Looking for the Possible Dance* is overturned in *So I Am Glad*, when the community pulls together after Savinien's beautifully and painstakingly crafted gardens are disastrously vandalised by a drug gang. As Jennifer returns from work she notices the communal energy created by the widely divergent members of the neighbourhood including the 'ladies Savinien had gardened for', 'Arthur's bakery boys', and 'the gentlemen Hell's Angels from halfway down the street'. The restored garden becomes 'the product of several imaginations within one plan'.[75] It appears, Jennifer notes, 'we had more friends that we imagined'.[76] Here community crisis raises communal sentiment, prompting a neighbourhood-wide response to the vandalism.

Despite such community efforts, though, Kennedy's works often criticise Scotland's socio-political position, seeing the country as both perpetrator and victim of its own ideological degradation. When Kennedy describes Margaret's childhood in *Looking for the Possible Dance*, she lists the educational system's 'Scottish Method (for the Perfection of Children)', one of whose tenets is that 'the history, language and culture of Scotland do not exist. If they did, they would be of no importance and might as well not'.[77] Jennifer echoes this sentiment in *So I Am Glad*, explaining that 'I grew up to believe myself the resident of a country within but not indistinguishable from Britain',[78] a belief that, Kennedy notes, was illusory under the pro-English Thatcher administration. 'You were continually being told these edicts from London about what you should be like and what you should enjoy and you should support England in cricket',[79] she says. Yet the erasure of Scottishness, including the replacement of Scottish language with Standard English, negatively reinforces a distinction that, she explains, the writing of Alasdair Gray and James Kelman broke through. Their work legitimised a vision of urban Scotland apart from romantic notions of 'very rural and plaintive'[80] Highland culture.

Kennedy also engages with the urban landscape, using it to investigate social conditions much as she intertwines family, personal, and cultural histories to explore her characters. In *Looking for the Possible Dance*, for example, Ian A. Bell notes that the Glaswegian setting allows her to 'deal powerfully with the effects of the male culture of violence in urban Scotland'.[81] When Colin ejects a con artist trying to sell fraudulent insurance to people at the Centre, he trespasses on gang jurisdiction. The man whose 'business' he disrupted retaliates by having him kidnapped, beaten, and crucified, nailing his hands and feet to the floor of an abandoned warehouse. 'This is our own small Terror, Colin', he explains. 'You can gather it every day from everywhere; post offices and court rooms, your evening paper, your evening streets. We just make our own use of it.'[82] *So I Am Glad*, too, uses the urban landscape as a background for the violent drug culture that plagues Glasgow. The 'ruined ground'[83] of the old railyards is where Savinien first encounters James. When Savinien returns to Jennifer's house, James destroys the garden, baiting him. Only when the recovered Savinien meets James on his own terms and duels with him does he restore his sense of self-worth and humanity. Savinien brings James to the point of death and then releases him, affirming life rather than death and humanity rather than the cruelty James represents.

Such explorations of the damage that larger social movements, legitimised or not, can cause are not limited to Scotland in Kennedy's works. In 'The Boy's Fat Dog', for example, she presents an unnamed narrator, pressed into guerilla service for an unidentified invading army. While he outlines the atrocities he has committed for his family, he explains the unwavering devotion he has to his cause and to a God who legitimates their actions by allowing them to continue. 'No one would lie about this', he avers. 'That would be more than a sin, that could never be forgiven'. The reasons for the war, 'written and spoken and we saw the photographs', convince him of the 'honesty' of his actions.[84] Although he feels anger at God and his family, an abstract rage at his actions – perhaps a suppressed recognition of their unnecessary viciousness – he expresses this anger when they raid villages, repurifying himself. 'It's good for me to let go that way',[85] he explains. While he realises a vague connection with the towns they destroy, recognising the farming com- munities and their daily routines, he can no longer relate to them on a personal level, speculating about their harvests in only an abstract way. Yet the end of the story offers a glimpse of remaining humanity and autonomy as he hopes for the black dog he sees in the village to escape. 'I think perhaps in the dark the dog won't get it', he thinks. 'Black dog, it could have a chance.'[86] Much as in 'A Perfect Possession', Kennedy allows us to see the thought processes of rational people who commit unthinkable acts, recognising that 'there are no monsters'.

Realms of the fantastic and social commentary

In 'Translations', Kennedy explores the exploitation and religious submission of a South American Indian tribe through the eyes of the Dead
Man, who watches the burning of his village and the degradation of his
fellow tribespeople in the New Mission to Indians. Yet his position in
the spirit world, possessed of the magic of the dead, allows him to escape
to the city where he sees pale, thin bodies similar to his own – a city of
the dead. While he has tried to destroy the spreading foreign influence,
killing the missionary of his village for 'infecting them all with Scotland'[87]
and enabling the burning of the village, he cannot stop the spread of
their influence. Instead, he uses his magic to escape the Mission and fly
to the city where he assists the living dead, delivering and burying infants
who have little chance of survival, for instance. 'Translations' employs
what Kennedy considers Alasdair Gray's contribution to Scottish literature – the move from straight realism to an exploration of social themes
through elements of the fantastic. 'You're seeing yourself and your culture
represented in fiction but it goes beyond that and becomes fantastic', she
explains. 'The fact that not only can we have realism'.[88] This use of the
fantastic allows Kennedy to blur distinctions between the real and the
unreal, experimenting with themes that become believable embedded
within realist narrative.

In 'The Mouseboks Family Dictionary', Kennedy creates a fictional
'tribe' whose emotional, material, and metaphysical existence is profiled
through various terms she lists and defines for the reader. As the defined
terms flesh out the Mousebok character, though, we see revealed the
darker or more ridiculous elements of people in general. In addition, the
profile she presents is plagued with guilt, greed, and a loathing of, yet
commitment to, a conservative morality play with common stereotypes
of Scottish character – parsimonious, self-righteous, and, as she explains
in *Looking for the Possible Dance*, convinced that 'guilt is good' and 'joy is
fleeting, sinful, and the forerunner of despair'.[89] In developing the
Mousebok description, Kennedy subtly insinuates issues of Scottish
character, as well as human flaws in the 'objective' and distant dictionary
format so that we, too, can examine our own potential pettiness and
absurdity at a distance. Only when we reflect on the character she
describes do those sly digs strike home.

In 'Christine' Kennedy focuses less on national attributes and
general human vices and instead on interpersonal relationships through
the character of Christine, the male narrator's former schoolmate. When

he meets her years later at a party, he realises that she can, literally, read his thoughts and emotions. While the recognition of this fact at first unsettles him, he comes to rely on that connection with her and the knowledge that she is watching over him. At the end of the story, at their last meeting, she gives him the image of a flower unfolding as he goes to sleep each night, to remind him of her presence. His need for that image and the emotional calm it lends him creates a bond between them, closer than any 'real' bond he can have. This emotional connection, the complete exposure and release of oneself, reflects the spiritual surrender Helen in 'Original Bliss' and Nathan in *Everything You Need* require for emotional fulfilment. The narrator of 'Christine' also has this need, although Christine must approach him so that he can realise and assuage it.

Similarly, *So I Am Glad* uses elements of the fantastic to create the relationship between Savinien and Jennifer. His literal presence allows her an expression of emotion that offers far-reaching effects. Savinien acts as an emotional counterpoint to Jennifer's calm. He feels everything, expresses everything, and manages to draw a similar emotional response from her as their relationship progresses. Even after he disappears when they travel to Sannois, France, the site of his original death, she cannot return to the calm she claims at the beginning of her narrative. Instead, she must express the emotional turmoil she now feels. 'You'll have read, I suppose, the opening of this book, about all of that calmness I no longer have. Sometimes the best beginning is a lie', she says. 'What do I have instead of the calm. A voice. I remember everything of one man's voice, not a part of it fades.'[90] Left with his emotive language, she must in turn reveal her own voice in the narrative she writes for us.

Writing and the role of the author

In effect, Jennifer writes to achieve self knowledge – her narrative is as much for her as it is for us. 'I sit here and forcibly run over the little bits of sandpaper and tin-tacks that my mind had softened, grown around, smoothed over. I'm here to make it sore again', she confesses. 'You see, I want to reverse or at least arrest the passage of time … I want to live again in minutes and hours which are gone and to forgo my present because it is less satisfactory.'[91] The problem, she notes, is that while writing allows her this stasis, it carries an 'unavoidable price. At the end of a page, a chapter, a day of work, I have to stop. I have to come back.'[92] Yet only by writing through her experiences with Savinien can she internalise and understand the experience. 'I will miss this and I will miss

Savinien and I will be glad',[93] she tells us at the end of her narrative. The narrator of 'Failing to Fall' undergoes a similar process, writing her story and hoping that, through writing it, she will understand the meaning of her experience and realise the missing elements of her life.

Kennedy addresses the writing process itself in a number of her works. For many of her characters, it represents a giving of self – a process difficult for characters who are often isolated. In 'The Seaside Photographer', the narrator writes through her memories of her father, addressing the narrative to him as a bittersweet eulogy to his fading years. She both blames and forgives, seeing all she knows of his story as well as the parts of his life that will always remain incomprehensible to her. 'If, in this world, I could, I would write you whole and well', she says. 'As it is, you are more and better now than ever you were then, a more beautiful and perfect breathing man. Nothing should dare touch you, not a thing. Only, the years and the years' hardness, they were out and waiting for you from the start. All I can do is write you words you cannot read and feel them between us'.[94] The narrative itself offers the writer a means of establishing peace and closure, much as Jennifer must write through her experience with Savinien before she can move forward.

In *Everything You Need*, Nathan, too, uses his writing as a means of emotional expression. Only through the account of his life that he writes can he reveal to Mary that he is her father. Yet the novel also addresses the concurrently creative and destructive process of writing as well as the inadequacies of language to effectively convey emotional meaning. Mary is caught in a web of linguistic betrayal as she struggles to hone her skill as a writer. Her mother lies to her about her father's death, her father conceals their relationship, and Nathan's publisher sends her letters, ostensibly from Nathan, to reacquaint her with her newly discovered father. Kennedy points to an example of language dysfunction when Mary tries to determine her Uncle Bryn's true state of health from his hospital.[95] In her first few calls she learns that he is a 'bit poorly' – a status that downgrades to 'quite poorly' and then, on her arrival at the hospital in Cardiff, to 'dead'. Yet Mary finds truth in writing; her unjaded feelings about her work contrast with the more cynical view Nathan and the other writers have of their work – a cynicism Nathan's hedonistic publisher, J. D., shares. Mary's belief in writing allows Nathan the creative strength to complete his final work, detailing his life and explaining himself to the daughter he cannot truly reach.

At the same time, Kennedy explains, these writers on the island are involved in a quest for a literary Grail. 'The question that you're meant to ask when you see the grail is "whom does the Grail serve?"', she says. For the writers on the island, the question becomes '"whom does the word serve?" – why do you do what you do? If you write as a vocation that must be a question that you answer. It's a part of yourself you have to know.'[96] When Nathan realises that his whodunnit horror novels, though immensely popular, do not answer that question, he turns instead to the final writing project he needs to complete – the only one that still has a meaningful answer to those questions. Mary and Nathan together complete the Grail sequence. As Nathan's writing wanes, so Mary's writing rises. Her tutelage under father's influence allows her to develop into the writer Nathan desired to be. She can answer the questions as he cannot.

Everything You Need's focus on the use of language returns to Kennedy's concern with empowered writing, particularly as it pertains to Scottish writing. The linguistic, and subject, default for many Scottish authors has been Scotland. 'There is this huge hunger for Celts' in the London publishing community, Kennedy explains,[97] which can bind writers at the same time that it offers them opportunities. As retired writer Monagh Cairns explains in Kennedy's story 'Warming My Hands and Telling Lies', 'disconnected from Scotland, I find I don't have much to write about. Scotland was my way in.'[98] Yet, she continues, 'the better Scottish writing gets, the less it will matter. The work will improve itself, it won't be competing with anything other than the best it can produce. It will be international.'[99] Kennedy reiterates this sentiment, suggesting that now Scottish writers can move out of Scotland without sacrificing identity. Like McLean, Galloway, and Banks, Kennedy, particularly in *Everything You Need*, explores ideas and characters that are not confined to Scottish issues or Scottish environments. The writing, as her character Monagh suggests, is becoming 'international'. As Gifford claims, these are writers who feel 'utterly confident of writing *from* Scotland, perhaps *about* Scotland, but by no means limited at all to Scotland'.[100]

Notes

1 C. March, 'Interview with A. L. Kennedy', *Edinburgh Review* 101 (1999), 107.
2 A. Smith, 'Four success stories', *Chapman* 74–5 (Autumn/Winter 1993), 181.
3 *Ibid.*, 192.
4 March, 'Interview with A. L. Kennedy', 109.
5 Although she throws a gender punch here and there. In 'Groucho's

Moustache', for example, the narrator, standing naked in front of Ian, debating their vulnerabilities, comments, 'I can't see any difference in status. We're about the same height. You're physically stronger, but, oh look, I can see the whole structure of society lining up behind you in the distance – it appears to be on your side.' A. L. Kennedy, 'Groucho's Moustache', in *Original Bliss* (London, Vintage [Jonathan Cape Ltd., 1997], 1998), 45.

6 C. March, 'Interview with Janice Galloway', *Edinburgh Review* 101 (1999), 88.

7 A. Smith, 'Four success stories', 180. Although Galloway's Joy in *The Trick Is to Keep Breathing* also presents a lesson in survival, much as Kennedy's characters do.

8 A. L. Kennedy, 'Sweet Memory Will Die', in *Night Geometry and the Garscadden Trains* (London, Phoenix [Polygon, 1990], 1995), 57.

9 A. L. Kennedy, 'Armaggedon Blue', in *Now That You're Back* (London, Vintage, [Jonathan Cape Ltd., 1994], 1995), 70.

10 *Ibid.*, 66.

11 *Ibid.*, 69.

12 *Ibid.*, 71.

13 A. L. Kennedy, 'Cap O'Rushes', in *Night Geometry and the Garscadden Trains* (London, Phoenix [Polygon, 1990], 1995), 112.

14 *Ibid.*, 113.

15 *Ibid.*, 117.

16 *Ibid.*, 121.

17 *Ibid.*, 120.

18 *Ibid.*, 121.

19 A. L. Kennedy, 'The Cupid Stunt', in *Original Bliss* (London, Vintage [Jonathan Cape Ltd., 1997], 1998), 147.

20 *Ibid.*, 148.

21 *Ibid.*, 150.

22 A. L. Kennedy, 'The Last', in *Night Geometry and the Garscadden Trains* (London, Phoenix [Polygon, 1990], 1995), 138.

23 Kennedy, 'Groucho's Moustache', 38.

24 *Ibid.*, 39.

25 *Ibid.*, 48–9.

26 March, 'Interview with A. L. Kennedy', 114.

27 A. L. Kennedy, 'A Perfect Possession', in *Now That You're Back* (London, Vintage [Jonathan Cape Ltd., 1994], 1995), 9.

28 *Ibid.*, 7.

29 March, 'Interview with A. L. Kennedy', 108.

30 A. L. Kennedy, 'Rockaway and the Draw', in *Original Bliss* (London, Vintage [Jonathan Cape Ltd., 1997], 1998), 10.

31 A. L. Kennedy, 'Failing to Fall, in *Now That You're Back* (London, Vintage [Jonathan Cape Ltd., 1994], 1995), 48.

32 *Ibid.*, 57.

33 A. L. Kennedy, 'Animal', in *Original Bliss* (London, Vintage [Jonathan Cape Ltd., 1997], 1998), 30.

34 A. L. Kennedy, 'Far Gone', in *Original Bliss* (London, Vintage [Jonathan Cape Ltd., 1997], 1998), 136.

35 *Ibid.*, 140.

36 A. L. Kennedy, 'Bix', in *Night Geometry and the Garscadden Trains* (London, Phoenix [Polygon, 1990], 1995), 97.

37 A. L. Kennedy, 'A Short Conversation Concerning the Rain in America', in *Original Bliss* (London, Vintage [Jonathan Cape Ltd., 1997], 1998), 91.

38 A. L. Kennedy, 'Night Geometry and the Garscadden Trains', in *Night Geometry and the Garscadden Trains* (London, Phoenix [Polygon, 1990], 1995), 30.

39 *Ibid.*, 31.

40 *Ibid.*, 32.

41 *Ibid.*, 34.

42 A. L. Kennedy, 'The Role of Notable Silences in Scottish History', in *Night Geometry and the Garscadden Trains* (London, Phoenix [Polygon, 1990], 1995), 71.

43 *Ibid.*, 72.

44 A. L. Kennedy, 'Breaking Sugar', in *Original Bliss* (London, Vintage [Jonathan Cape Ltd., 1997], 1998), 109.

45 A. L. Kennedy, 'Like a City in the Sea', in *Now That You're Back* (London, Vintage, [Jonathan Cape Ltd., 1994], 1995), 192.

46 Smith, 'Four success stories', 180.

47 March, 'Interview with A. L. Kennedy', 117.

48 Kennedy, 'Original Bliss', in *Original Bliss* (London, Vintage [Jonathan Cape Ltd., 1997], 1998), 162.

49 *Ibid.*, 181.

50 We learn that his lung cancer has relapsed.

51 D. McMillan, 'Constructed out of bewilderment: stories of Scotland', in I. A. Bell (ed.), *Peripheral Visions: Images of Nationhood in Contemporary Scottish Fiction* (Cardiff, University of Wales Press, 1995), 95. McMillan sees *Looking for the Possible Dance* as a text that supports such a connection with Banks's *The Crow Road* – with Margaret's 'search for self-coherence' providing a 'female gendered version[]' of Banks' 'historicized modernity'. *Ibid.*

52 M. Burgess, 'Disturbing words: Rose, Galloway and Kennedy', in H. Kidd (ed.), *Calemadonnas: Women and Scotland* (n.p., Gairfish, 1994), 100.

53 A. L. Kennedy, 'Now That You're Back', in *Now That You're Back* (London, Vintage [Jonathan Cape Ltd., 1994], 1995), 236.

54 *Ibid.*, 246.

55 A. L. Kennedy, 'Bracing Up', in *Now That You're Back* (London, Vintage, [Jonathan Cape Ltd., 1994], 1995), 88.

56 *Ibid.*, 90.
57 *Ibid.*, 99.
58 A. L. Kennedy, *So I Am Glad* (London, Vintage [Jonathan Cape Ltd. 1995], 1996), 4.
59 *Ibid.*, 6.
60 *Ibid.*, 22.
61 *Ibid.*, 71.
62 *Ibid.*, 104.
63 *Ibid.*, 72.
64 *Ibid.*, 131.
65 *Ibid.*
66 *Ibid.*, 129.
67 *Ibid.*, 180.
68 Much as Colin's disappearance years earlier was necessary for him to gain emotional maturity and independence.
69 A. L. Kennedy, *Looking for the Possible Dance* (London, Vintage [Martin Secker & Warburg, Ltd. 1993], 1998), 175.
70 D. Gifford, 'Imagining Scotlands: the return to mythology in modern Scottish fiction', in S. Hagemann (ed.), *Studies in Scottish Fiction: 1945 to Present* (Frankfurt am Main, Peter Lang GmbH, 1996), 44.
71 *Ibid.*, 217.
72 Gifford, 'Imagining Scotlands', 44.
73 Unlike Jean in 'Didacus', who submits to her employer's pawings in order to keep her job – what Margaret would have had to do to stay at the Community Centre.
74 Kennedy, *Looking for the Possible Dance*, 225.
75 Kennedy, *So I Am Glad*, 236.
76 *Ibid.*, 238.
77 Kennedy, *Looking for the Possible Dance*, 15.
78 Kennedy, *So I Am Glad*, 188.
79 March. 'Interview with A. L. Kennedy', 111.
80 *Ibid.*, 102.
81 I. A. Bell, 'Imagine living there: form and ideology in contemporary Scottish fiction', in S. Hagemann (ed.), *Studies in Scottish Fiction: 1945 to Present* (Frankfurt am Main, Peter Lang GmbH, 1996), 220.
82 Kennedy, *Looking for the Possible Dance*, 230.
83 Kennedy, *So I Am Glad*, 177.
84 A. L. Kennedy, 'The Boy's Fat Dog', in *Now That You're Back* (London, Vintage [Jonathan Cape Ltd., 1994], 1995), 147.
85 *Ibid.*, 150.
86 *Ibid.*, 151.
87 A. L. Kennedy, 'Translations', in *Night Geometry and the Garscadden Trains* (London, Phoenix [Polygon, 1990], 1995), 20.
88 March, 'Interview with A. L. Kennedy', 103.
89 Kennedy, *Looking for the Possible Dance*, 15.

90 Kennedy, *So I Am Glad*, 280.

91 *Ibid.*, 186.

92 *Ibid.*, 187.

93 *Ibid.*, 280.

94 A. L. Kennedy, 'The Seaside Photographer', in *Night Geometry and the Garscadden Trains* (London, Phoenix [Polygon, 1990], 1995), 126.

95 March, 'Interview with A. L. Kennedy', 117.

96 *Ibid.*, 118.

97 *Ibid.*, 110.

98 A. L. Kennedy, 'Warming My Hands and Telling Lies', in *Now That You're Back* (London, Vintage [Jonathan Cape Ltd., 1994], 1995), 163–4.

99 *Ibid.*, 165.

100 D. Gifford, 'At last – the real Scottish literary renaissance?', *Books in Scotland* 34 (1990), 2.

Conclusion

Continuing legacies

The issues that Welsh, McLean, Warner, Banks, Galloway, and Kennedy examine also play out in the works of other contemporary Scottish writers, who create additional facets to the concept of 'Scottish writing'. Jimmy Boyle, Ajay Close, Des Dillon, and Dilys Rose, for example, offer explorations of the urban underworld, elements of the macabre and the fantastic, and gender issues that echo the concerns these six writers present. In addition, other strands of contemporary Scottish writing by Alan Massie, Robin Jenkins, and George Mackay Brown illustrate the diversity of Scottish literature and connections to previous generations of Scottish writers.

Jimmy Boyle's *Hero of the Underworld* drops us into the nightmarish world of Hero, a veritable prisoner at The Institution – the local insane asylum. Abused by a series of malicious and sadistic keepers, he befriends a motley assortment of other inmates as they stage an escape to the city and attempt to rebuild their lives. Joined by other 'social misfits', Hero and his accomplices manage to thwart the inspector and the underground crime ring pursuing them in order to steal enough money to retire from the city to a farm with a prize bull they have rescued from a local abattoir.

Through the course of the novel, Boyle explores various elements of street life that compliment the urban world Welsh proffers, ranging from the local hard man – who is laid low by a head-butt from Hero's midget friend – to the judge and the psychiatrist they blackmail into releasing fellow inmates. In the process, Boyle offers a city peopled with a cast of horrific, comic, and melancholic characters, ranging from necrophiliacs and petty 'mafioso' to single mothers and lonely undertakers. As Hero travels towards the safety and security he craves he recognises that everyone around him is walking wounded. 'Since I got

out of The Institution, I've never met one person who is normal', Hero
comments. 'Sure I've met people, and initially it's been fine, and just when
I think they're nice, they show another side of themselves, reveal some
bizarre or weird habit.' Boyle's vision suggests that life inside The
Institution differs only marginally from life outside; it rests on a means
to escape the psychological shackles Hero sees binding both friends and
enemies. At the same time, Boyle's nightmarish images of street crime,
the prison system, and its corruption reflect his own criminal record in
Gorbals as a teenager, and his subsequent imprisonment (and eventual
release), for a murder he did not commit.

Des Dillon also offers the streets of working-class Scotland but
spins them into a wonderland of excitement and danger through the eyes
of his child narrator in *Me and Ma Gal* and *Itchycooblue*. In *Itchycooblue*,
Dillon transforms the city estates into a land of adventure through which
Derrick travels in search of a moorhen's egg to add to the collection his
father, dying of asbestosis, keeps. Much like Morvern in Warner's *These
Demented Lands* encounters representatives of the contemporary Highlands and Islands as she traverses the reinvented 'traditional Scotland',
Derrick and his friend Gal cross the city, encountering the hard men and
working-class women that people McLean's and Welsh's novels.

In their travels, Derrick offers a pantheon of characters and places
that conflate the fantasyland he sees with the harsher realities those
places reveal. He and Gal lead Mackenzie, the gang leader pursuing
them, into the path of The Bricklayer, a demented man who slings
bricks from the railroad tracks at passers-by. Later, he and Gal play at
the Echo – the massive sewer pipe from the city that empties out into the
Burn – and discover a field of *itchycooblue* they walk through – an open
receptacle for the very asbestos that is killing Derrick's father. Yet by
offering this view of the city through Derrick's imaginative narration,
Dillon's *Itchycooblue* puts a fantastic spin onto lives traditionally depicted
as meagre and bleak, illustrating the vibrancy that co-exists with the
social problems that plague the urban estates.

Ajay Close's vision of Glasgow eschews the fantastic, matter-of-
factly depicting the problems that plague the city such as unemployment
and violent underground crime and corruption. 'Everyone's a hard man
these days', Nan realises in *Official and Doubtful*. 'In lowlife bars across
the city, accountants and lecturers huddle up to stickmen and hoods.'[2]
Yet such depictions function as a backdrop environment for her
middle-class, near-middle-age women narrators in *Official and Doubtful*
and *Forspoken*. Instead, Close focuses on introspection, exploring the

interpersonal relationships her characters seek and their troubled paths toward personal healing.

Like Kennedy's Jennifer in *So I Am Glad*, Close's Tracy in *Forspoken* and Nan in *Official and Doubtful* appear somewhat aloof, partially isolated from the people surrounding them – observers even in the midst of events that centre on them. In large part this distance stems from their struggles to reconcile their lives with the uncertainty that faces them. In *Official and Doubtful*, Nan has assumed a new identity in Scotland to at once escape and come to terms with the legacy of her abusive marriage, which has resulted in her killing her husband. As she develops serendipitous relationships with Imogene, a famous feminist writer, Cal, a successful entrepreneur, and Danny, a Labour MP, she begins to rebuild her own shattered identity. By the end of the novel, she is ready to return to England and face the charges against her.

In *Forspoken*, Tracy similarly faces her past as her sister, Samantha, reappears in Scotland after living in America to remind her of the scars left by their unorthodox, 'hippie' childhood. In the process, Tracy is left to question her relationship with Drew, a lapsed minister-cum-television personality, and her own sense of self. Nan's and Tracy's inquiries are less an investigation into Scottishness than they are about exploring personal identity, of which Scotland and the city in which they live make up only one, though significant, part.

Dilys Rose addresses 'Scottishness' as a sometimes backdrop for her focus on gender issues and gender identity. Instead, like Galloway, she explores the difficulties women face in their relationships with men and in the societal standards to which they are held – a 'broad yet very personal sympathetic feminism'.[3] In 'Before Oscar', for example, the formerly trim Belinda feels her marriage faltering after the birth of her son has left her overweight and worn. 'She, the mother, the wife, the would-be-if-she-were-asked lover. Was it possible to be all three?' she wonders. 'Was it even worth attempting?'[4] In 'New York', a Scottish woman unsuccessfully tries to fend off the advances of a bartender who has plied her with drinks on her first night in the city.

In addition, Rose moves abroad from Scottish landscapes, exploring troubles facing a working-class American woman in 'I Can Sing, Dance, Rollerskate', impoverished Mexican streetchildren dreaming of reaching Texas in 'Our Lady of the Pickpockets', and mismatched travellers to Central America in 'Maya'. Rather than focusing on locations and geographies, she comments on the disconnections among people, much as McLean explores the loneliness and isolation that afflict people. In

'Princess', Robert exists from weekend to weekend to visit his daughter, Sharon, who has been in his ex-wife's custody since their divorce. In 'Little Black Lies', Sonny questions his sexual identity as he moves from a teenager to an older man, considering heterosexuality for the first time in his life. The personal crises Rose presents illustrate the problems people have relating to one another.

Other strands of contemporary Scottish fiction

Yet other contemporary Scottish writers explore different avenues, drawing more closely on traditional styles and themes rather than the youth and rave culture that drives the works of Welsh, for example, or leaks into the Highlands and Islands of Warner and McLean. George Mackay Brown's works, for example, display the lyricism of language and cadence that Lewis Grassic Gibbon explored decades earlier. His focus on Celtic and Nordic heritage and folklore, and everyday existence in the Highlands and Islands, speaks to the lives McLean begins to explore in *Blackden*.

In *Beside the Ocean of Time*, for example, Mackay Brown explores life in the Orkney Islands during the mid-twentieth century through the eyes of Thorfinn, a boy during the 1930s. As his life progresses, he dreams of himself within the folklore on which he is raised – the Nordic adventurers who peopled the Orkneys, the Island and Highland resistance to British government and the Navy press-gangs, and the selkies – the enchanted seal-people of the ocean surrounding the island. These fantasies intermingle with Thorfinn's experience of day-to-day life in the islands. In the process, Mackay Brown offers the mingling of folklore and history with contemporary life, as Thorfinn, now an accomplished writer, returns to the now-abandoned island to write his novels amidst his own memories and the cultural memories the island holds for him.

Alan Massie's work, on the other hand, investigates some of the increasingly troubled traditional class conceptualisations that may linger in contemporary Scotland. In *One Night in Winter*, Massie offers Dallas Graham, a now middle-aged antique dealer who remembers a series of incidents leading up to the murder of a prominent Scottish nationalist, Fraser Donnelly, in north-east Scotland twenty years earlier. As Dallas's story unfolds, the schism between the classes emerges at various points, revealing Dallas's exploitation of his life as the son of the local 'laird' during his university years, thriving on champagne, and that upbringing's conflict with his emerging friendship with Jimmy, Donnelly's chauffeur, as well as Caroline's 'slumming' with Donnelly's companions that leads to her rape and descent into insanity. At the end of the novel, Dallas returns with his teenage son to north-east Scotland and shows him their crumbling estate – a dusty relic like the bric-a-brac and antiques that sit unsold in his shop. In the process, Massie reveals the slow decay of the class system and the growing pains Dallas has witnessed during the past two decades.

This variety of narratives offered by contemporary Scottish writers reveals the multiplying divergent directions Scottish literature is taking. The availability of 'non-traditional' styles and issues has moved Scottish literature out of easy classifications of parochialism and rusticity, and instead into an increasingly mainstream, multinational readership. As a result, an increasingly volatile Scottish literary scene finally has come to reflect the multi-faceted Scottish experience.

Notes

1   J. Boyle, *Hero of the Underworld* (London, Serpent's Tail, 1999), 183–4.
2   A. Close, *Official and Doubtful* (London, Minerva [Martin Secker & Warburg Limited, 1996], 1997), 7.
3   D. Gifford, 'Contemporary fiction II', in D. Gifford and D. McMillan (eds), *A History of Scottish Women's Writing* (Edinburgh, Edinburgh University Press, 1997), 628.
4   D. Rose, 'Before Oscar', in *Our Lady of the Pickpockets* (London, Minerva [Martin Secker & Warburg Limited, 1989], 1990), 59.

Bibliography

Introduction

Baker, Simon, '"Wee stories with a working-class theme": The reimagining of urban realism in the fiction of James Kelman', in S. Hagemann (ed.), *Studies in Scottish Fiction: 1945 to Present* (Frankfurt am Main, Peter Lang, 1996), 235–50.

Bell, Ian A., 'New writing in Scotland', *British Book News* (Feb. 1987), 72–3.

—— 'Imagine living there: form and ideology in contemporary Scottish fiction', in S. Hagemann (ed.), *Studies in Scottish Fiction: 1945 to Present* (Frankfurt am Main, Peter Lang, 1996), 217–33.

Craig, Cairns, 'Resisting arrest: James Kelman', in G. Wallace and R. Stevenson (eds), *The Scottish Novel Since the Seventies: New Visions, Old Dreams* (Edinburgh, Edinburgh University Press, 1993), 99–114.

Dixon, Keith, 'Talking to the people: a reflection on recent Glasgow fiction', *Studies in Scottish Literature* 28 (1993), 92–104.

—— 'Making sense of ourselves: nation and community in modern Scottish writing', *Forum for Modern Language Studies* 29.4 (Oct. 1993), 359–68.

Freeman, Alan, 'Ghosts in sunny Leith: Irvine Welsh's *Trainspotting*', in S. Hagemann (ed.), *Studies in Scottish Fiction: 1945 to Present* (Frankfurt am Main, Peter Lang, 1996), 251–62.

Galloway, Janice, 'Different oracles: me and Alasdair Gray', *Review of Contemporary Fiction* 15.2 (Summer 1995), 193–6.

Gifford, Douglas, 'Imagining Scotlands: the return to mythology in modern Scottish fiction', in S. Hagemann (ed.), *Studies in Scottish Fiction: 1945 to Present* (Frankfurt am Main, Peter Lang, 1996), 17–49.

—— 'Contemporary Scottish fiction I', in D. Gifford and D. McMillan (eds), *A History of Scottish Women's Writing* (Edinburgh, Edinburgh University Press, 1997), 579–603.

Hagemann, Susanne, 'Introduction', in S. Hagemann (ed.), *Studies in Scottish Fiction: 1945 to Present* (Frankfurt am Main, Peter Lang, 1996), 7–15.

Hassan, Gerry, *The New Scotland* (London, The Fabian Society, 1998).

Kelman, James, *Some Recent Attacks* (Stirling, A. K. Press, 1992).

—— *How Late It Was, How Late* (London, Secker & Warburg, 1994).

Malzhan, Manfred, 'The industrial novel', in C. Craig (ed.), *The History of Scottish Literature, v. 4: Twentieth Century*, 229–42.

March, Cristie, 'An interview with Janice Galloway', *Edinburgh Review* 101 (1999), 85–98.

—— 'An interview with A. L. Kennedy', *Edinburgh Review* 101 (1999), 99–119.

McMillan, Dorothy, 'Constructed out of bewilderment: stories of Scotland', in I. A. Bell, (ed.), *Peripheral Visions: Images of Nationhood in Contemporary British Fiction* (Cardiff, University of Wales Press, 1995), 80–99.

Redhead, Steve, 'Celtic trails: Alan Warner', in *Repetitive Beat Generation* (Edinburgh, Rebel Inc., 2000), 127–34.

—— 'Rebel rebel: Kevin Williamson', in *Repetitive Beat Generation* (Edinburgh, Rebel Inc., 2000), 153–61.

Robertson, James, 'Bridging styles: a conversation with Iain Banks' [*Radical Scotland* 42 (Dec. 1989/Jan. 1990)], 11 July 2000, available at www.phlebas.com/text/interv4.html.

Wallace, Gavin, 'Introduction', in G. Wallace and R. Stevenson (eds), *The Scottish Novel Since the Seventies: New Visions, Old Dreams* (Edinburgh, Edinburgh University Press, 1993), 1–7.

—— 'Voices in empty houses: the novel of damaged identity', in G. Wallace and R. Stevenson (eds), *The Scottish Novel Since the Seventies: New Visions, Old Dreams* (Edinburgh, Edinburgh University Press, 1993), 217–31.

Chapter 1

Freeman, Alan, 'Ghosts in sunny Leith: Irvine Welsh's *Trainspotting*', in S. Hagemann (ed.), *Studies in Scottish Fiction: 1945 to Present* (Frankfurt am Main, Peter Lang, 1996), 251–62.

Hagemann, Susanne, 'Introduction', in S. Hagemann (ed.), *Studies in Scottish Fiction: 1945 to Present* (Frankfurt am Main, Peter Lang, 1996), 7–15.

Jamieson, Gill, 'Fixing the city: arterial and other spaces in Irvine Welsh's fiction', in G. Norquay and G. Smyth (eds), *Space and Place* (Liverpool, John Moores University Press, 1997), 217–26.

Maley, Willy, 'You'll have had your theatre', 1 June 2000, available at www.spikemagazine.com/0199welshplay.htm.

Marshall, Gary, 'Dirty work', 1 June 2000, available at www.spikemagazine.com/0399filth.htm.

Mitchell, Chris, 'Love is a many splintered thing', 1 June 2000, available at www.spikemagazine.com/spikeecs.htm.

Redhead, Steve, 'Introduction: the repetitive beat generation – live', in S. Redhead (ed.), *Repetitive Beat Generation* (Edinburgh, Rebel Inc., 2000), xi–xxviii.

—— 'Post-punk junk: Irvine Welsh', in S. Redhead (ed.), *Repetitive Beat Generation* (Edinburgh, Rebel Inc., 2000), 137–50.

—— 'Rebel rebel: Kevin Williamson', in *Repetitive Beat Generation* (Edinburgh, Rebel Inc., 2000), 153–61.

Strachan, Zoe, 'Queerspotting', 1 June 2000, available at www.spikemagazine. com/0599queerspotting.htm.

Welsh, Irvine, *Trainspotting* (New York, W. W. Norton & Company, Inc. [Martin Secker & Warburg Ltd., 1993], 1996).

—— *Marabou Stork Nightmares* (London, W. W. Norton & Company, Ltd. [1995], 1997).

—— 'Eurotrash', in *The Acid House* (London, W. W. Norton & Company, Ltd. [Jonathan Cape Ltd., 1994], 1995), 10–31.

—— 'Stoke Newington Blues', in *The Acid House* (London, W. W. Norton & Company, Ltd. [Jonathan Cape Ltd., 1994], 1995), 32–41.

—— 'Where the Debris Meets the Sea', in *The Acid House* (London, W. W. Norton & Company, Ltd. [Jonathan Cape Ltd., 1994], 1995), 87–92.

—— 'The House of John Deaf', in *The Acid House* (London, W. W. Norton & Company, Ltd. [Jonathan Cape Ltd., 1994], 1995), 99–102.

—— 'The Two Philosophers', in *The Acid House* (London, W. W. Norton & Company, Ltd. [Jonathan Cape Ltd., 1994], 1995), 108–17.

—— 'Disnae Matter', in *The Acid House* (London, W. W. Norton & Company, Ltd. [Jonathan Cape Ltd., 1994], 1995), 118–19.

—— 'The Granton Star Cause', in *The Acid House* (London, W. W. Norton & Company, Ltd. [Jonathan Cape Ltd., 1994], 1995), 120–36.

—— 'Snowman Building Parts for Rico the Squirrel', in *The Acid House* (London, W. W. Norton & Company, Ltd. [Jonathan Cape Ltd., 1994], 1995), 137–44.

—— 'A Smart Cunt', in *The Acid House* (London, W. W. Norton & Company, Ltd. [Jonathan Cape Ltd., 1994], 1995), 177–289.

—— 'Lorraine Goes to Livingston', in *Ecstasy* (London, W. W. Norton & Company, Ltd. [Jonathan Cape Ltd., 1996], 1996), 1–72.

—— 'Fortune's Always Hiding', in *Ecstasy* (London, W. W. Norton & Company, Ltd. [Jonathan Cape Ltd., 1996], 1996), 73–150.

—— 'The Undefeated', in *Ecstasy* (London, W. W. Norton & Company, Ltd. [Jonathan Cape Ltd., 1996], 1996), 151–276.

—— 'A Fault on the Line', in H. Ritchie (ed.), *New Scottish Writing* (London, Bloomsbury Publishing PLC, 1996), 48–54.

—— *Filth* (W. W. Norton & Company, Ltd. [Jonathan Cape Ltd., 1998], 1998).

Chapter 2

Gifford, Douglas, 'Imagining Scotlands: the return to mythology in modern Scottish fiction', in S. Hagemann (ed.), *Studies in Scottish Fiction: 1945 to Present* (Frankfurt am Main, Peter Lang, 1996), 17–49.

—— 'Contemporary Scottish fiction I', in D. Gifford and D. McMillan (eds), *A History of Scottish Women's Writing* (Edinburgh, Edinburgh University Press, 1997), 579–603.

Lawrence, Alexander, 'Duncan McLean: Scottish writer', 11 July 2001, available at www.freewilliamsburg.com/still_fresh/mclean.htr.

Redhead, Steve, 'Introduction: the repetitive beat generation – live', in S. Redhead (ed.), *Repetitive Beat Generation* (Edinburgh, Rebel Inc., 2000), xi–xxviii.

—— 'Bunker man: Duncan McLean', in S. Redhead (ed.), *Repetitive Beat Generation* (Edinburgh, Rebel Inc., 2000), 101–9.

McLean, Duncan, 'When God Comes and Gathers His Jewels', in *Bucket of Tongues* (London, W. W. Norton & Company Ltd., 1992), 1–18.

—— 'Cold Kebab Breakfast', in *Bucket of Tongues* (London, W. W. Norton & Company Ltd., 1992), 19–28.

—— 'A/deen Soccer Thugs Kill All Visiting Fans', in *Bucket of Tongues* (London, W. W. Norton & Company Ltd., 1992), 29–42.

—— 'The Doubles', in *Bucket of Tongues* (London, W. W. Norton & Company Ltd., 1992), 45–50.

—— 'After Guthrie's', in *Bucket of Tongues* (London, W. W. Norton & Company Ltd., 1992), 51–6.

—— 'New Year', in *Bucket of Tongues* (London, W. W. Norton & Company Ltd., 1992), 57–60.

—— 'Headnip', *Bucket of Tongues* (London, W. W. Norton & Company Ltd., 1992), 61–72.

—— 'Doubled Up With Pain', in *Bucket of Tongues* (London, W. W. Norton & Company Ltd., 1992), 73–8.

—— 'Bod Is Dead', in *Bucket of Tongues* (London, W. W. Norton & Company Ltd., 1992), 79–86.

—— 'Quality Control', in *Bucket of Tongues* (London, W. W. Norton & Company Ltd., 1992), 107–12.

—— 'Hours of Darkness', in *Bucket of Tongues* (London, W. W. Norton & Company Ltd., 1992), 113–54.

—— 'Three Nasty Stories', in *Bucket of Tongues* (London, W. W. Norton & Company Ltd., 1992), 155–72.

—— 'Lurch', in *Bucket of Tongues* (London, W. W. Norton & Company Ltd., 1992), 175–92.

—— 'Loaves and Fishes, Nah', in *Bucket of Tongues* (London, W. W. Norton & Company Ltd., 1992), 187–96.

—— 'The Druids Shite It, Fail to Show', in *Bucket of Tongues* (London, W. W. Norton & Company Ltd., 1992), 197–218.

—— 'Shoebox', in *Bucket of Tongues* (London, W. W. Norton & Company Ltd., 1992), 219–28.

—— 'Tongue', in *Bucket of Tongues* (London, W. W. Norton & Company Ltd., 1992), 231–8.

—— 'Lucky To Be Alive', in *Bucket of Tongues* (London, W. W. Norton & Company Ltd., 1992), 239–45.

—— *Blackden* (London, Martin Secker & Warburg Limited, 1994).

—— 'Singing Mrs Murphy', in H. Ritchie (ed.), *New Scottish Writing* (London, Bloomsbury Publishing PLC, 1996), 186–95.

—— *Bunker Man* (London, W. W. Norton & Company, Ltd. [Jonathan Cape Ltd., 1995], 1997).

—— *Lone Star Swing* (W. W. Norton & Company, Ltd. [Jonathan Cape Ltd., 1997], 1997).

—— 'Introduction: getting an edge', in *Plays I* (London, Methuen Publishing Limited, 1999), ix–xviii.

—— *Julie Allardyce*, in *Plays I* (London, Methuen Publishing Limited, 1999), 2–86.

—— *One Sure Thing*, in *Plays I* (London, Methuen Publishing Limited, 1999), 88–93.

—— *Rug Comes to Shuv*, in *Plays I* (London, Methuen Publishing Limited, 1999), 96–106.

—— *Blackden*, in *Plays I* (London, Methuen Publishing Limited, 1999), 108–57.

—— *I'd Rather Go Blind*, in *Plays I* (London, Methuen Publishing Limited, 1999), 160–9.

Chapter 3

Gifford, Douglas, 'Ambiguities and ironies', *Books in Scotland* 62 (Summer 1997), 1–10.

March, Cristie, 'Interview with Janice Galloway', *Edinburgh Review* 101 (1999), 85–98.

Mulvey, Laura, 'Visual pleasure and narrative cinema', *Screen* 16.3 (1975), 1–16.

Redhead, Steve, 'Introduction: the repetitive beat generation – live', in S. Redhead (ed.), *Repetitive Beat Generation* (Edinburgh, Rebel Inc., 2000), xi–xxviii.

—— 'Celtic trails: Alan Warner', in S. Redhead (ed.), *Repetitive Beat Generation* (Edinburgh, Rebel Inc., 2000), 127–34.

Strachan, Zoe, 'Queerspotting', 1 June 2000, available at www.spikemagazine.com/0599queerspotting.htm.

Warner, Alan, *Morvern Callar* (New York, Anchor Books [1995], 1997).

—— *These Demented Lands* (London, Vintage [1997], 1998).

—— *The Sopranos* (London, Jonathan Cape Ltd., 1998).

Williamson, Kevin, 'Introducing Rebel Inc.', 1 June 2000, available at www.canongate.net/rebel/rip.taf?_n=6.

—— 'Kevin Williamson on the classics', 1 June 2000, available at www.canongate.net/rebel/rip.taf?_n=7.

Chapter Four

Banks, Iain, *The Wasp Factory* (London, Simon & Schuster, 1984).

—— *The Bridge* (London, Abacus [Macmillan Limited 1986], 1999).

—— *Espedair Street* (London, Abacus [Macmillan Limited, 1987], 1998).

—— *Canal Dreams* (London, Abacus [Macmillan Limited 1989], 1996).

—— *Complicity* (London, Abacus [Little, Brown and Company, 1993], 1998).

—— *The Crow Road* (London, Abacus [Scribners, 1993], 1998).

—— *Whit* (London, Abacus [Little, Brown and Company, 1995], 1998).

—— *A Song of Stone* (London, Scribner [Abacus, 1997], 1999).

—— *The Business* (London, Abacus [Little, Brown and Company, 1999], 2000).

Banks, Iain M., 'A few notes on the Culture' [posted www.rec.arts.sf, 10 Aug. 1994], 11 July 2000, available at www.soft.net.uk/theziggy/books/ibanks/culture/html.

—— *Consider Phlebas* (London, Orbit [MacMillan, 1987], 1999).

—— *The Player of Games* (New York, HarperPaperbacks [St. Martin's Press, 1989], 1990).

—— *Use of Weapons* (London, Orbit [Macdonald & Co. Ltd, 1990], 1999).

—— *Feersum Endjinn* (London, Orbit [1994], 1995).

—— *Against a Dark Background* (London, Orbit [1995], 1998).

—— *Excession* (London, Bantam [Orbit, 1996], 1998).

—— *Inversions* (London, Orbit [1998], 1999).

Barry, Kevin, 'Happy being grim' [*The Irish Times*, 18 Feb. 1997], 11 July 2000, available at www.phlebas.com/text/banksint20.html.

Fay, Liam, 'Depraved heart' [*Hotpress*, May 1996], 11 July 2000, available at www.phlebas.com/text/banksint05.html.

Gifford, Douglas, 'Imagining Scotlands: the return to mythology in modern Scottish fiction', in S. Hagemann (ed.), *Studies in Scottish Fiction: 1945 to Present* (Frankfurt am Main, Peter Lang, 1996), 17–49.

'Great Uncle Iain', [*Edinburgh Student Newspaper*, 6 Feb. 1997], 11 July 2000, available at www.phlebas.com/text/banksint19.html.

MacGillivray, Alan, 'The worlds of Iain Banks', *Laverock* (1996), 22–7.

McKenzie, Simon, 'Scottish writer Iain Banks spoke with Simon McKenzie' [*Time Off*, May 1995], 11 July 2000, available at www.phlebas.com/text/banksint10.html.

Melia, Sally Ann, 'Very likely impossible, but oh, the elegance...' [*Science Fiction Chronicle*, Oct. 1994], 11 July 2000, available at www.phlebas.com/text/banksint02.html.

Mitchell, Chris, 'Getting used to being God', 11 July 2000, available at www.spikemagazine.com/0996banks.htm.

Morton, Oliver, 'Iain Banks spoke with Oliver Morton' [*Wired*, Jun. 1996], 11 July 2000, available at www.phlebas.com/text/banksint13.html.

Nicholls, Stan, 'Man of the Culture' [*Starlog*, Dec. 1994], 11 July 2000, available at www.phlebas.com/text/banksint03.html.

Riach, Alan, 'Nobody's children: orphans and their ancestors in popular
    Scottish fiction', in S. Hagemann (ed.), *Studies in Scottish Fiction: 1945
    to Present* (Frankfurt am Main, Peter Lang, 1996), 51–83.
Robertson, James, 'Bridging styles: a conversation with Iain Banks' [*Radical
    Scotland* 42 (Dec. 1989/Jan. 1990)], 11 July 2000, available at www.
    phlebas.com/text/interv4.html.
Yates, Robert, 'A wee hard kernel of cynicism', *The Observer*, 20 Aug. 1995, 16.

Chapter 5

Bell, Ian A., 'Imagine living there: form and ideology in contemporary
    Scottish fiction', in S. Hagemann (ed.), *Studies in Scottish Fiction: 1945
    to Present* (Frankfurt am Main, Peter Lang, 1996), 217–33.
Burgess, Moira, 'Disturbing words: Rose, Galloway, and Kennedy', H. Kidd
    (ed.), *Calemadonnas: Women and Scotland* (Gairfish, 1994), 92–102.
Coombe, Stella, 'Stella Coombe interviews Janice Galloway', *Harpies and
    Quines* 1 (May/June 1992), 26–9.
Elphinstone, Margaret, 'Contemporary feminist fantasy in the Scottish
    literary tradition', C. Gonda (ed.), *Tea and Leg-Irons* (London, Open
    Letters, 1992), 45–59.
Galloway, Janice, 'Blood', in *Blood* (London, Minerva [Martin Secker &
    Warburg Limited, 1991], 1992), 1–9.
—— 'Love in a Changing Environment', in *Blood* (London, Minerva
    [Martin Secker & Warburg Limited, 1991], 1992), 17–19.
—— 'Frostbite', in *Blood* (London, Minerva [Martin Secker & Warburg
    Limited, 1991], 1992), 20–8.
—— 'It Was', in *Blood* (London, Minerva [Martin Secker & Warburg
    Limited, 1991], 1992), 32–5.
—— 'David', in *Blood* (London, Minerva [Martin Secker & Warburg
    Limited, 1991], 1992), 36–9.
—— 'Into the Roots', in *Blood* (London, Minerva [Martin Secker &
    Warburg Limited, 1991], 1992), 58–63.
—— 'Breaking Through', in *Blood* (London, Minerva [Martin Secker &
    Warburg Limited, 1991], 1992), 64–9.
—— 'Fair Ellen and the Wanderer Returned', in *Blood* (London, Minerva
    [Martin Secker & Warburg Limited, 1991], 1992), 70–6.
—— 'Need for Restraint', in *Blood* (London, Minerva [Martin Secker &
    Warburg Limited, 1991], 1992), 82–9.
—— 'Plastering the Cracks', in *Blood* (London, Minerva [Martin Secker &
    Warburg Limited, 1991], 1992), 90–102.
—— 'The Meat', in *Blood* (London, Minerva [Martin Secker & Warburg
    Limited, 1991], 1992), 108–9.
—— 'Fearless', in *Blood* (London, Minerva [Martin Secker & Warburg
    Limited, 1991], 1992), 110–15.
—— 'Scenes from the Life No. 27: Living In', in *Blood* (London, Minerva

[Martin Secker & Warburg Limited, 1991], 1992), 116–23.

—— 'A Week with Uncle Felix', in *Blood* (London, Minerva [Martin Secker & Warburg Limited, 1991], 1992), 130–79.

—— 'Valentine', in *Where You Find It* (London, Vintage [Jonathan Cape Ltd., 1996], 1997), 1–14.

—— 'Where You Find It', in *Where You Find It* (London, Vintage [Jonathan Cape Ltd., 1996], 1997), 15–18.

—— 'Sonata Form', in *Where You Find It* (London, Vintage [Jonathan Cape Ltd., 1996], 1997), 19–36.

—— 'After the Rains', in *Where You Find It* (London, Vintage [Jonathan Cape Ltd., 1996], 1997), 59–70.

—— 'Bisex', in *Where You Find It* (London, Vintage [Jonathan Cape Ltd., 1996], 1997), 85–92.

—— 'Peeping Tom', in *Where You Find It* (London, Vintage [Jonathan Cape Ltd., 1996], 1997), 93–108.

—— 'Babysitting', in *Where You Find It* (London, Vintage [Jonathan Cape Ltd., 1996], 1997), 109–18.

—— 'Someone Had To', in *Where You Find It* (London, Vintage [Jonathan Cape Ltd., 1996], 1997), 119–26.

—— 'A Proper Respect', in *Where You Find It* (London, Vintage [Jonathan Cape Ltd., 1996], 1997), 127–38.

—— 'The Bridge', in *Where You Find It* (London, Vintage [Jonathan Cape Ltd., 1996], 1997), 139–56.

—— 'Tourists from the South Arrive in the Independent State', in *Where You Find It* (London, Vintage [Jonathan Cape Ltd., 1996], 1997), 157–64.

—— 'Last Thing', in *Where You Find It* (London, Vintage [Jonathan Cape Ltd., 1996], 1997), 173–80.

—— 'Proposal', in *Where You Find It* (London, Vintage [Jonathan Cape Ltd., 1996], 1997), 193–212.

—— 'Six Horses', in *Where You Find It* (London, Vintage [Jonathan Cape Ltd., 1996], 1997), 213–21.

—— 'Different oracles: me and Alasdair Gray', *Review of Contemporary Fiction* 15.2 (1995), 193–6.

—— *Foreign Parts* (Normal, IL, Dalkey Archive Press [Jonathan Cape Ltd., 1994], 1995).

—— *The Trick Is to Keep Breathing* (Normal, IL, Dalkey Archive Press [Polygon 1989], 1995).

—— 'Objective truth and the grinding machine', 6 June 2000, available at www.galloway.1to1.org/objective.html.

—— 'Singing outside heaven', 6 June 2000, available at www.galloway.1to1.org/Singing.html.

—— 'Balancing the books', 6 June 2000, available at www.galloway.1to1.org/books.html.

Gifford, Douglas, 'Imagining Scotlands: the return to mythology in modern

Scottish fiction', in S. Hagemann (ed.), *Studies in Scottish Fiction: 1945 to Present* (Frankfurt am Main, Peter Lang, 1996), 17–49.

Huguet, Josiane Paccaud, 'Breaking through cracked mirrors: the short stories of Janice Galloway', 6 June 2000, available at www.galloway.1to1.org Josiane.html.

March, Cristie, 'Interview with Janice Galloway', *Edinburgh Review*, 101 (1999), 85–98.

Norquay, Glenda, 'The fictions of Janice Galloway: "weaving a route through chaos"', in G. Norquay and G. Smyth (eds), *Space and Place* (Liverpool, John Moores University Press, 1997), 323–30.

Rose, Gillian, *Feminism and Geography: The Limits of Geographical Knowledge* (Minneapolis, University of Minnesota Press, 1993).

Roy, James Charles, 'Landscape and the Celtic soul', *Eire-Ireland* 31.3–4 (Autumn–Winter 1996), 228–54.

Smith, Ali, 'Four success stories', *Chapman* 74–5 (Autumn/Winter 1993), 177–92.

Chapter 6

Bell, Ian A., 'Imagine living there: form and ideology in contemporary Scottish fiction', in S. Hagemann (ed.), *Studies in Scottish Fiction: 1945 to Present* (Frankfurt am Main, Peter Lang, 1996), 217–33.

Burgess, Moira, 'Disturbing words: Rose, Galloway and Kennedy', in H. Kidd (ed.), *Calemaddonas: Women and Scotland* (Gairfish, 1994), 92–102.

Gifford, Douglas, 'At last – the real Scottish literary renaissance?', *Books in Scotland* 34 (1990), 1–4.

—— 'Imagining Scotlands: the return to mythology in modern Scottish fiction', in S. Hagemann (ed.), *Studies in Scottish Fiction: 1945 to Present* (Frankfurt am Main, Peter Lang, 1996), 17–49.

Kennedy, A. L., 'Tea and Biscuits', in *Night Geometry and the Garscadden Trains* (London, Phoenix [Polygon, 1990], 1993), 1–8.

—— 'Translations', in *Night Geometry and the Garscadden Trains* (London, Phoenix [Polygon, 1990], 1993), 9–23.

—— 'Night Geometry and the Garscadden Trains', in *Night Geometry and the Garscadden Trains* (London, Phoenix [Polygon, 1990], 1993), 24–34.

—— 'The Moving House', in *Night Geometry and the Garscadden Trains* (London, Phoenix [Polygon, 1990], 1993), 35–41.

—— 'Didacus', in *Night Geometry and the Garscadden Trains* (London, Phoenix [Polygon, 1990], 1993), 47–51.

—— 'Sweet Memory Will Die', in *Night Geometry and the Garscadden Trains* (London, Phoenix [Polygon, 1990], 1993), 52–61.

—— 'The Role of Notable Silences in Scottish History', in *Night Geometry and the Garscadden Trains* (London, Phoenix [Polygon, 1990], 1993), 62–72.

—— 'The High Walk', in *Night Geometry and the Garscadden Trains*

(London, Phoenix [Polygon, 1990], 1993), 73–81.

—— 'Star Dust', in *Night Geometry and the Garscadden Trains* (London, Phoenix [Polygon, 1990], 1993), 82–91.

—— 'Bix', in *Night Geometry and the Garscadden Trains* (London, Phoenix [Polygon, 1990], 1993), 92–101.

—— 'The Poor Souls', in *Night Geometry and the Garscadden Trains* (London, Phoenix [Polygon, 1990], 1993), 102–8.

—— 'Cap O'Rushes', in *Night Geometry and the Garscadden Trains* (London, Phoenix [Polygon, 1990], 1993), 109–121.

—— 'The Seaside Photographer', in *Night Geometry and the Garscadden Trains* (London, Phoenix [Polygon, 1990], 1993), 122–6.

—— 'The Last', in *Night Geometry and the Garscadden Trains* (London, Phoenix [Polygon, 1990], 1993), 127–38.

—— 'A Perfect Possession', in *Now That You're Back* (London, Vintage [Jonathan Cape Ltd., 1994], 1995), 1–10.

—— 'Christine', in *Now That You're Back* (London, Vintage [Jonathan Cape Ltd., 1994], 1995), 11–28.

—— 'Failing to Fall', in *Now That You're Back* (London, Vintage [Jonathan Cape Ltd., 1994], 1995), 41–62.

—— 'Armaggedon Blue', in *Now That You're Back* (London, Vintage [Jonathan Cape Ltd., 1994], 1995), 63–72.

—— 'Bracing Up' in *Now That You're Back* (London, Vintage [Jonathan Cape Ltd., 1994], 1995), 88.

—— 'The Mouseboks Family Dictionary', in *Now That You're Back* (London, Vintage [Jonathan Cape Ltd., 1994], 1995), 107–24.

—— 'Friday Payday', in *Now That You're Back* (London, Vintage [Jonathan Cape Ltd., 1994], 1995), 125–42.

—— 'The Boy's Fat Dog', in *Now That You're Back* (London, Vintage [Jonathan Cape Ltd., 1994], 1995), 143.

—— 'Warming My Hands and Telling Lies', in *Now That You're Back* (London, Vintage [Jonathan Cape Ltd., 1994], 1995), 153–76.

—— 'Like a City in the Sea', in *Now That You're Back* (London, Vintage [Jonathan Cape Ltd., 1994], 1995), 177–96.

—— 'Now That You're Back', in *Now That You're Back* (London, Vintage [Jonathan Cape Ltd., 1994], 1995), 225–48.

—— 'Rockaway and the Draw', in *Original Bliss* (London, Vintage [Jonathan Cape Ltd., 1997], 1998), 1–18.

—— 'Animal', in *Original Bliss* (London, Vintage [Jonathan Cape Ltd., 1997], 1998), 19–32.

—— 'Groucho's Moustache', in *Original Bliss* (London, Vintage [Jonathan Cape Ltd., 1997], 1998), 33–50.

—— 'A Short Conversation Concerning the Rain in America', in *Original Bliss* (London, Vintage [Jonathan Cape Ltd., 1997], 1998), 81–92.

—— 'The Snowbird', in *Original Bliss* (London, Vintage [Jonathan Cape Ltd., 1997], 1998), 93–106.

—— 'Breaking Sugar', in *Original Bliss* (London, Vintage [Jonathan Cape Ltd., 1997], 1998), 107–24.

—— 'Far Gone', in *Original Bliss* (London, Vintage [Jonathan Cape Ltd., 1997], 1998), 125–40.

—— 'The Cupid Stunt', in *Original Bliss* (London, Vintage [Jonathan Cape Ltd., 1997], 1998), 141–50.

—— 'Original Bliss', in *Original Bliss* (London, Vintage [Jonathan Cape Ltd., 1997], 1998), 151–311.

—— *Looking for the Possible Dance* (London, Vintage [Martin Secker & Warburg, Ltd., 1993], 1998).

—— *So I Am Glad* (London, Vintage [Jonathan Cape Ltd., 1995], 1996).

—— *Everything You Need* (London, Vintage [Jonathan Cape Ltd., 1999], 2000).

March, Cristie, 'Interview with Janice Galloway', *Edinburgh Review* 101 (1999), 85–98.

—— 'Interview with A. L. Kennedy', *Edinburgh Review* 101 (1999), 99–119.

McMillan, Dorothy, 'Constructed out of bewilderment: stories of Scotland', in I. A. Bell (ed.), *Peripheral Visions: Images of Nationhood in Contemporary Scottish Fiction* (Cardiff, University of Wales Press, 1995), 80–99.

Smith, Ali, 'Four success stories', *Chapman* 74–5 (Autumn/Winter 1993), 177–92.

Conclusion

Boyle, Jimmy, *Hero of the Underworld* (London, Serpent's Tail, 1999).

Brown, George Mackay, *Beside the Ocean of Time* (London, Flamingo [John Murray Publishers Ltd, 1994], 1995).

Close, Ajay, *Official and Doubtful* (London, Minerva [Secker & Warburg, 1996], 1997).

—— *Forspoken* (London, Secker & Warburg, 1998).

Dillon, Des, *Me and Ma Gal* (Argyll, Argyll Publishing [1995], 1996).

—— *Itchycooblue* (London, Headline Book Publishing, 1999).

Gifford, Douglas, 'Contemporary Fiction II', in D. Gifford and D. McMillan (eds), *A History of Scottish Women Writers* (Edinburgh, Edinburgh University Press, 1997), 604–29.

Massie, Alan, *One Night in Winter* (London, Futura Publications [The Bodley Head Ltd, 1984], 1985).

Rose, Dilys, 'Our Lady of the Pickpockets', in *Our Lady of the Pickpockets* (London, Minerva [Martin Secker & Warburg Limited, 1989], 1990), 1–8.

—— 'Maya', in *Our Lady of the Pickpockets* (London, Minerva [Martin Secker & Warburg Limited, 1989], 1990), 9–18.

—— 'New York', in *Our Lady of the Pickpockets* (London, Minerva [Martin Secker & Warburg Limited, 1989], 1990), 21–6.

—— 'I Can Sing, Dance, Rollerskate', in *Our Lady of the Pickpockets* (London, Minerva [Martin Secker & Warburg Limited, 1989], 1990), 27–33.

—— 'Before Oscar', in *Our Lady of the Pickpockets* (London, Minerva [Martin Secker & Warburg Limited, 1989], 1990), 51–63.

—— 'Little Black Lies', in *Our Lady of the Pickpockets* (London, Minerva [Martin Secker & Warburg Limited, 1989], 1990), 103–11.

—— 'Princess', in *War Dolls* (London, Review [1998], 1999), 141–53.

Index